ROBERTO

MAR

13

RODRIGUEZ

P9-APB-181

SILVER BURDETT English

Nancy Nickell Ragno
Marian Davies Toth
Betty G. Gray

SILVER BURDETT & GINN

MORRISTOWN, NJ • NEEDHAM, MA

Atlanta, GA • Cincinnati, OH • Dallas, TX • Menlo Park, CA • Northfield, IL

Acknowledgments

Cover: Imagery for Silver Burdett

Contributing Artists: Michael Adams; Charles Berger; Harry Borgman; Ray Burns; Penny Carter; Eulala Conner; Carolyn Croll; René Daly; Diane Dawson; Marie DeJohn; Roberta Eagan; Robin Eaton; Shelly Freshman; Paulette Giguere; Joan Goodman; Paul Harvey; Meryl Henderson; Chris Holzer; Robert Jackson; John Jones; Jane Kendall; Jan Palmer; Karen Pellaton; Norma Rahn; Sally Schaedler; Steven Schindler; Den Schofield; George Ulrich; Herman Vestal; James Watling; Jane Yamada; Lane Yerkes.

Photographs: Unit 1 3: Bob & Clara Calhoun/Bruce Coleman. 23–34: Silver Burdett. 35: *l.*, *t.r.* Victoria Beller-Smith for Silver Burdett; *b.r.* Silver Burdett. 36–37: Victoria Beller-Smith for Silver Burdett. 38: E.R. Degginger; except *m.r.* Phil Degginger. 41: Silver Burdett. **Unit 2** 47: E.R. Degginger. 74–75: Cary Wolinsky/Stock, Boston. 77–78: Silver Burdett. **Unit 3** 85–103: Silver Burdett. 107: *t.* J.H. Carmichael, Jr./ Bruce Coleman; *m.* E.R. Degginger; *b.* Silver Burdett. 108: © Larry Mulvehill/Photo Researchers, Inc. 109: *t.* Silver Burdett; *b.l.* © Jerry Wachter/Photo Researchers, Inc.; *b.r.* © Syd Greenberg/Photo Researchers, Inc. 112: Silver Burdett. 113: B.G. Silberstein/Shostal Associates. **Unit 4** 117: Imagery for Silver Burdett. 138–139: Victoria Beller-Smith for Silver Burdett. 144: Silver Burdett. 145: Pablo Picasso, *First Steps*, Yale University Art Gallery, Gift of Stephen Carlton Clark. **Unit 5** 153: Imagery for Silver Burdett. 178–181: Silver Burdett **Unit 6** 187–223: Silver Burdett **Unit 7** 231: Barbara Kirk for Silver Burdett. 248: Ray Manley/Shostal Associates. 251: Walter Chandoha. 258: Silver Burdett. 259: Shostal Associates; except *m.l.*, *m.r.* E.R. Degginger **Unit 8** 263: © Michal Heron, 1981. 284–291: Silver Burdett.

Contributing Writers: Judy Brim; Michael Quinn

Acknowledgments continued on page 300

© 1987 Silver Burdett Company. All rights reserved. Printed in the United States of America. This publication, or parts thereof, may not be reproduced in any form by photographic, electrostatic, mechanical, or any other method, for any use, including information storage and retrieval, without written permission from the publisher.   ISBN 0-382-10333-5

CONTENTS

UNIT ONE

GRAMMAR   Sentences   **2**

GRAMMAR	**1** What Is a Sentence?	**4**
GRAMMAR	**2** Word Order in Sentences	**6**
GRAMMAR/MECHANICS	**3** Statements and Questions	**8**
GRAMMAR/MECHANICS	**4** Commands and Exclamations	**10**
GRAMMAR	**5** Sentence Parts	**12**
GRAMMAR	**6** Subjects in Sentences	**14**
GRAMMAR	**7** Predicates in Sentences	**16**
VOCABULARY	**8** Synonyms	**18**
	Grammar Review	**20**

Grammar and Writing Workshop:
Sentence Combining   **22**

COMPOSITION   Classifying

STUDY SKILLS	**9** Alphabetical Order	**24**
STUDY SKILLS	**10** Finding Words in a Dictionary	**26**
STUDY SKILLS	**11** Using a Dictionary	**28**
STUDY SKILLS/WRITING	**12** Using a Thesaurus	**30**
WRITING	**13** What Is a Paragraph?	**32**
WRITING	**14** The Writing Process: A Photo Essay	**34**
PREWRITING/WRITING/ REVISING/PUBLISHING	**15** Writing Project: Writing a Paragraph	**38**

Worktable: A Class Dictionary   **42**
Building Bridges to Science   **43**

Checkpoint: Unit 1   **44**

UNIT TWO

GRAMMAR · Nouns 46

GRAMMAR	**1** What Is a Noun?	48
GRAMMAR/SPELLING	**2** Singular Nouns and Plural Nouns	50
GRAMMAR/SPELLING	**3** Spelling Plural Nouns	52
GRAMMAR/MECHANICS	**4** Singular Possessive Nouns	54
GRAMMAR/MECHANICS	**5** Plural Possessive Nouns	56
VOCABULARY	**6** Compounds	58
	Grammar Review	60

Grammar and Writing Workshop:
Writing with Nouns 62

COMPOSITION · Narrating

LITERATURE	**7** Reading a Story	64
LITERATURE/WRITING	**8** Time Order in Stories	70
MEDIA AWARENESS/SPEAKING	**9** Telling About a TV Show	72
PREWRITING/WRITING/	**10** Writing Project:	
REVISING/PUBLISHING	Writing a Story	74

Worktable: A Paper-Plate Mask 78
Building Bridges to Mathematics 79

Checkpoint: Unit 2 80

CUMULATIVE REVIEW: Units 1—2 82

UNIT THREE

GRAMMAR *Nouns*   84

GRAMMAR	**1** Common Nouns and Proper Nouns	86
MECHANICS	**2** Capital Letters for Names and Titles	88
MECHANICS	**3** Capital Letters for Place Names	90
MECHANICS	**4** Capital Letters for Calendar Words	92
MECHANICS	**5** Using Commas	94
VOCABULARY	**6** Context Clues	96
	Grammar Review	98

Grammar and Writing Workshop:
Writing with Proper Nouns   100

COMPOSITION *Creating*

LITERATURE/SPEAKING	**7** Reading Poetry Aloud	102
LITERATURE/LISTENING	**8** Listening for Comparisons in Poetry	104
LITERATURE/WRITING	**9** Writing Comparisons	106
PREWRITING/WRITING/	**10** Writing Project:	
REVISING/PUBLISHING	Writing a Poem	108

Worktable: A Concrete Poem   112
Building Bridges to Social Studies   113

Checkpoint: Unit 3   114

UNIT FOUR

GRAMMAR *Pronouns*   116

GRAMMAR   **1** What Is a Pronoun?   118

GRAMMAR   **2** Subject Pronouns   120

GRAMMAR   **3** Object Pronouns   122

GRAMMAR   **4** Possessive Pronouns   124

USAGE   **5** Using *I* and *me*   126

VOCABULARY   **6** Homophones   128

Grammar Review   130

Grammar and Writing Workshop:
Writing with Pronouns   132

COMPOSITION *Reasoning*

THINKING SKILLS   **7** *Who, What, When, Where,* and *Why*   134

THINKING SKILLS   **8** Solving Problems   136

THINKING SKILLS   **9** Messages Without Words   138

PREWRITING/WRITING/ REVISING/PUBLISHING   **10** Writing Project:
Writing a Mystery Story   140

Worktable: A Picture Riddle   144

Building Bridges to Art   145

Checkpoint: Unit 4   146

CUMULATIVE REVIEW: Units 1—4   148

UNIT FIVE

GRAMMAR Verbs   **152**

GRAMMAR	**1** What Is a Verb?	**154**
GRAMMAR/USAGE	**2** Verbs in the Present	**156**
USAGE	**3** Making Pronouns and Verbs Agree	**158**
GRAMMAR	**4** Verbs in the Past	**160**
GRAMMAR/SPELLING	**5** Spelling Verbs in the Present	**162**
GRAMMAR/SPELLING	**6** Spelling Verbs in the Past	**164**
VOCABULARY	**7** Prefixes	**166**
	Grammar Review	**168**

Grammar and Writing Workshop:
Writing with Verbs   **170**

COMPOSITION Informing

SPEAKING/LISTENING	**8** Giving and Following Directions	**172**
SPEAKING/LISTENING	**9** Using the Telephone	**174**
WRITING/MECHANICS	**10** Writing a Friendly Letter	**176**
PREWRITING/WRITING/ REVISING/PUBLISHING	**11** Writing Project: Writing Directions	**178**

Worktable: A Puzzle Greeting Card   **182**
Building Bridges to Science   **183**

Checkpoint: Unit 5   **184**

UNIT SIX

GRAMMAR *Verbs* 186

GRAMMAR	**1** Reviewing Action Verbs	188
GRAMMAR/USAGE	**2** Verbs with Special Past Forms	190
GRAMMAR	**3** The Verb *be*	192
USAGE	**4** Using the Forms of *be*	194
GRAMMAR	**5** Main Verbs and Helping Verbs	196
USAGE	**6** Using Irregular Verbs	198
USAGE	**7** Using Irregular Verbs	200
MECHANICS	**8** Contractions	202
VOCABULARY	**9** Suffixes	204
	Grammar Review	206

Grammar and Writing Workshop:
Writing with Verbs 208

COMPOSITION *Researching*

STUDY SKILLS	**10** Choosing a Topic	210
STUDY SKILLS	**11** Using the Library	212
STUDY SKILLS	**12** Using the Parts of a Book	214
STUDY SKILLS	**13** Using an Encyclopedia	216
STUDY SKILLS/WRITING	**14** Using Your Own Words	218
PREWRITING/WRITING/	**15** Writing Project:	
REVISING/PUBLISHING	Writing a Report	220

Worktable: "What's the Answer?" 224
Building Bridges to Social Studies 225

Checkpoint: Unit 6 226

CUMULATIVE REVIEW: Units 1–6 228

UNIT SEVEN

GRAMMAR *Adjectives*   **230**

GRAMMAR **1** What Is an Adjective?   **232**

GRAMMAR **2** Adjectives That Tell *How Many*   **234**

GRAMMAR **3** Adjectives That Tell *What Kind*   **236**

GRAMMAR/USAGE **4** Adjectives That Compare   **238**

USAGE **5** Using *a, an,* and *the*   **240**

VOCABULARY **6** Antonyms   **242**

Grammar Review   **244**

Grammar and Writing **Workshop:**
Writing with Adjectives   **246**

COMPOSITION *Describing*

LITERATURE/WRITING **7** Using Details to Describe   **248**

WRITING **8** Describing What You See and Hear   **250**

WRITING **9** Describing What You Taste, Smell, and Touch **252**

PREWRITING/WRITING/ **10** Writing Project:
REVISING/PUBLISHING Writing a Description   **254**

Worktable: A Collage   **258**

Building Bridges to Science   **259**

Checkpoint: Unit 7   **260**

UNIT EIGHT

GRAMMAR   *Sentences*   262

GRAMMAR	**1** Nouns in Sentences	264
GRAMMAR	**2** Verbs in Sentences	266
GRAMMAR	**3** Adverbs	268
GRAMMAR	**4** Adverbs That End in *-ly*	270
MECHANICS	**5** Using Commas in a Series	272
MECHANICS	**6** Contractions	274
VOCABULARY	**7** Homographs	276
	Grammar Review	278

Grammar and Writing Workshop:
Sentence Combining   280

COMPOSITION   *Persuading*

LISTENING/THINKING SKILLS	**8** Listening for Facts and Opinions	282
SPEAKING/LISTENING	**9** Sharing Opinions	284
WRITING/MECHANICS	**10** Writing a Book Report	286
PREWRITING/WRITING/ REVISING/PUBLISHING	**11** Writing Project: Writing an Advertisement	288

Worktable: A Safety Poster   292
Building Bridges to Health   293

Checkpoint: Unit 8   294

CUMULATIVE REVIEW: Units 1—8   296

REVIEW AND PRACTICE HANDBOOKS   **301**
  Grammar Handbook   **302**
  Young Writer's Handbook   **348**

THESAURUS   **367**

INDEX   **385**

Grammar

Sentences

Composition

Classifying

Buried Treasure

How do squirrels remember
when woods are white with snow
where they hid the pine cones
they buried months ago?

Sometimes they remember,
and sometimes they do *not.*
Look at all the seedlings
from cones the squirrels forgot!

—*Aileen Fisher*

1 — What Is a Sentence?

> • A **sentence** is a group of words that tells a complete thought.

Read the groups of words below. Some groups are sentences. Some groups are not sentences.

Sentences	1. Many families enjoy the circus.
	2. Circuses began many years ago.
	3. People could see all kinds of animals.

Not Sentences	4. On parade.
	5. Elephants and monkeys.
	6. Stand on horses.

Word groups 1, 2, and 3 are sentences. Each sentence tells about the circus. Each sentence tells a complete thought about something.

Word groups 4, 5, and 6 are not sentences. They do not tell complete thoughts.

Skills Tryout

Tell which of these word groups are sentences.

1. P.T. Barnum started the first American circus.
2. Was the greatest showman of all time.
3. He took Tom Thumb to cities everywhere.
4. Forty inches tall and weighed seventy pounds.
5. Jumbo was the biggest elephant in the world.

Practice

Read each word group. For each pair, write the word group that is a sentence.

1. **a.** Most large circuses have three rings.
   b. Became larger over the years.
2. **a.** The clowns stay together in Clown Alley.
   b. Brightly colored clothes and feathers.
3. **a.** Hard to make the people laugh.
   b. Today clowns are part of the circus.
4. **a.** Many funny clown policemen.
   b. Some clowns do tricks on horseback.
5. **a.** There are three kinds of clowns.
   b. Baggy pants, white face, and tramp.
6. **a.** Juggling, riding, and other things to learn.
   b. There is a school for clowns in Venice, Florida.
7. **a.** No two clowns can dress up exactly alike.
   b. Some funny faces and some sad faces.
8. **a.** White face and a floppy hat to wear.
   b. Emmett Kelly was a famous clown with sad eyes.
9. **a.** Clowns perform between the main acts.
   b. A very important job.
10. **a.** Dan Rice was the first great American clown.
    b. Invited to visit President Abraham Lincoln.

Application SPEAKING

Tell about a circus you have seen or heard about. Try to use sentences that tell complete thoughts.

Word Order in Sentences

> ● The words in a sentence must be in an order that makes sense.

One group of words below tells about the picture and makes sense.

brown I a see cow.   <u>I see a brown cow.</u>

The underlined group of words makes sense. The words in this sentence are in the right order.

Changing the order of words sometimes changes the meaning of a sentence. Which sentence below tells about the picture?

The <u>cow</u> followed the <u>calf</u>.
The <u>calf</u> followed the <u>cow</u>.

Skills Tryout

Use each group of words below to make a sentence.

1. has The bell a cow.
2. spots has calf The.
3. clover chew Cows.
4. wants calf The dinner.
5. to barn They walk the.
6. red The is barn.

Practice

A. Use each group of words to make a sentence. Write each sentence.

1. We animals have.
2. pony small The is.
3. big The are dogs.
4. A mice cat chases.
5. quack ducks Our.
6. Hens eggs lay.
7. crows The rooster.
8. are pigs fat Six.
9. sheep gives A wool.
10. farm our love I.

B. Change the order of the underlined words in each sentence. Notice how the meaning changes. Write each new sentence.

EXAMPLE: The <u>cat</u> jumped in front of the <u>kitten</u>.
ANSWER: The kitten jumped in front of the cat.

11. The <u>turkey</u> chased the <u>goose</u>.
12. My <u>aunt</u> looked at my <u>puppy</u>.
13. The <u>pony</u> was bigger than the <u>calf</u>.
14. The <u>barn</u> is behind the <u>house</u>.
15. The <u>dog</u> ran after the <u>cat</u>.

Application WRITING SENTENCES

Write a sentence about each farm animal named below. Cut each sentence apart and mix up the words. Ask someone to put the groups of words back together to make sense.

lamb   chicken   horse

3 Statements and Questions

- The first word of a sentence begins with a **capital letter**.
- A **statement** is a sentence that tells something. It ends with a period (**.**).
- A **question** is a sentence that asks something. It ends with a question mark (**?**).

Read each sentence below. Notice that each sentence begins with a capital letter.

1. Jan read about Christopher Columbus.
2. Who was Christopher Columbus?

Sentence 1 tells something. It is a statement. The mark at the end is a period.

Sentence 2 asks about something. It is a question. What is the mark at the end?

Skills Tryout

Tell if each sentence is a statement or a question.

1. Where was Columbus born?
2. Columbus was born in Italy.
3. How many ships did he have?
4. Columbus had three small ships.
5. Columbus thought the world was round.

Practice

A. Read each sentence. Write *statement* if it tells something. Write *question* if it asks something.

1. How many times did Columbus sail from Spain?
2. He made four trips to look for new lands.
3. How long did his first trip take?
4. Columbus sailed for more than two months.
5. Columbus was a great sailor.

B. Write each sentence. Begin each sentence with a capital letter. Use periods and question marks correctly.

6. where did Christopher Columbus land
7. he landed on islands near Florida
8. who paid for his voyages
9. the queen of Spain gave him money
10. columbus was looking for India
11. he wanted to bring back spices
12. why were spices so important in 1492
13. people used spices to keep food safe
14. they also used spices to make perfume
15. did Columbus find cinnamon and pepper

Application WRITING SENTENCES

Look at the picture of Christopher Columbus. Write two statements and two questions about the picture.

4 — Commands and Exclamations

- A **command** is a sentence that gives an order. It ends with a period (**.**).
- An **exclamation** is a sentence that shows strong feeling. It ends with an exclamation mark (**!**).

Read each sentence below. Notice that each sentence begins with a capital letter.

Throw the ball to me.
I love baseball games!

The first sentence gives an order. It is a command. What mark is at the end?

The second sentence shows strong feeling. It is an exclamation. What mark is at the end?

Skills Tryout

Tell if each sentence below is a command or an exclamation.

1. The runner is out!
2. Watch the player on first base.
3. Give the bat to Jill.
4. This is a close game!
5. Show Mario your new catcher's mitt.

Practice

A. Read each sentence below. Write *command* if it gives an order. Write *exclamation* if it shows strong feeling.

1. Eileen saw a great baseball team!
2. Tell me which team she saw.
3. What exciting players the Atlanta Braves are!
4. Tell me if Eileen saw the catcher.
5. He is such a terrific player!

B. Each sentence below is a command or an exclamation. Write each sentence correctly.

6. how thrilling the World Series game was
7. it was won by a grand-slam home run
8. name the teams in California
9. one player hit three home runs
10. show Mark your baseball cards
11. what a great place New York is
12. visit the Baseball Hall of Fame
13. tell me how to get there
14. we can't wait to see the museum
15. borrow a map from my older sister

Application WRITING SENTENCES

Write two commands and two exclamations. Use one of the words below in each sentence.

baseball   pitcher   score   strike

Sentence Parts

- A sentence has two parts. The **subject** names someone or something. The **predicate** tells what the subject is or does.

Read each sentence below. The blue part is the subject. It names someone or something. The green part is the predicate. It tells what the subject is or does.

1. The children ride to the library.
2. They are returning some books.
3. The red book is due today.

The children is the subject in sentence 1. The predicate is *ride to the library*. What are the subjects in sentences 2 and 3? What are the predicates in sentences 2 and 3?

Skills Tryout

Name the subject in each sentence below. Then name the predicate.

1. Maria | read a book about bicycles.
2. She | saw a funny picture.
3. An old bicycle | had a huge front wheel.
4. The seat | was very high.
5. The rider | looked frightened.

Practice

A. Read each sentence. Write *subject* if the subject is underlined. Write *predicate* if the predicate is underlined.

1. Bicycles <u>are used all over the world</u>.
2. <u>Some riders</u> travel for days on bicycles.
3. <u>France</u> has a long race every year.
4. The race <u>is over two thousand miles long</u>.
5. Many people <u>ride through five countries</u>.
6. <u>They</u> pedal over high mountains.
7. <u>We</u> saw pictures of the race.
8. Whole families <u>were watching the race</u>.
9. <u>A boy</u> was waving a flag at the riders.
10. The flag <u>was red, white, and blue</u>.

B. Write each sentence. Draw a line between the subject and the predicate.

11. Some early bicycles had no pedals.
12. Riders pushed with their feet.
13. One old bicycle had wooden wheels.
14. The ride was bumpy and uncomfortable.
15. The bicycle was called a boneshaker.

Application WRITING SENTENCES

Write four sentences about bicycles. Make up a subject or predicate for each sentence part below.

a. My bicycle ____.
b. ____ had a blue bike.
c. ____ rode fast.
d. A girl ____.

6 — Subjects in Sentences

> • The **subject** of a sentence names someone or something.

Read these sentences about the picture. The subject of each sentence is in blue.

1. **A jumbo jet** flew over the city.

2. **Jeffrey** flew over the city.

A jumbo jet is the subject of sentence 1. *Jeffrey* is the subject of sentence 2.

The subject of the sentence below is missing. What subject can you add to tell something else about the picture?

_____ flew over the city.

Skills Tryout

The subject is underlined in each sentence below. Think of a different subject. Say each new sentence.

1. A bird can fly.
2. Jets can fly fast.
3. My kite flies high.
4. Planes fly over towns.
5. A helicopter landed.
6. The crow flew away.

Practice

A. The subject is underlined in each sentence. Think of a different subject. Write each new sentence. Then underline the subject.

EXAMPLE: The robin flew away without a sound.
ANSWER: Three geese flew away without a sound.

1. The eagle has very strong wings.
2. Crows can fly for hours.
3. My kite got caught in the tree.
4. The plane was in the air for ten hours.
5. The glider landed in the middle of a field.

B. Add a subject to each word group below. Write each complete sentence.

6. ___ went to the airport.
7. ___ carried a heavy suitcase.
8. ___ fastened their seat belts.
9. ___ pressed his nose to the window.
10. ___ fell asleep after the plane took off.
11. ___ was served for lunch during the trip.
12. ___ flew to Chicago last week.
13. ___ rode in a very small airplane once.
14. ___ waved at the plane from the ground.
15. ___ picked us up at the airport.

Application WRITING SENTENCES

Write three sentences about things that fly. Be sure that each sentence has a different subject.

7 — Predicates in Sentences

> ● The predicate of a sentence tells what the subject is or does.

Read the two sentences below. The predicate of each sentence is in green.

1. The pumpkin is my favorite plant.

2. Joan grows many vegetables.

The predicate tells what the subject is or does. In sentence 1 *is my favorite plant* is the predicate. It tells what the pumpkin is. In sentence 2 *grows many vegetables* is the predicate. It tells what Joan does.

The predicate of the sentence below is missing. What predicate can you add to complete the sentence?

My family ____.

Skills Tryout

The predicate is underlined in each sentence. Think of a different predicate. Say each new sentence.

1. The garden is in the backyard.
2. Joan pulls out many weeds.
3. She wears thick gloves and a hat.
4. The flowers have a wonderful smell.
5. A worm crawls through the dirt.

Practice

A. The predicate is underlined in each sentence. Think of a different predicate. Write each new sentence. Then underline the predicate.

EXAMPLE: Sunshine helps a garden grow.
ANSWER: Sunshine is good for plants.

1. A garden needs good, rich soil.
2. Carrots grow under the ground.
3. Three watermelons grew last year.
4. A rake is an important tool.
5. Some plants grow on thick vines.

B. Add a predicate to each word group below. Write each complete sentence.

6. A beautiful butterfly ____.
7. The rain ____.
8. Red juicy tomatoes ____.
9. Tall corn plants ____.
10. Tiny ladybugs ____.
11. A hungry rabbit ____.
12. A pumpkin pie ____.
13. My older brother ____.
14. Green leafy lettuce ____.
15. Tasty peppers ____.

Application WRITING SENTENCES

Write three sentences about food. Be sure that each sentence has a different predicate.

Synonyms

> ● **Synonyms** are words that have almost the same meaning.

Yvonne's class visited the zoo. She wrote these sentences about an animal she saw.

Kanga has <u>strong</u> legs.
Her legs are <u>powerful</u>.

Kanga is <u>fast</u>.
She moves <u>quickly</u>.

The underlined words in each pair of sentences are synonyms. They mean almost the same thing. *Powerful* is a synonym for *strong*. What is a synonym for *quickly*?

Skills Tryout

Read each sentence. Name the synonym in ( ) for the underlined word.

1. Kanga's baby is <u>tiny</u>. (small, furry)
2. The <u>baby</u> is called a joey. (weak, infant)
3. Kanga <u>carries</u> him everywhere. (feeds, takes)
4. His eyes are <u>shut</u>. (brown, closed)
5. The joey is <u>afraid</u>. (scared, hungry)

Practice

A. Read each sentence. Write the synonym in ( ) for the underlined word.

1. Kanga has <u>beautiful</u> brown eyes. (lovely, clear)
2. Her <u>broad</u> tail helps her jump. (soft, wide)
3. Kangaroos can move <u>quickly</u>. (fast, quietly)
4. Kanga's joey <u>sleeps</u> in her pouch. (naps, drinks)
5. The pouch is like a <u>bag</u>. (tail, sack)
6. Kanga <u>enjoys</u> living in the zoo. (leaves, likes)
7. She eats <u>tasty</u> meals there. (delicious, many)
8. She is <u>happy</u> when children visit. (sleepy, glad)
9. Kanga is usually <u>quiet</u>. (brave, silent)
10. She does not like <u>chilly</u> weather. (cold, rainy)

B. Write each sentence below. Use a synonym from the box in place of the underlined word.

| ~~small~~   great   ~~traveled~~   ~~named~~   odd |

11. Kanga <u>came</u> to our zoo from Australia.
12. Australia has <u>unusual</u> animals.
13. Koala bears are <u>tiny</u>.
14. Wild dogs are <u>called</u> dingoes.
15. It seems like a <u>wonderful</u> country.

Application USING LANGUAGE

Write each sentence twice. Use a different synonym each time.

a. I am ___ today.   **b.** We had a ___ ride.

Word Order in Sentences *pages 4–7*

A. Write each group of words in the right order to make a sentence.

1. a Fay letter wrote.
2. cap Ari his lost.
3. movie We a saw.
4. Grandpa book the read.
5. its The tail chased cat.

Statements and Questions *pages 8–9*

B. Each sentence below is a statement or a question. Write each sentence correctly.

6. do you have any pets
7. my brother fed the fish in the tank
8. one goldfish is three years old
9. are goldfish made of gold
10. they look like gold in the sunlight

Commands and Exclamations *pages 10–11*

C. Each sentence below is a command or an exclamation. Write each sentence correctly.

11. liz can't wait until her birthday
12. show Jean your new watch
13. look for Joe at the park
14. tell me where the library is
15. what a terrific day it is for a picnic

Subjects and Predicates in Sentences *pages 12–17*

D. Write *subject* if the subject is underlined. Write *predicate* if the predicate is underlined.

16. <u>My teacher</u> visited the Grand Canyon.
17. Many hikers <u>climbed the steep trails</u>.
18. Some people <u>rode mules</u>.
19. <u>The Colorado River</u> crosses the Grand Canyon.
20. Ms. Reynolds <u>camped near the river</u>.
21. <u>Two curious raccoons</u> visited her campsite.
22. They <u>turned over a trash can</u>.

E. Add subjects to word groups **23–26**. Add predicates to word groups **27–30**. Write each complete sentence.

23. ___ laughed.
24. ___ talked to me.
25. ___ ran away.
26. ___ smells good.

27. The student ___.
28. Dogs ___.
29. A balloon ___.
30. The soldier ___.

Synonyms *pages 18–19*

F. Write the synonym in ( ) for the underlined word.

31. Our garden is <u>big</u>. (large, nice)
32. We grow <u>tasty</u> vegetables. (delicious, strange)
33. Many <u>tiny</u> creatures live there. (happy, small)
34. Grasshoppers <u>leap</u> all day. (sing, jump)
35. A <u>noisy</u> cricket chirps at night. (shiny, loud)

See also Handbook pages 302–313.

Sentence Combining

> ● Sentences that repeat words can be combined.

Read the sentences below.

    A. Phillip laughed at the movie.
    B. His friend laughed at the movie. (and)
A + B. Phillip and his friend laughed at the movie.

Sentence A tells what Phillip did. Sentence B tells that his friend did the same thing. But sentence A + B gives both of these ideas in one sentence.

Sentence A + B was made by combining, or joining, sentence A and sentence B. The repeated words in sentence B were removed. *His friend* was joined to sentence A with the word *and*. One longer, strong sentence took the place of two short sentences.

Other sentences can be combined in this way.

    C. Sandra saw a movie star.
    D. Sandra got his autograph. (and)
C + D. Sandra saw a movie star and got his autograph.

Sentence C and sentence D each tell one thing that Sandra did. Sentence C + D was made by combining sentence C and sentence D. The repeated word in sentence D was removed. The new words were joined to sentence C with the word *and*.

Combine-a-Pair Combine each pair of sentences below. Use the clues in ( ) the way they were used on page 22. Write each new sentence.

1. Annette made a movie.
   Randy made a movie. (**and**)
2. Her brother wrote the story for the movie.
   I wrote the story for the movie. (**and**)
3. Bobby brought a movie camera.
   Bobby showed us how it worked. (**and**)
4. Our class heard about the film.
   Our class wanted to help. (**and**)
5. The movie was eight minutes long.
   The movie had no sound. (**and**)

No-Clue Time Combine each pair of sentences without clues. Remember to use the word *and*. Write each new sentence.

6. Mark saw an exciting movie.
   Tracy saw an exciting movie.
7. Good movies are fun.
   Good movies tell us about our world.
8. Actors study hard.
   Actors learn their lines.
9. Directors make movies.
   Writers make movies.
10. Directors help the actors.
    Directors show them what to do.

9 Alphabetical Order

> • **Alphabetical order** is the order of the letters in the alphabet.

Rosa collects postcards. She has postcards from every state. First she put the cards in groups by states. Then she put the states in alphabetical order. Now she can easily find any card she wants!

Alphabetical order is a useful way to list words. Dictionaries list words in alphabetical order. Telephone books list names this way, too. In what other places is alphabetical order used?

Using Alphabetical Order
a b c d e f g h i j k l m n o p q r s t u v w x y z

1. Look at the first letter of each word. Use the first letter of each word to put the words in order.

   <u>A</u>laska   <u>C</u>olorado   <u>D</u>elaware

2. If the first letters are the same, use the second letter of each word.

   O<u>h</u>io   O<u>k</u>lahoma   O<u>r</u>egon

3. If the first and second letters are the same, use the third letter.

   Mi<u>c</u>higan   Mi<u>n</u>nesota   Mi<u>ss</u>ouri

Tell how to put these words in alphabetical order.

1. Vermont
2. Georgia
3. Arkansas
4. Arizona
5. Virginia
6. Nevada

Practice

A. Write each list of words in alphabetical order.

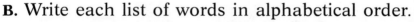

1. state, town, city, world
2. Nebraska, Kansas, Utah, Kentucky
3. river, stream, bay, sea
4. cottage, cabin, house, hut
5. Asia, Africa, Australia, America

B. Write each list of words in alphabetical order.

6. hill, hall, hen, huge, howl
7. growl, grain, grin, grumble, green
8. belt, best, begin, beet, beauty
9. slow, sleet, school, slump, seat
10. cheese, clash, cellar, comb, chase

Application USING STUDY SKILLS

List five things that belong together. For example, list five colors or five insects or five sports. Write your list in alphabetical order. Then ask a friend to tell why the five things belong together.

10 — Finding Words in a Dictionary

- The words in a dictionary are in alphabetical order.
- **Guide words** show the first word and the last word on a dictionary page.

A dictionary has information about words. The words are listed in alphabetical order. To find a word quickly, think of a dictionary as having three parts. The word *antelope* is found in the front part. The word *unicorn* is found in the back. Where will you find the word *ostrich*?

Middle: h, i, j, k, l, m, n, o, p

Front: a, b, c, d, e, f, g

Back: q, r, s, t, u, v, w, x, y, z

Two words called guide words appear at the top of each dictionary page. They are the first and last words on the page. Every word on the page comes between the guide words.

leopard	311	level

The word *lesson* comes between the guide words shown. Which word below would also appear on this page?

label   letter   lend

Skills Tryout

Tell if each word below is found in the front, the middle, or the back of a dictionary.

1. illness
2. clever
3. television
4. western
5. flute
6. guitar
7. legend
8. jingle
9. sluggish

Practice

A. Write each word. Then write *front, middle,* or *back* to show where it is found in a dictionary.

  1. manner   2. effort   3. storm   4. harp

B. Read each word. Write the pair of guide words it comes between.

  5. racer   rabbit–radar   relish–repeat
  6. comet   class–coat   color–cone
  7. violin   very–video   vine–vision

C. Read each pair of guide words. Write the word that would appear on the same page.

  8. capital–close   canyon   clean   crayon
  9. eggplant–elephant   eighty   east   enemy
  10. zigzag–zone   zebra   zipper   zoom

Application USING STUDY SKILLS

Have a friend write three words. See how quickly you can find each word in a dictionary.

11 — Using a Dictionary

> ● A dictionary gives spellings and meanings of words.

Words that are explained in a dictionary are **entry words.** They are listed in alphabetical order in dark type. The entry words have spaces between syllables.

The dictionary gives the meaning for each entry word. Some words have more than one meaning. Each meaning is numbered. Sometimes an **example sentence** shows how a word is used.

Read the dictionary entries below. Tell which entry words have more than one meaning.

---

pic co lo   A small flute with a high shrill sound.

pick le   1. Salt water, vinegar, or other liquid used to preserve food. 2. Cucumber preserved in pickle. 3. Trouble or difficulty. *We were in a pickle with that flat tire.*

pic nic   1. An outdoor meal or party. *They had a picnic in the park.* 2. To go on a trip with a meal. *We picnic at the lake often.*

pie   A round pastry with a fruit, meat, or cream filling.

pil low   A case filled with feathers or other soft material.

pinch   1. To squeeze between finger and thumb. *She pinched herself to be sure she was awake.* 2. To press or squeeze so that it hurts. *My shoes pinch my feet.* 3. A tiny amount; a bit. *The soup needs a pinch of salt.*

Skills Tryout

Answer the questions from the dictionary entries.

1. How many entry words are listed?
2. Which entry includes two meanings?
3. Which meaning of *pickle* has an example sentence?
4. How many meanings does *piccolo* have?

Practice

A. Write your answer from the dictionary entries.

1. Which two entry words have three meanings?
2. Which two entry words name foods?
3. Which word is a synonym for "a tiny amount"?
4. Which kind of pastry can have a meat filling?
5. Which word names a musical instrument?
6. Which entry has two example sentences?
7. Which word means "case filled with feathers"?

B. Write each sentence. Then write the numeral
for the meaning that *pickle* has in the sentence.

8. I ate a pickle with my sandwich.
9. Grandma soaked the green peppers in pickle.
10. Did you see what a pickle we were in?

Application USING STUDY SKILLS

Look in a dictionary. Find three words that
begin with the letter *p*. Write one meaning for
each word. Then make up an example sentence.

12 — Using a Thesaurus

> ● A **thesaurus** contains lists of synonyms.

A thesaurus is a book of synonyms. Like a dictionary, it lists entry words in alphabetical order. For each entry word many synonyms, or words that have almost the same meaning, are listed. The last part of the entry lists words that mean the opposite of the entry word. Words that have opposite meanings are antonyms.

Writers can look up words and choose synonyms that make their sentences more interesting.

Study the thesaurus entry below.

Entry word	**small**—not big in size or number; the opposite of large.
Example sentence	She saw a <u>small</u> kitten in the tree.
Synonyms	*little*—small in size or number. Have you seen my <u>little</u> notebook?
	petite—small in body size or height. Some clothes come in <u>petite</u> sizes.
	pocket-sized—small; miniature. He carries a <u>pocket-sized</u> radio in his book bag.
	tiny—very small in size; not giant. That <u>tiny</u> bird makes a soft sound.
	weak—small or soft. Her voice sounded <u>weak</u>.
Antonyms	ANTONYMS: big, giant, great, huge, large

Skills Tryout

Use the entry on page 30 to answer the questions.

1. What is the entry word? What is the example sentence?
2. How many synonyms are listed?
3. Which words mean the opposite of *small*?

Practice

A. Choose a different synonym to replace *small* in each sentence below. Write each new sentence.

1. The *small* ant ran across the strawberry.
2. A *small* voice called me.
3. Can you see the *small* dots on the glass?
4. Some clothes are made to fit *small* people.
5. I carry a *small* dictionary with me.

B. Turn to the Thesaurus on page 367. Choose a word to replace *bad* in each sentence below.

6. Those puppies aren't *bad.*
7. My math grade is *bad.*
8. There was a *bad* storm.
9. We made a *bad* decision.
10. Too much sun may be *bad* for you.

Application USING STUDY SKILLS

Pick a word from the Thesaurus in the back of your book. Write a sentence for each synonym.

13 — What Is a Paragraph?

- A **paragraph** is a group of sentences about one main idea.
- The **topic sentence** tells the main idea.

You know that a sentence tells a complete thought. Sometimes the thought is simple. One sentence can tell everything you want to say about it. But what if you want to say more? What if you want to give examples or explain? Then you need to write a group of sentences. You need to write a paragraph.

A paragraph is a group of sentences about one main idea, or topic. Usually one sentence in the paragraph tells what the main idea is. That sentence is called the topic sentence. It is often the first sentence of the paragraph. All the other sentences add details about the main idea.

Here is a paragraph. Notice that the first word is *indented*, or moved in. You indent to show where a new paragraph begins.

A googol is a very large number. It is the number 1 with a hundred zeros after it. A nine-year-old boy named the googol. His uncle, a mathematician, asked him to think of a name for this very big number. The boy said, "Name it a googol!"

Tell about the example paragraph on page 32.

1. What is the topic sentence?
2. Which sentences add details?
3. Give a title for the paragraph.

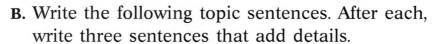

Practice

A. Write each of these as a paragraph. Remember to indent. Underline each topic sentence.

1. A nanosecond is a small amount of time. It is smaller than a second. In fact, there are one billion nanoseconds in one second!
2. Light moves with amazing speed! It travels at 186,282 miles a second. In one year it travels more than 5½ million million miles!
3. Astronomers use mathematics. They use math to find out how far away the stars are. They use it to find the size and paths of the stars.

B. Write the following topic sentences. After each, write three sentences that add details.

4. Our classroom is a busy place.
5. There are many sounds in the school yard.

Application USING WRITING SKILLS

Write about helping an adult. Include a topic sentence and three detail sentences.

14 — The Writing Process

Have you ever written a poem? Have you ever written a story or a letter?

What happens when you write? Think about it. Can you describe what happens when you write?

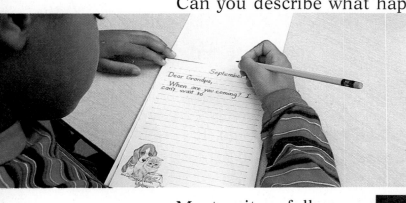

Most writers follow four steps:

1. They get ideas. (prewriting)
2. They write down their ideas. (writing)
3. They make some changes and rewrite. (revising)
4. They share what they have written. (publishing)

These steps are called "the writing process." You can read more about it on the next three pages. Does it sound like what happens when you write?

1. Prewriting

Prewriting is getting ideas. How do you get ideas to write about? Here are a few ways:

- Notice how a thing looks. Notice how it smells, sounds, tastes, or feels. Write what you noticed.
- Read a poem or a story. Write what it makes you think of or feel like.
- Ask someone some questions. Ask about something they have done or know about. Write what they say.

There are many ways to get an idea to write about. One idea is all you need to start.

2. Writing

Don't worry if you have only one idea. Start to write. Then you will get more ideas.

Keep on writing as long as you are getting ideas. Don't worry about spelling. Don't worry about being neat. When you have written down all of your ideas, stop. You have written your first draft.

WRITER'S HINT: As you write, it helps to know your purpose. Purpose is the reason for writing.

Are you telling a make-believe story?

Are you giving facts about something?

You will write better if you remember your purpose.

3. Revising

Always read what you have written. You may see ways to make it better. You may think of something you left out. You may want to use some different words.

Changing your writing to make it better is called revising.

4. Publishing

Publishing is sharing what you have written. There are many ways to share. You can read aloud a story you wrote. You can mail a letter. You can put a poem on the bulletin board.

If you want someone to read your writing, be polite. Look for spelling errors and other mistakes. (This is called proofreading.) Fix the mistakes. Give your reader a neat and correct copy to read.

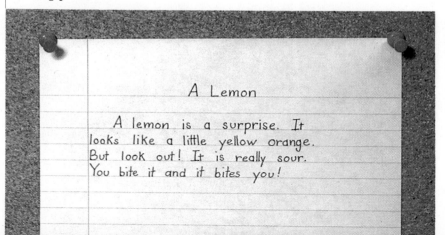

A Lemon

A lemon is a surprise. It looks like a little yellow orange. But look out! It is really sour. You bite it and it bites you!

15 — Writing a Paragraph

- A **paragraph** may tell how things in a group are alike.

In this lesson you will use an important thinking skill—*classifying.* You will study animals and put them into groups. Then you will write a paragraph telling your classmates about one group. As you work you will see how writing helps you to think.

1. Prewriting

Study the animals in the pictures.

Which animals are alike in some way? Put them into a group. See how many different groups you can think of. Then talk about the animal groups with your classmates. List the different groups on the board. Tell how the animals in each group are alike.

▶ Choose one group of animals for your topic. Then write a plan for your paragraph. Under *Main Idea* tell how the animals are alike. Under *Details* list the animals in the group.

Main Idea:
Some animals live in shells.
Details:
giant turtle
snail
hermit crab

2. Writing

How will you begin your paragraph? Take the main idea in your paragraph plan. Use it to write a topic sentence. You could write a question: "Did you know that some animals have shells for houses?" You could write a statement: "Three different kinds of animals live in shells."

▶ Write the topic sentence of your paragraph. Follow the topic sentence with detail sentences. The detail sentences should tell about each animal in your group.

3. Revising

▶ Read your paragraph to someone. How can it be improved? Use this checklist for help.

Revision Checklist

- Does my topic sentence tell the main idea?
- Did I follow the topic sentence with detail sentences?
- Did I tell how the animals in my group are alike?
- Are my sentences complete thoughts?

Look at the editing marks on the next page. Writers use these marks to make changes. See how these marks are used in the sample paragraph. The paragraph was improved by making each sentence a complete thought.

¶Three different kinds of animals ^live in shells. The giant turtle ^carries a house on its (bak) back. The tiny (snale) snail ^does the same

Three different kinds of animals live in shells. The giant turtle carries a house on its back. The tiny snail does the same thing. Most unusual of all is the hermit crab. It runs from one shell to another looking for a house.

►Make changes to improve your paragraph. Use the editing marks to make changes.

4. Publishing

►Share your paragraph with the class. First check it for errors. Use the Proofreading Checklists on this page to help you. Use the editing marks to make corrections.

Proofreading Checklist
- **Is the first word of the paragraph indented?**
- **Does each sentence begin with a capital letter?**
- **Does each sentence have the correct punctuation mark at the end?**
- **Is each word spelled correctly?**
- **Have I used my best handwriting?**

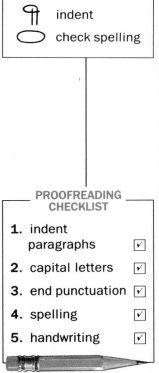

EDITING MARKS

∧ add

⌢ indent

◯ check spelling

►Make a class bulletin board. Hang up one picture of each animal shown on page 38. Display your paragraph on the bulletin board. Take time to read and enjoy your classmates' paragraphs.

PROOFREADING CHECKLIST

1. indent paragraphs ☑
2. capital letters ☑
3. end punctuation ☑
4. spelling ☑
5. handwriting ☑

Writing Project

A Class Dictionary

Ortiz, Alicia, 1. A friendly girl with sparkling brown eyes. 2. A girl who loves to play soccer. 3. A girl who is a whiz at math. 4. A girl who was born in Dallas, Texas.

Put your dictionary skills to work. Make a class dictionary. Write a dictionary entry about someone else. You may need to ask that person some questions. Use the information you get for your "definitions."

Use the entry shown above as your example. Notice that you write the last name first. Maybe the person can give you a photo. If not, you may wish to draw an illustration.

When all the entries are done, collect the pages. Help to put them in alphabetical order. Your class dictionary is finished!

Science

In a science book you read many new words, such as *molecule*. Familiar words, such as *work*, may have a special meaning in science. You will need to look up such words in a dictionary. Your science book may have a dictionary at the back. It is called a *glossary*.

Pluto

▶ Try out your dictionary skills for science. The underlined word in each sentence below has a special meaning in science. Look up the word. Write the meaning it has in the sentence.

Neptune

1. The earth's <u>crust</u> is its thinnest layer.
2. The earth's <u>core</u> may be liquid metal.
3. <u>Matter</u> takes up space.
4. The earth's <u>mantle</u> is a layer of heavy rock.

Uranus

Saturn

Speakers at Work A *planetarium* is a building where people study the sun, the stars, and the planets. People who work in a planetarium tell visitors how these bodies move in space. They explain the order of the planets. This means the order of the planets from the sun.

Jupiter

Mars

Earth

Venus

Mercury

▶ You try it. Tell about the order of the planets in two ways. First name them in their order from the sun. Then name them in alphabetical order.

Sun

Sentences   *pages 4–17*

A. Write *yes* if the word group is a sentence.
Write *no* if the word group is not a sentence.

1. Tom flew a kite.
2. A strong wind.
3. Ran on the grass.
4. The string broke.

B. Write each group of words in sentence order.

5. new a pet I have.
6. has rain The stopped.
7. missed bus Alice the.
8. in Clams live the sea.

C. Write each sentence correctly. Use a capital
letter and put the correct mark at the end.

9. where is your friend
10. all birds have wings
11. pass the potatoes
12. how hot the sun is

D. Write *subject* if the subject is underlined. Write
predicate if the predicate is underlined.

13. Jill wrote a poem.
14. My tooth is loose.
15. The movie starts soon.
16. The monkey made faces.

Synonyms   *pages 18–19*

E. Write the synonym in ( ) for the underlined word.

17. feel (see, touch)
18. quick (fast, fun)
19. shout (yell, whisper)
20. tired (glad, sleepy)

Dictionary   *pages 24–29*

F. Read each pair of guide words. Write the word in (   ) that would appear on the same page.

21. egg—end (elf, eat)
22. sag—sew (sip, sat)
23. bull—bun (bump, but)
24. odd—old (one, off)

G. Read the dictionary entries. Answer each question.

hoard To store away money or goods. **hoarse** Having a rough, low voice; husky.	25. Which word is a synonym for "husky"? 26. What is the meaning of *hoard*?

Thesaurus   *pages 30–31*

H. Read the thesaurus entry. Answer the questions.

funny—causing laughter. My kitten does <u>funny</u> tricks. *hilarious*—extremely funny. *witty*—clever and amusing. **ANTONYM**: boring	27. What is the entry word? 28. What is the antonym for the entry word?

Paragraphs   *pages 32–33*

I. Write the topic sentence below. After it, write two sentences that add details.

   We use water in many different ways.

See also Handbook pages 302–313, 348.

2

Grammar
Nouns

Composition
Narrating

Moon

I have a white cat whose name is Moon;
He eats catfish from a wooden spoon,
And sleeps till five each afternoon.

Moon goes out when the moon is bright
And sycamore trees are spotted white
To sit and stare in the dead of night.

Beyond still water cries a loon,
Through mulberry leaves peers a wild baboon
And in Moon's eyes I see the moon.

—*William Jay Smith*

1 — What Is a Noun?

> ● A **noun** names a person, place, or thing.

Chen saw a film about the seashore. Then he wrote these sentences.

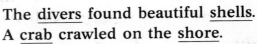

The <u>divers</u> found beautiful <u>shells</u>.
A <u>crab</u> crawled on the <u>shore</u>.

The underlined words in Chen's sentences are nouns. They name persons, places, and things. The word *divers* names persons. The words *crab* and *shells* name things. The word *shore* names a place.

Look at the underlined noun in the sentence below. Tell if it names a person, a place, or a thing.

We saw <u>Betty</u> dive.

Skills Tryout

Find the nouns in these sentences.

1. The family went to the beach.
2. Some joggers ran on the sand.
3. Ann built a castle.
4. Seaweed floated in the water.
5. Fish swam near the shore.

Practice

A. One of the words in each pair is a noun. Write the nouns.

1. towel, hot
2. under, clams
3. later, seashore
4. Erin, walked
5. sun, above

6. scary, lobster
7. shark, salty
8. starfish, bumpy
9. roared, shells
10. sand, when

B. Write each sentence below. Underline the nouns.

11. Tommy and Paul swam in the ocean.
12. Their eyes hurt.
13. The water tasted like salt.
14. Birds walked along the rocks.
15. A gull carried a fish in its mouth.
16. A family had lunch at the beach.
17. The children unfolded a blanket.
18. Sand was in their shoes.
19. A surfer rode on the waves.
20. The surfboard was made of wood.

Application WRITING SENTENCES

Write about a trip to the beach. Write one sentence with a noun that names a place. Write one sentence with a noun that names a person. Write one sentence with a noun that names a thing. Underline these three nouns.

2 — Singular Nouns and Plural Nouns

- A **singular noun** names one person, place, or thing.
- A **plural noun** names more than one person, place, or thing.
- Add *-s* to form the plural of most nouns.

Notice the underlined nouns in these sentences.

1. **They looked at a <u>star</u>.**
2. **The bright <u>stars</u> twinkled.**

The noun *star* in sentence 1 names one thing. It is a singular noun. The noun *stars* in sentence 2 names more than one thing. It is a plural noun. Most plural nouns are formed by adding *-s* to a singular noun.

Skills Tryout

Read each sentence. Tell if each underlined noun is a singular noun or a plural noun.

1. The <u>sun</u> is a very bright <u>star</u>.
2. The <u>planets</u> travel around the <u>sun</u>.
3. We saw three <u>satellites</u> last <u>month</u>.
4. <u>Comets</u> look like flaming <u>balls</u> with <u>tails</u>.
5. <u>Saturn</u> is the <u>planet</u> that has <u>rings</u> around it.

Practice

A. Read each sentence. Write *singular* if the underlined word is a singular noun. Write *plural* if the underlined word is a plural noun.

1. <u>Meteors</u> are pieces of stone in space.
2. In Arizona a large <u>meteor</u> fell to the ground.
3. It made a huge <u>hole</u> in the ground.
4. Some <u>visitors</u> took pictures.
5. My <u>brothers</u> looked through a telescope.
6. They saw the <u>planet</u> named Jupiter.
7. Jupiter has four large <u>moons</u>.
8. Jupiter is much larger than <u>Earth</u>.
9. No <u>person</u> from Earth has been to Jupiter.
10. It would take many <u>years</u> to get there.

B. Write each sentence. Use the correct form of the noun in ( ).

11. Mars is the red ——. (planet, planets)
12. Mercury has long, bright ——. (day, days)
13. A —— on Mercury is very cold. (night, nights)
14. The Milky Way is made of many ——. (star, stars)
15. Earth has only one ——. (moon, moons)

Application WRITING SENTENCES

Pretend to take a ride through outer space. Write some sentences about your ride. Use the plural form of each noun below.

cloud   spaceship   light   planet

3 — **Spelling Plural Nouns**

- Add -*es* to form the plural of nouns that end in *s*, *x*, *ch*, or *sh*.

- If a noun ends in a consonant and *y*, change the *y* to *i* and add -*es* to form the plural.

The words *class*, *ax*, *bunch*, and *leash* are singular nouns. They end in *s*, *x*, *ch*, and *sh*. The plural of these nouns is formed by adding -*es*.

class	ax	bunch	leash
classes	axes	bunches	leashes

Some singular nouns end in a consonant and *y*. To form the plural, change the *y* to *i* and add -*es*.

pony	strawberry
ponies	strawberries

A few words change their spelling to form the plural.

woman	man	foot
women	men	feet

Skills Tryout

Spell the plural form of each singular noun below.

1. penny
2. lunch
3. crash

4. glass
5. man
6. fox

Practice

A. Write the plural of each singular noun.

1. dress
2. party
3. bush
4. woman
5. ash

6. baby
7. ranch
8. butterfly
9. church
10. tax

B. Write each sentence below. Use the plural form of the noun in ( ).

11. Many ____ have Thanksgiving parades. (city)
12. The marchers' ____ get very tired. (foot)
13. We sat on ____ and watched a parade. (bench)
14. Some ____ have special dinners. (family)
15. We set the table with nice ____. (dish)
16. The plates were packed in two big ____. (box)
17. Leslie poured water into tall ____. (glass)
18. Kelly ate some ____. (cranberry)
19. Lee and I broke the wishbone and made ____. (wish)
20. We'll eat turkey ____ next week. (sandwich)

Application WRITING SENTENCES

Use the plural of each noun below in a sentence. You may draw a picture to go with one of your sentences.

baby   bush   branch   fox   man

4 — Singular Possessive Nouns

> ● A **possessive noun** shows ownership.
>
> ● To form the possessive of a singular noun, add an apostrophe and *s* ('**s**).

Some forms of nouns show that the person or thing named owns something. Read this sentence.

A peacock's tail is beautiful.

The word *peacock's* is a possessive noun. It shows that something belongs to the peacock. In this sentence, what belongs to the peacock?

Now read these sentences.

Tammy's aunt has a pet shop.
Mrs. Allen's canary sings all day.

The words *Tammy's* and *Mrs. Allen's* are possessive nouns. Each noun names one person. An apostrophe and *s* was added to *Tammy* and *Mrs. Allen* to form possessive nouns.

| Tammy | Mrs. Allen |
| Tammy's | Mrs. Allen's |

Skills Tryout

Spell the possessive form of each singular noun.

1. cousin
2. gull
3. Susan
4. boy
5. rooster
6. duck

Practice

A. Write the possessive form of each singular noun.

1. Eric
2. lady
3. boy
4. owl
5. king
6. grandfather
7. Ms. Elliott
8. parrot
9. hen
10. Dr. Ray

B. Write each sentence below. Use the possessive form of the noun in ( ).

EXAMPLE: We looked at ___ book. (Marco)
ANSWER: We looked at Marco's book.

11. ___ favorite bird is the kiwi. (Ellen)
12. The ___ feathers look like hair. (kiwi)
13. The kiwi is the ___ enemy. (worm)
14. The peacock is the ___ cousin. (chicken)
15. The ___ feathers are beautiful. (peacock)
16. Once ___ uncle saw an eagle in a tree. (Ralph)
17. The ___ nest was very large and high. (eagle)
18. My ___ book is about ostriches. (friend)
19. An ___ neck is long and thin. (ostrich)
20. ___ garden has a birdbath. (Miss Gold)

Application WRITING SENTENCES

Write three sentences. Use the possessive form of each singular noun below.

parakeet   Mr. Cohn   owl

> • To form the possessive of a plural noun that ends in s, add an apostrophe (').

Plural nouns have a special form to show ownership. Read these sentences.

1. **The boys play in the school band.**
2. **The boys' trumpets are made of brass.**

In sentence 1 *boys* is a plural noun. It ends in *s*. In sentence 2 *boys'* is a possessive noun. It ends with an apostrophe.

The plural possessive *boys'* shows that something belongs to the boys. What belongs to the boys?

Study the nouns in the chart. Notice how the plural possessive nouns are formed.

Plural Nouns	Plural Possessive Nouns
girls twins cities	girls' twins' cities'

Skills Tryout

Spell the possessive form of each plural noun.

1. players
2. actors
3. girls
4. dancers
5. cats
6. artists

Practice

A. Write the possessive form of each plural noun.

1. parents
2. boys
3. sisters
4. dogs
5. runners
6. teachers
7. writers
8. speakers
9. friends
10. families

B. Write each sentence below. Use the possessive form of the plural noun in ( ).

11. The ___ clarinets look alike. (twins)
12. The ___ stands are metal. (musicians)
13. The ___ feet move to the music. (players)
14. Those ___ voices are too soft. (singers)
15. The ___ songs were familiar to us. (students)
16. We watched both ___ marching bands. (schools)
17. Janet liked the ___ uniforms. (bands)
18. The ___ uniforms looked colorful. (marchers)
19. The ___ buttons were shining brightly. (jackets)
20. Two ___ hats blew off in the wind. (girls)

Application WRITING SENTENCES

Write three sentences about the musicians named below. Use the possessive form of each plural noun.

singers   drummers   choirs

6 — Compounds

> ● A **compound** is a word formed from two words.

Some words are formed from two smaller words. The new word is called a compound. Read these sentences.

1. Lisa carried her <u>sailboat</u> to the park.
2. She wore her <u>raincoat</u> and boots.

In sentence 1 *sailboat* is a compound. It is formed from *sail* and *boat.* What two words form the compound *raincoat* in sentence 2?

The two smaller words in each compound help to tell what the compound means.

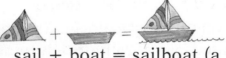

sail + boat = sailboat (a boat that sails)

rain + coat = raincoat (a coat for rain)

Skills Tryout

Say the two words that form each compound.

1. railroad
2. barnyard
3. skyscraper

4. grandfather
5. driveway
6. doghouse

Practice

A. Write the two words that form each compound.

EXAMPLE: storybook

ANSWER: story + book

1. airplane
2. notebook
3. spaceship
4. headache
5. campfire

6. watermelon
7. football
8. snowflake
9. sunshine
10. shoelace

B. Write the compound in each sentence below. Then write the two words that form the compound.

11. Ken's dad works on a steamship.
12. Keisha lives near the airport.
13. The newsboy delivered our paper.
14. Gary's skateboard has a green stripe.
15. Amanda jogged until sunset.
16. My cousin needed a wheelchair last month.
17. She broke her foot in our backyard.
18. Rhoda saw a picture of a houseboat.
19. The bedroom was very small.
20. We went fishing in a rowboat.

Application USING LANGUAGE

Use each pair of words below to form a compound. Write a sentence using each compound.

motor + boat

high + way

stop + light

road + side

Singular Nouns and Plural Nouns *pages 48–51*

A. Copy each sentence. Underline each singular noun. Draw a circle around each plural noun.

1. The boys picked apples at a farm.
2. My sister has new boots.
3. The officer blew a whistle at the cars.
4. The players rode a bus to the game.
5. The nurse talked to the students.

Spelling Plural Nouns *pages 52–53*

B. Write the plural form of each noun.

6. egg
7. wish
8. man
9. story
10. box

11. dress
12. inch
13. foot
14. tax
15. strawberry

Singular Possessive Nouns *pages 54–55*

C. Write the possessive form of each singular noun.

16. horse
17. doctor
18. Diana
19. Mrs. Lyon

20. pilot
21. elephant
22. brother
23. Perry

Plural Possessive Nouns *pages 56–57*

D. Write the possessive form of each plural noun.

24. teams
25. turtles
26. cousins
27. girls
28. uncles
29. monkeys
30. families

E. Write each sentence below. Use the possessive form of the noun in ( ).

31. That ___ eyes are green. (kitten)
32. My ___ house has a front porch. (aunt)
33. Many ___ barns are red. (farmers)
34. ___ friend brought a game to play. (Jason)
35. All the new ___ eyes are still shut. (puppies)
36. The ___ meeting lasted one hour. (teachers)
37. My ___ class reunion is in July. (sister)

Compounds *pages 58–59*

F. Write the two words that form each compound.

38. steamboat
39. mailbox
40. eggplant
41. campfire
42. raincoat
43. snowflakes
44. toothache
45. highway

See also Handbook pages 314–319.

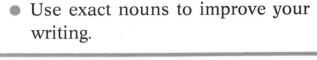

> ● Use exact nouns to improve your writing.

Read the sentences below.

1. Frank was frightened by an animal.
2. Frank was frightened by a lizard.

Sentence 1 tells us that Frank was frightened by an animal. But was he frightened by a butterfly? A goldfish? Sentence 1 does not tell exactly what kind of animal frightened Frank.

Sentence 2 tells exactly what kind of animal scared Frank. *Lizard* is an <u>exact</u> noun. It makes sentence 2 clearer than sentence 1.

Exact nouns are used in two of the sentences below.

My relative visited us.　　We went into the building.
My aunt visited us.　　　We went into the store.

Try to use exact nouns in your own writing. They help to tell the reader exactly what you mean.

The Noun Game　Look at the list of nouns below. Think of more exact nouns for each one. Write at least three exact nouns for each word.

game	insect	room
flower	fruit	clothes

Grammar
and Writing
Workshop

The Noun Switch Write each sentence. Use a more exact noun for the underlined word. Use a word from the Noun Bank, or use a noun of your own.

```
─────────── Noun Bank ───────────
  kitten    lunch    parakeet   bait    grin
  runner    frown    bottles    cans    boxer
```

1. My <u>pet</u> won first prize at the pet show.
2. I packed <u>stuff</u> for our fishing trip.
3. A famous <u>athlete</u> visited our gym class.
4. I knew how Pete felt from the <u>look</u> on his face.
5. Somebody filled our playground with <u>junk</u>.

Change-a-Noun Write each sentence. Change the underlined noun to a more exact noun.

6. That store sells <u>toys</u>.
7. A small <u>animal</u> scampered by.
8. We went to the new <u>building</u> on our block.
9. The door closed with a loud <u>sound</u>.
10. A <u>person</u> gave us directions to the park.

Using the Thesaurus

Suppose you could take a trip somewhere. Where would you go? Write three sentences about a trip, but don't use the word *trip*. Find the entry for *trip* in the Thesaurus. It begins on page 367. Use three different synonyms for *trip* in your sentences.

> ● In most stories, the main character must solve a problem.

Read this story to find out how good sense can be used to solve a problem. Some words in the story are underlined. Their meanings are given at the bottom of each page.

The Practical Princess

by Jay Williams

Princess Bedelia was as lovely as the moon shining upon a lake full of water lilies. She was as graceful as a cat leaping. And she was also extremely practical.

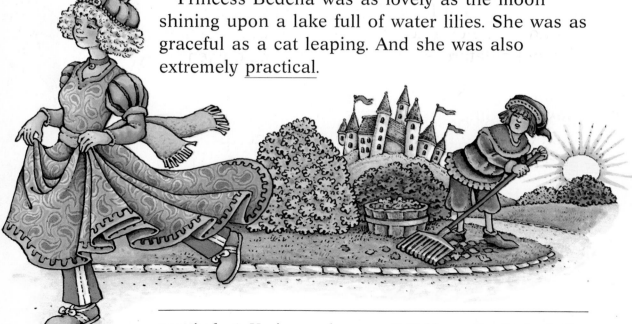

---

practical 1. Having good sense. 2. Taking action instead of daydreaming.

When she was born, three fairies came to her cradle to give her gifts as was usual in that country. The first fairy gave her beauty. The second gave her <u>grace</u>. But the third, who was a wise old creature, said, "I give her <u>common sense</u>."

"I don't think much of that gift," said King Ludwig, raising his eyebrows. "What good is common sense to a princess? All she needs is <u>charm</u>."

Nevertheless, when Bedelia was eighteen years old, something happened that made the king change his mind.

---

grace Beauty of movement.
common sense Good sense; good judgment.
charm The power to please or delight others.

A dragon moved into the neighborhood. He settled in a dark cave on top of a mountain, and the first thing he did was to send a message to the king. "I must have a princess to devour," the message said, "or I shall breathe out my fiery breath and destroy the kingdom."

Sadly, King Ludwig called together his councillors and read them the message. "Perhaps," said the Prime Minister, "we had better advertise for a knight to slay the dragon. That is what is generally done in these cases."

"I'm afraid we haven't time," answered the king. "The dragon has only given us until tomorrow morning. There is no help for it. We shall have to send him the princess."

Princess Bedelia had come to the meeting because, as she said, she liked to mind her own business, and this was certainly her business. "Rubbish!" she said. "Dragons can't tell the difference between princesses and anyone else. Use your common sense. He's just asking for me because he's a snob."

---

devour   Eat up; destroy.
councillors   People chosen to give advice.
Prime Minister   Main adviser to a king or head of state.
slay   Strike; kill.
snob   A person who likes only people who are rich or high in rank.

"That may be so," said her father, "but if we don't send you along, he'll destroy the kingdom."

"Right!" said Bedelia. "I see I'll have to deal with this myself." She left the <u>council chamber</u>. She got the largest and <u>gaudiest</u> of her state robes, stuffed it with straw, and tied it together with string. Into the center of the bundle she packed about a hundred pounds of gunpowder. She got two strong young men to carry it up the mountain for her. She stood in front of the dragon's cave and called, "Come out! Here's the princess!" The dragon came blinking and <u>peering</u> out of the darkness. Seeing the bright robe covered with gold and silver <u>embroidery</u>, and hearing Bedelia's voice, he opened his mouth wide.

---

council chamber   A room where meetings are held.
gaudiest   Showiest; flashiest.
peering   Looking searchingly.
embroidery   Fancy designs on cloth made by stitching with colored thread.

At once, at Bedelia's signal, the two young men swung the robe and gave it a good <u>heave</u>, right down the dragon's throat. Bedelia threw herself flat on the ground, and the two young men ran.

As the gunpowder met the flames inside the dragon, there was a tremendous explosion.

Bedelia got up, dusting herself off. "Dragons," she said, "are not very bright."

She left the two young men sweeping up the pieces, and she went back to the castle to have her <u>geography</u> lesson, for as you know, she was very practical.

heave   The act of throwing with great effort.
geography   The study of the earth's surface; the study of maps of the earth.

About the Story

1. What happened when Bedelia was a baby?
2. What happened when Bedelia was eighteen years old?
3. In a fairy tale, what character usually kills the dragon? How do you know?
4. A story builds up to the most exciting part. What was the most exciting part of this story?
5. What did Bedelia prove about the gift of common sense?

Activities

Try acting out the story of "The Practical Princess." You will need a narrator and these characters: Princess Bedelia, King Ludwig, three fairies, the dragon, councillors, the Prime Minister, and two young men.

Here are some ways to act out the story.

- One person, the narrator, reads the story aloud. The characters act out the story without speaking.

- The characters read the words that are in quotation marks. They also perform actions. A narrator reads the rest of the story.

- The characters get together first and talk about what they want to do and say. Then they act out the story, using their own words. After that a new set of characters is chosen. They act out the story, using their own words.

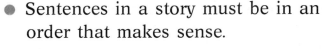

- Sentences in a story must be in an order that makes sense.
- Words such as *first, next, then, finally, soon, later,* and *last* help put a story in order.

Read what Gino told his friend Sammy John about the story "Jack and the Beanstalk."

Jack climbed the beanstalk. Jack planted seeds outside his window. He took the golden harp and ran away. Jack cut down the beanstalk. A beanstalk began to grow. It grew and grew until it reached the sky. He saw a giant with a golden harp.

Do you think Sammy John understood Gino's story? Did Gino's story make sense?

Now read the story again. Notice how the underlined words help put the story in order.

<u>First</u> Jack planted seeds outside his window. <u>Then</u> a beanstalk began to grow. It grew and grew until it reached the sky. <u>Next</u> Jack climbed the beanstalk. <u>Soon</u> he saw a giant with a golden harp. <u>Later</u> he took the golden harp and ran away. <u>Finally</u> Jack cut down the beanstalk.

Read the story. Tell which seven words help put the story in an order that makes sense.

Two friends built a fort. First they gathered some wood. Then they put the walls together. Next they added a roof and a door. They put on a doorknob last. Finally it was finished. Later they made up a password. Soon they will have a meeting there.

Practice

The sentences below tell about the story "The Practical Princess" on page 64. Write the sentences in the right order. Watch for clue words.

1. The dragon wanted to devour a princess.
2. Soon Princess Bedelia had a plan.
3. When Princess Bedelia was born, three fairies gave her gifts.
4. Later a dragon moved into the neighborhood.
5. Then the king and his councillors held a meeting to decide what to do.
6. Finally Princess Bedelia and some young men destroyed the dragon with gunpowder.

Application TELLING A STORY

Think of a story you really enjoyed. Share it with a friend. Be sure to tell the story in the right order.

9

Telling About a TV Show

> • Not all TV shows are alike. Some are about real life. Others are make-believe stories.

Paul and Ellie talked about TV shows they had seen. One of the shows was about a car. The other show was about campers. Read these paragraphs about the shows.

I saw a show about a magic car! It started, and it took itself to a gas station. It told the clerk it was thirsty. Then it chased some bank robbers. Every once in a while, the car would float through the air. Finally the little car went back to its own garage. Its owner never even knew it had left!

I saw a show about campers in the winter snow. First their gear got wet when their canoe overturned. Then one camper slipped on an icy rock and twisted an ankle. They waited for hours before help came. Finally someone heard their frightened calls. At last a helicopter rescued them. It ended happily after all!

Skills Tryout

Tell the answer to each question below. Use the paragraphs about the TV shows.

1. Which show told about something that could happen in real life?
2. Which show told a make-believe story?

Practice

A. Write the answer to each question. Use the paragraphs about the TV shows on page 72.

> 1. Which words help put the paragraph about the magic car in order?
> 2. Which words help put the paragraph about the campers in order?

B. Write *real* or *make-believe* for each TV show described below.

> 3. flying elephants deliver mail in Kansas
> 4. an airline pilot loses her suitcase on a bus
> 5. Spinner Spider has a school for ladybugs
> 6. a famous chef shows how to bake onion rolls
> 7. Mr. Tatum buys a talking trumpet
> 8. a supermarket runs out of candles during a power failure
> 9. a group of singers tours the United States
> 10. two tigers decide to turn into kittens

Application SPEAKING

Think of a TV show you watched. Share it with a classmate. Be sure to tell what happened in the right order. Ask your classmate to decide if the show you watched was about something real or make-believe.

10 — Writing a Story

> ● A **story** tells what happens. It tells how the character solves a problem.

Writing Project

"Once upon a time, long ago and far away … ." Many stories begin that way. Do those words make you curious? Do you want to know what happened?

Through the ages people have enjoyed stories. In this lesson you will write your own story to read to the class. You will see how a picture and your imagination can make you a storyteller.

1. Prewriting

You will need an idea for your story. A picture can give you just the idea you need. Try it with this picture.

Imagine you are stepping into the picture. Think about these questions:

Where are you going?
Why are you going there?
Who do you meet?
What is going to happen?
What will you do?
How do you feel?

▶ The answers to the questions will help you create a story. Talk about the questions with your classmates. Write down your favorite answer to each question.

2. Writing

There are many ways to begin a story. Here are three story beginnings you can use:

- Once upon a time …
- One day I stepped into a picture …
- Once long ago, …

▶ Write your story as if you were telling it to someone. Use your favorite answers to the questions about the picture. Tell how your character solves a problem. Write your story quickly to get all your ideas on paper.

3. Revising

▶ Read your story to someone who would like to listen. What did your listener think of your story? How can it be improved? This checklist will give you help.

Revision Checklist
- Did I tell what happened?
- Did I tell how the character solves a problem?
- Did I tell my readers how I felt?
- Did I choose the best words?

Read the sample. Notice how choosing the best words made the story better.

Once long ago, the king of a ~~big~~ **huge** ~~cassel~~ **castle** ~~asked~~ **invited** me to come to a **feast** ~~meal~~. Was the

Once long ago, the king of a huge castle invited me to come to a feast. Was the king trying to trick me? No one had ever been able to find the secret road to the king's castle. I started up the steep hill in front of the castle and stumbled over a rock. The rock was covering a deep hole. My heart pounded as I peeked into the hole and spotted the king's secret road!

▶ Now use the editing marks to make changes in your story.

4. Publishing

▶ Proofread your story. Place a ruler under the first line. Read one line at a time. Slide the ruler down as you read. This makes it easier to check your work. Use the Proofreading Checklist on this page or the one in the Young Writer's Handbook on page 355. Use the editing marks to make corrections.

▶ Illustrate your story, if you wish. Then read your story to your classmates. Do you enjoy reading aloud? Read your story to a younger child or someone at home.

EDITING MARKS

—— cross out

∧ add

¶ indent

◯ check spelling

PROOFREADING CHECKLIST

1. indent paragraphs ☑
2. capital letters ☑
3. end punctuation ☑
4. spelling ☑
5. handwriting ☑

Writing Project

A Paper-Plate Mask

Make a paper-plate mask of your favorite story character. You and your classmates can then wear your masks to act out stories.

Draw a face and color it. Cut out holes for the eyes. Then punch a small hole on each side of the plate. The holes should be a little above the eyes. Put a string through the holes to hold the mask on.

If you wish, glue on yarn or paper curls for hair. You might use a paper bag instead of a paper plate for your mask.

Mathematics

In this unit you used words to tell a story. Did you know that numbers can tell a story, too? Here is an example.

Polly walked dogs to earn money. Altogether she had five dogs to walk. The graph below shows how many she walked each day, Monday through Friday.

▶ Try it. Use the graph to tell a story. Tell how many dogs Polly walked on Monday, on Tuesday, on Wednesday, and so on.

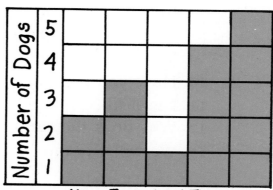

Writers at Work People who take surveys use numbers each day to record their findings. Survey takers gather information. They ask such questions as: *Is the city getting larger, or smaller? How many people ride buses to work?*

▶ Try it. Ask your classmates a question that can be answered with a number. Examples: *How many states have you lived in? How many sisters do you have? How many pencils are in your desk?* Record the results. Then tell the class what you found out.

Nouns   *pages 48–57*

A. One of the words in each pair is a noun.
Write the nouns.

1. book, around
2. after, school
3. candle, now
4. soft, clock
5. glad, tree
6. door, bad

B. Write *singular* or *plural* for each underlined noun.

7. Jimmy took <u>pictures</u> at the parade.
8. Everyone brought a <u>blanket</u> to the picnic.
9. Woodchucks live in <u>holes</u> underground.
10. Have you ever tried catching <u>butterflies</u>?
11. Carol filled her <u>glass</u> with water.
12. Why does the <u>sun</u> go down at night?
13. We will buy the <u>tickets</u> this afternoon.

C. Write the plural form of each noun.

14. lunch
15. dish
16. ax
17. baby
18. man
19. wish
20. fox
21. bench
22. foot

D. Write the possessive form of each noun.

23. Tom
24. friend
25. Mr. Ling
26. aunts
27. Stacy
28. students
29. zebra
30. girls
31. hen

Checkpoint: Unit 2

Compounds   *pages 58–59*

E. Write the two words that form each compound.

32. sunrise   34. toothpaste
33. bluebird   35. newspaper

Stories   *pages 64–73*

F. Write *real* or *make-believe* for each TV show described below.

36. firefighters rescue people from a burning house
37. a talking mouse tricks a curious cat
38. elves help a shoemaker finish his work
39. a girl takes her first airplane ride
40. a duck teaches a fish how to fly

G. Write four words that help to put the story in order.

Tracy made a birthday card for Sam. First she found some paper and crayons. Then she wrote a birthday message on the card. Finally the card was finished. Soon Tracy will give the card to Sam.

H. Imagine that you are writing a story about a boy named Rick who finds a lost puppy in the park. Write four sentences that tell what Rick does with the puppy.

See also Handbook pages 314–319.

Checkpoint: Unit 2

Sentences   *pages 4–17*

A. Write *yes* if the word group is a sentence. Write *no* if the word group is not a sentence.

1. Liz ran quickly.
2. Two other girls.
3. Across the field.
4. He won the race.

B. Write each group of words in sentence order.

5. big Owls birds are.
6. likes skate Pam to.
7. lunch his Tom made.
8. found I penny the.

C. Write each sentence correctly. Use a capital letter and put the correct mark at the end.

9. open the window
10. how cold the wind is
11. we ride the bus
12. can you see me
13. what a big cat that is
14. wear your sneakers
15. will you be late
16. she plays the flute

D. Write *subject* if the subject is underlined. Write *predicate* if the predicate is underlined.

17. We <u>laughed at the funny joke</u>.
18. <u>Ken and his friend</u> waved to us.
19. Our class <u>will march in the parade</u>.
20. A little girl <u>rang the doorbell</u>.
21. <u>Two green trucks</u> drove over the bridge.
22. <u>My dog</u> barked at the strange sound.

Cumulative Review

Nouns *pages 48–57*

E. Write the noun in each pair of words.

23. across, book   **25.** candle, about
24. mitten, loud   **26.** thin, coat

F. Write *singular* if the underlined noun is singular. Write *plural* if the underlined noun is plural.

27. <u>Robins</u> live in our oak tree.
28. My <u>sister</u> likes to dance.
29. How many <u>cherries</u> did you eat?
30. Andy wrote <u>letters</u> to his friends.
31. Ben did not wear his new <u>hat</u>.
32. Did you see the <u>giraffe</u>?

G. Write the plural form of each noun.

33. dress   **37.** party
34. family   **38.** tax
35. bush   **39.** woman
36. sandwich **40.** dish

H. Write the possessive form of each noun.

41. turkey   **44.** teachers
42. ladies   **45.** children
43. Mr. Smith **46.** chair

Grammar
Nouns

Composition
Creating

George Washington

I wonder if George Washington
Was very fond of books,
And if he liked to hunt and fish
And wade in little brooks.

I wonder if his pockets bulged
Like mine with precious things,
With marbles, cookies, tops, and balls,
And nails, and glass, and strings.

I wonder if he whistled tunes
While mending broken toys—
My father says George Washington
Was much like other boys.

—Winifred Catherine Marshall

Common Nouns and Proper Nouns

> ● A **common noun** names any person, place, or thing.
>
> ● A **proper noun** names a particular person, place, or thing.

A noun names a person, place, or thing. Some nouns name a particular person, place, or thing. Read these sentences. The nouns are underlined.

1. The <u>woman</u> was born in this <u>country</u>.
2. <u>Clara Barton</u> was born in <u>America</u>.

In sentence 1 *woman* and *country* are common nouns. They do not tell which woman or which place is named. In sentence 2 *Clara Barton* and *America* are proper nouns. They name a particular person and a particular place.

Some proper nouns have more than one word. Find the proper nouns below. Each important word in a proper noun begins with a capital letter.

Grant Public School   desk   **Statue of Liberty**

Skills Tryout

Tell if each noun is a common noun or a proper noun.

1. Los Angeles
2. building
3. Gulf of Mexico
4. tree
5. school
6. Cozy Inn

Practice

A. Copy the underlined nouns from the sentences below. Write *common* beside each common noun. Write *proper* beside each proper noun.

1. <u>Clara Barton</u> lived in the <u>United States of America</u>.
2. She taught at a <u>school</u> in <u>New Jersey</u>.
3. She helped the <u>soldiers</u> who were injured.
4. <u>Clara</u> began the <u>American Red Cross</u>.
5. Our <u>city</u> named <u>Barton Park</u> after her.
6. In <u>December</u> there was a <u>flood</u> in <u>Riverdale</u>.
7. Some <u>families</u> lost their <u>homes</u>.
8. Many <u>people</u> needed <u>help</u>.
9. The <u>workers</u> served <u>meals</u> at <u>Tracy Hospital</u>.
10. A <u>man</u> read a <u>story</u> to some <u>children</u>.

B. Each sentence below has two nouns. Write them. Then write *common* or *proper* beside each noun.

EXAMPLE: Stacy is a nurse.

ANSWER: Stacy, proper   nurse, common

11. A nurse cares for people.
12. Amy Jones works at a hospital.
13. Some doctors visit schools.
14. The dentist checks the students.
15. Sara works at Cook School.

Application WRITING SENTENCES

Write three sentences about your city or town. Use at least one proper noun in each sentence.

2 Capital Letters for Names and Titles

> ● Each word in the name of a person or pet begins with a capital letter.

The names of people and pets are proper nouns.

John Arthur Reese　　**Lassie**　　**Alex**

Each word in each name begins with a capital letter.

Titles are sometimes used with the names of people. Notice the underlined titles below.

<u>Mrs.</u> Paula Bay　　<u>Mr.</u> Phil Uno　　<u>Miss</u> Leah Kaye
<u>Ms.</u> Tamara Juris　　<u>Dr.</u> Mary Jo Smith

Some titles are abbreviations. An **abbreviation** is a shortened form of a word. For instance, *Dr.* is the abbreviation for *Doctor.* Many abbreviations begin with a capital letter and end with a period.

An **initial** is the first letter of a name. An initial may stand for a person's name. It is written with a capital letter and is followed by a period.

Joe <u>C.</u> West　　<u>T. R.</u> Jackson　　<u>S.</u> Byron

Skills Tryout

Tell how to write each name correctly.

1. ms c rice
2. rin tin tin
3. sue ann lang
4. dr james r black
5. l r beck
6. trigger

Practice

A. Write each name correctly.

1. debra e bowles
2. p f lupa
3. mr nathan p davis
4. miss l k bloom
5. rodney thomas lewis
6. k r randall
7. dr juanita diaz
8. sandy c gates
9. mrs brenda zak
10. ms gail ong

B. Write each sentence correctly.

11. mrs nancy rose trains dogs.
12. We took our puppy named j j to her class.
13. I saw barbara tracy and her gray poodle.
14. Her dog is named smoky.
15. The trainer is mr k g benton.
16. He helped miss t payne with her collie.
17. The collie ran to dr evans.
18. The smallest dog belongs to ray brown.
19. His terrier is named tiny terry.
20. The spotted dog belongs to ms rachel wolfe.
21. My brother jerry likes books about dogs.
22. His favorite author is albert p terhune.
23. Have you met miss p adams?
24. She and craig ellis work at the pet shop.
25. She sold a puppy to c w shay.

Application WRITING SENTENCES

Write three sentences about familiar people and pets. Use initials, titles, and abbreviations.

> ● Each word in the name of a street, town, city, or state begins with a capital letter.

Names of particular places are proper nouns. Look at the underlined proper nouns in these sentences. Notice that each word in each name begins with a capital letter.

My cousins live on North Bell Road in Phoenix. Phoenix and Tucson are cities in Arizona.

Look at the map below. Find the place names. How does each word in each name begin?

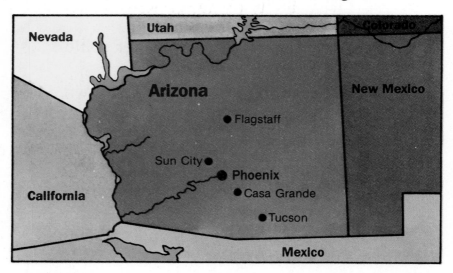

Skills Tryout

Tell how to write each place name correctly.

1. glendale
2. yuma
3. new mexico
4. valley road
5. second street
6. central avenue

Practice

A. Write these place names correctly.

1. nevada
2. grand canyon drive
3. safford
4. denver
5. peach springs

6. lincoln avenue
7. colorado
8. san francisco
9. east balboa way
10. south dakota

B. Write these sentences correctly.

11. Kevin lives in new jersey.
12. He read about arizona, the forty-eighth state.
13. He learned about an empty town named jerome.
14. Every year a city named prescott has a rodeo.
15. The rodeo parade begins on main street.
16. There is a museum near tucson.
17. A city called yuma is close to california.
18. There are copper mines near tucson and miami.
19. florida also has a city named miami.
20. A big park in mesa is near university avenue.

Application WRITING SENTENCES

Write a complete sentence to answer each question. Use proper nouns.

a. What is the name of your state?
b. What city would you like to visit?
c. What street is your school on?
d. What is another city or town in your state?

Capital Letters for Calendar Words

- The name of a day or month begins with a capital letter.
- The name of a holiday or special day begins with a capital letter.

Look at the calendar for February. The names of the month and the days begin with capital letters.

February

Sunday	Monday	Tuesday	Wednesday	Thursday	Friday	Saturday
			National Freedom Day 1	Groundhog Day 2	3	4
5	6	7	8	9	10	National Inventors' Day 11
Lincoln's Birthday 12	13	Valentine's Day 14	Susan B. Anthony Day 15	16	17	18

Find the names of holidays and special days on the calendar. How does each word in each name begin?

Skills Tryout

Read the sentences below. Find the names of days, months, holidays, and special days. Tell how to write these names correctly.

1. Susan B. Anthony was born in february.
2. Sally made a poster for lincoln's birthday.
3. The last monday in may is memorial day.
4. On arbor day our class planted trees.
5. Every tuesday and thursday we go to the library.

Practice

A. Find the names of days, months, holidays, and special days. Write these names correctly.

1. Christine's party is next wednesday.
2. My little brother was born in may.
3. Calvin's birthday is on groundhog day.
4. Did you see the parade on thanksgiving day?
5. Every saturday Larry has a piano lesson.
6. Helen Keller was born in june.
7. Some schools open in august.
8. Banks are closed on washington's birthday.
9. In Norway mother's day is in february.
10. The first moon landing was in july of 1969.

B. Write each sentence correctly.

11. The first day of may is bird day in some states.
12. Our class made cards for valentine's day.
13. Our school opens the tuesday after labor day.
14. In Canada thanksgiving day is in october.
15. columbus day is also called discovery day.

Application   FILLING OUT FORMS

Copy the form below. Fill out the form to win a free birthday toy. Use capital letters correctly.

BIRTHDAY DRAWING FOR FREE TOY
Name _____ Phone _____
Birthday _____ Age _____

5 — Using Commas

> - Use a comma after *yes* or *no* at the beginning of a sentence.
> - Use a comma after the name of a person spoken to.

A comma (,) is a special mark that is used in sentences. It tells you to stop for a moment between words. Read the sentences below. Notice the commas.

1. Jonathan, have you seen the school play yet?
2. No, I do not have a ticket.
3. Tanya, you know what the play is about.
4. Yes, it is about a magic nutcracker.

Sentences 1 and 3 begin with the names of persons. Jonathan and Tanya are being spoken to. A comma comes after each name.

In sentences 2 and 4 the commas come after the words *yes* and *no*.

Skills Tryout

Tell where a comma is needed in each sentence.

1. Mrs. Kwam tell us the story.
2. Yes the nutcracker is a toy soldier.
3. Valerie did you bring the album to school?
4. No you can listen to it tomorrow.
5. Danny look at the colorful costumes.

Practice

A. Write the sentences. Use commas where they are needed.

1. Tina are you going to dance in the program?
2. Cliff let's watch her practice.
3. Peter play the music for the sugarplum fairies.
4. Alicia show us the costume you will wear when you play the part of Clara.
5. Tony go see the play about the nutcracker.

B. Write a sentence to answer each question below. Begin each sentence with *Yes* or *No*. Use commas where they are needed.

EXAMPLE: Do you like music?
ANSWER: Yes, I do like music.
   (or)   No, I do not like music.

6. Did you try for a part in the program?
7. Have you heard the orchestra play?
8. Do you play a musical instrument?
9. Do you like to sing?
10. Would you like to take dance lessons?

Application WRITING SENTENCES

Pretend that you are a talking toy. Your friends don't know who you are. Write three sentences that will give them clues and help them to recognize you. Begin each sentence with a different name followed by a comma.

> ● A **context clue** helps you understand the meaning of a new word.

Read the sentences below.

1. Beth is a <u>brilliant</u>, or very intelligent, girl.
2. That stone is <u>brilliant</u>, not dull.

The word *brilliant* has more than one meaning. You must read all of each sentence to get the right meaning. In sentence 1 *very intelligent* is a clue that *brilliant* means "smart." In sentence 2 *not dull* is a clue that *brilliant* means "shiny," the opposite of *dull.*

Clues to meaning may also be in other sentences.

The town was <u>deserted</u>. It was empty.

The second sentence helps you to know that *deserted* means "empty."

Skills Tryout

Tell what you think each underlined word means.

1. Very heavy rain will <u>damage</u>, not help, the plants.
2. The large pool was <u>shallow</u>, instead of deep.
3. She drank hot chicken <u>broth</u>, a clear soup.
4. The roof <u>collapsed</u>. It had to be repaired.
5. David <u>devoured</u> his meal. The plate was clean.

Practice

A. Read each sentence or group of sentences. Write what you think the underlined word means.

1. The airplane began to <u>descend</u>. The wheels were lowered to help it land.
2. The pilot received <u>instructions</u> from the tower. He could hear the directions on his radio.
3. The pilot <u>maneuvered</u>, or moved, the plane to the gate.
4. The plane came to a <u>gradual</u>, not sudden, stop.
5. The passengers began to <u>disembark</u>. Finally everyone was off.
6. The flight had been <u>uneventful</u> and dull.

B. Write what you think each underlined word means.

7. Be careful and <u>mind</u> the baby when Mom leaves.
8. Yes, you may turn on the TV. She doesn't <u>mind</u>.
9. I'm in a hurry. I can only wait for one <u>second</u>.
10. Al didn't win, but he placed <u>second</u> in the race.

Application USING LANGUAGE

Each sentence below gives a clue to the meaning of the underlined word. Write the underlined words. After each word, write the clue.

a. They wore strange, <u>outlandish</u> costumes.
b. He was <u>generous</u>, not selfish, like his sister.
c. The class was so noisy, I couldn't hear above the <u>racket</u>.

Common Nouns and Proper Nouns *pages 86–87*

A. Write the nouns. Then write *common* or *proper* beside each noun.

1. Lonnie Gray
2. coyote
3. West Germany
4. Fresno State College
5. ranch
6. Grand Hotel
7. theater
8. Montreal Expos

B. Write each sentence. Underline each common noun. Draw a circle around each proper noun.

9. The South Pole is covered with ice and snow.
10. Dr. Reed looked at the sick puppy.
11. The team played at Grant School.
12. My relatives live in Switzerland.
13. Heidi wants to visit this country.
14. Samantha rode her bicycle on Oak Avenue.

Capital Letters for Names and Titles *pages 88–89*

C. Write each sentence. Use capital letters and periods correctly.

15. My piano teacher is mr ted hauser.
16. We saw dr steven b pearl at the beach.
17. My cousin eddie has a cat named hot shot.
18. Did mrs r caruso call you yet?
19. I think ms angela duran won the contest.
20. This book is about george washington carver.

Capital Letters for Place Names and Calendar Words *pages 90–93*

D. Write each place name or calendar word correctly.

21. kansas city
22. south elm street
23. january
24. grandparent's day
25. rhode island

Using Commas *pages 94–95*

E. Write the sentences. Use commas where they are needed.

26. Pauline have you ever seen a windmill?
27. Yes Golden Gate Park has several windmills.
28. Ivan tell us about your trip.
29. No we are not having pizza for lunch today.
30. Yes I would like to go skating with you.

Context Clues *pages 96–97*

F. Write what you think each underlined word means.

31. Too much salt <u>spoiled</u> the soup. It tasted awful.
32. The storm <u>demolished</u> the treehouse. We had to build it again.
33. The pilot <u>contacted</u> the control tower by radio to ask directions.
34. The sun's <u>glaring</u> light hurt her eyes. Gina put on sunglasses.
35. He is a <u>loyal</u> friend. He stands by me.

See also Handbook pages 320–321, 356–361.

Writing with Proper Nouns

> ● Use proper nouns to add detail to your writing.

Grammar and Writing Workshop

Read the sentences below.

1. We flew to the city and saw the sights.
2. We flew to Washington, D.C., and saw the White House and the Capitol.

Sentence 1 tells us that sights were seen in a city. Sentence 2 is a stronger, better sentence. It tells us the exact sights that were seen. It tells us the exact city, too. The proper nouns *Washington, D.C.*, *White House*, and *Capitol* tell important details in sentence 2.

The Proper Noun Game Look at the list of nouns below. Each one could be replaced by proper nouns.

Copy the list. Then write at least three proper nouns for each common noun.

EXAMPLE: country
ANSWER: France, United States of America, Mexico

hero	store	state
singer	teacher	school

Compare your list with a classmate's list. Did you write any of the same proper nouns?

The Proper Noun Switch Write at least two proper nouns for each underlined word below. Use words from the Proper Noun Bank, or use proper nouns of your own.

```
┌──────────────── Proper Noun Bank ─────────────────┐
│ Boston    Royals           Albert Einstein   Mercury │
│ Jupiter   Susan B. Anthony  Dodgers           Chicago │
└────────────────────────────────────────────────────┘
```

1. The city is known for its fine museums.
2. We saw a fine portrait of a famous American.
3. I built a model of a planet last week.
4. Rick might play for the baseball team someday.

Add-a-Proper Noun The subject of the paragraph below is you! Write the paragraph. Use proper nouns to complete the sentences.

I was born in the month of ___. I live on ___ in the town of ___. ___ is one of my best friends. My favorite actor is ___.

Using the Thesaurus

Find the Thesaurus entry for *leader*. Write each sentence. Use a different synonym for *leader* in each.

a. The leader gave orders to the troops.
b. Who is the leader of that tribe of American Indians?
c. Zubin Mehta is the leader of an orchestra.
d. The country honored its leader.

Reading Poetry Aloud

> ● Many poems are fun to read aloud and listen to.

Read these poems aloud just to enjoy them.

How to Eat a Poem

Girls: Don't be polite.
Boys: Bite in.
Girls: Pick it up with your fingers and lick the juice that may run down your chin.
Boys: It is ready and ripe now, whenever you are.

All: You do not need a knife or fork or spoon or plate or napkin or tablecloth.

Solo 1: For there is no core
Solo 2: or stem
Solo 3: or rind
Solo 4: or pit
Solo 5: or seed
Solo 6: or skin
　　　　to throw away.
　　　　—*Eve Merriam*

April Rain Song

Solo 1: Let the rain kiss you.
Solo 2: Let the rain beat upon your head with silver liquid drops.
Solo 3: Let the rain sing you a lullaby.

All: The rain makes still pools on the sidewalk. The rain makes running pools in the gutter.
Solo 4: The rain plays a little sleep-song on our roof at night—

All: And I love the rain.
　　　　—*Langston Hughes*

from **Knitted Things**

Group 1: There was a witch who knitted things:
           Elephants and playground swings.
Solo: She knitted rain,
           She knitted night,
           But nothing really came out right.
Group 2: The elephants had just one tusk
           And night looked more
           Like dawn or dusk.
                                    —*Karla Kuskin*

Who Has Seen the Wind?

Group 1: Who has seen the wind?
               Neither I nor you:
           But when the leaves hang trembling
           The wind is passing through.

Group 2: Who has seen the wind?
               Neither you nor I:
           But when the trees bow down their heads
           The wind is passing by.
                                    —*Christina Georgina Rossetti*

About the Poems

Rhyming words end with the same sounds: *sun*
and *done, clean* and *green, cricket* and *ticket.*

1. Name the words that rhyme in the poem
   about knitted things.
2. Do any of the lines in "April Rain Song" rhyme?

Activity

Look through a poetry book. Find a poem you
really like. Practice reading it aloud. Then share it.

8 Listening for Comparisons in Poetry

> ● Poems often contain comparisons.

Listen to these poems. Listen for comparisons. A **comparison** tells how one thing is like another.

1. Frog

The spotted frog
Sits quite still
On a wet stone;

He is green
With a luster
Of water on his skin;

His back is mossy
With spots, and green
Like moss on a stone;

His gold-circled eyes
Stare hard
Like bright metal rings;

When he leaps
He is like a stone
Thrown into the pond;

Water rings spread
After him, bright circles
Of green, circles of gold.
—*Valerie Worth*

2. The Rains of Spring
Arranged by Olive Beaupré Miller

The rains of spring
Which hang to the branches
Of the green willow,
Look like pearls upon a string.
—*Lady Ise*

3. A Modern Dragon

A train is a dragon that roars through the dark.
He wriggles his tail as he sends up a spark.
He pierces the night with his one yellow eye,
And all the earth trembles when he rushes by.
—*Rowena Bastin Bennett*

About the Poems

Poem 1 **1.** What is the frog's green color like?
        2. What are his gold-circled eyes like?

Poem 2 **3.** What looks like "pearls upon a string"?

Poem 3 **4.** What is the train compared to?
        5. What is the train's "one yellow eye"?

Activities

A. Choose one of these: a frog, raindrops, a train. Make up your own comparison about what you choose. Tell how it looks or sounds or feels like something else. You might also compare how it moves.

B. Read the poems below. Answer the questions.

> In spring the chirping
> frogs sing like birds ... in summer
> they bark like old dogs.
> —*Onitsura*

Central Park Tourney

Cars
In the Park
With long spear lights
Ride at each other
Like armored knights.
—*Mildred Weston*

What do the frogs sing like? What do they bark like? What are the cars in the park like?

9 — Writing Comparisons

> ● The words *like* and *as* may be used to compare things.

In Lesson 8 you listened for comparisons that poets wrote. You may not be a poet, but you use comparisons, too. You use them when you say things like this: *I'm as hungry as a bear. ... Amy swims like a fish. ... Your hands are like ice!*

Read the poem below.

Whispers

Whispers
    tickle through your ear
    telling things you like to hear.

Whispers
    are as soft as skin
    letting little words curl in.

Whispers
    come so they can blow
    secrets others never know.
                —*Myra Cohn Livingston*

What is a whisper compared to in the second verse of the poem? How are the two things alike?

Skills Tryout

Tell how each of the things below can be compared to something else. Compare their colors, shapes, or the way they look.

1. a football
2. a STOP sign
3. a mouse
4. a snowflake
5. a carrot
6. a leaf

Practice

Write each group of words. Complete the comparisons.

EXAMPLE: as orange as …
ANSWER: as orange as the blazing sun

1. as blue as …
2. a sailboat that looks like …
3. pale green like …
4. as bright red as …
5. the round moon that looks like …
6. a butterfly that looks like …
7. as fast as …
8. an umbrella that looks like …
9. golden like …
10. as slippery as …

Application WRITING COMPARISONS

Choose one of the shells. Write some sentences to tell what it looks like. Make comparisons. Tell what else has the same color or colors. Tell what its shape reminds you of.

10 — Writing a Poem

Writing Project

> ● A **poem** may use comparisons to "paint" a word picture.

You have been reading and listening to poems. Now you will be the poet. You will write a poem about your favorite month or time of the year. In your poem you will use comparisons to "paint" word pictures. Then you and your classmates will make a poetry calendar.

1. Prewriting

▶ What will you write about? Ask yourself: *What time of year do I like best? Do some months remind me of special things?* Then choose a favorite month or time of year for your poem.

▶ Close your eyes and picture yourself in your favorite time of year. What do you see? Hear? Feel? Smell? Taste? Jot down your ideas as quickly as you can. Write down words and groups of words. Use the pictures of the seasons for ideas.

Look at the list you made. What did you write about? What did it remind you of? Write comparisons for some of the things on your list.

2. Writing

▶ Write the first line of your poem. There are many ways to begin. Here are three examples:

- My favorite month (time of year) is …
- The best thing about ___ is …
- ___ reminds me of many things.

Finish your poem by writing comparisons. Start each comparison on a new line. Begin each line with a capital letter, even if it's not a sentence. This will make it look like a poem.

3. Revising

▶ Read your poem and listen. Listen for word pictures and comparisons. Can you improve your poem? This checklist will help you.

Revision Checklist

- Did I name my favorite month or time of year?
- Did I tell what I could see, hear, feel, smell, or taste?
- Do my comparisons "paint" word pictures?
- Is every word in the poem needed?

Read the sample. Notice how the poem was improved by taking out words that were not needed.

> My favorite month ~~of all months~~ is ⟨Januaury,⟩ *January*
>
> With ~~soft~~ snow like a soft blanket of ∧ clouds *fluffy*

My favorite month is January,
With snow like a soft blanket of fluffy clouds
And ice shining like stars on tree branches.
The wind sounds like whispers in the dark.
It feels like cold fingers against my cheek.

▶ Use the editing marks to make your changes. This is *your* poem. Make it pleasing to you.

4. Publishing

▶ Proofread your poem. Use the Proofreading Checklist on this page or the one in the Young Writer's Handbook on page 355. Make corrections, using the editing marks.

▶ Make a poetry calendar for your classroom. Write the name of each month on a card. Put the cards on a bulletin board with the months in the right order. Draw or cut out pictures to go with each month. Display your poem under the month or time of year you wrote about.

EDITING MARKS

— cross out

∧ add

◯ check spelling

PROOFREADING CHECKLIST

1. indent paragraphs ☑
2. capital letters ☑
3. end punctuation ☑
4. spelling ☑
5. handwriting ☑

Writing Project

A Concrete Poem

A concrete poem uses the shape of the words to show the poem's idea. This kind of poetry may take many shapes and forms. Select the one you like best. Write a concrete poem of your own.

1. Draw a word so that it looks like what it says.

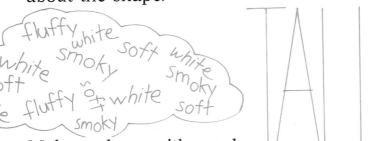

2. Fill a shape with words or sounds that tell about the shape.

3. Make a shape with words.

Social Studies

In social studies you learn facts about how people live in cities. Poetry can help you *feel* what it is like to live in a city. Read this poem. Then tell what it says about city living.

I See a Thousand Roofs

The wall around our roof
Is quite secure.
Mother asked the Superintendent
To be sure.

We stand as closely as we can
Beside our roof wall . . .
I cannot see the street cars
Or taxis at all.

But I can see a thousand
Other roofs like ours,
And rolling steam and smoke,
And pointed towers.

—*James S. Tippett*

Writers at Work   Some people who work in public relations write slogans. A slogan is a saying or a group of words that tells a message. A good slogan gets our attention about something. "I ♥ New York" is a slogan you may have seen.

▶ Try it. Write a slogan for a town, city, state, or school. Make it a two-line poem if you wish.

Nouns   *pages 86–87*

A. Write the underlined nouns. Then write *common* or *proper* beside each noun.

1. The World Trade Center is in New York City.
2. Two apples rolled off the table.
3. Maria ate lunch at Tony's Sandwich Shop.
4. The Chicago White Sox is my favorite team.
5. Andy flew on an airplane to Miami.
6. Melissa goes to classes at the Smith School.

Capital Letters and Periods   *pages 88–93*

B. Write each name correctly.

7. ms lisa k miller
8. george washington
9. cinderella
10. miss e donahoe

11. ann c weston
12. christopher robin
13. dr seuss
14. mrs tina levine

C. Write each sentence. Use capital letters correctly.

15. Sara traveled to texas on halloween.
16. In january I go skating every tuesday.
17. Ed played silly tricks on april fools' day.
18. Jo's family moved to pine street last friday.
19. The first monday in september is labor day.
20. Our class celebrated lincoln's birthday.

Commas *pages 94–95*

D. Write each sentence. Use commas correctly.

21. Yes the Grand Canyon is in Arizona.
22. Amanda where is your red jacket?
23. No I have not eaten lunch yet.
24. Juan please return this book to the library.

Context Clues *pages 96–97*

E. Write what you think each underlined word means.

25. A loud clap of thunder <u>startled</u> Liz.
26. The book had colorful <u>illustrations</u> of flowers.
27. The mail carrier delivered a heavy brown <u>parcel</u>.
28. May I listen to one <u>final</u> story before bedtime?

Poetry *pages 102–107*

F. Write each group of words. Complete the comparisons.

29. as blue as ...   31. sweet like ...
30. cold like ...   32. as soft as ...

G. Write the incomplete rhyme below. Finish the last line, ending with a rhyming word.

The curious cat climbed up the tree
And _____.

See also Handbook pages 320–321, 356–361.

Grammar
Pronouns

Composition
Reasoning

Little

I am the sister of him
And he is my brother.
He is too little for us
To talk to each other.

So every morning I show him
My doll and my book;
But every morning he still is
Too little to look.

—*Dorothy Aldis*

1 — What Is a Pronoun?

> ● A **pronoun** takes the place of a noun or nouns.

You know that nouns name persons, places, and things. Sometimes other words are used instead of nouns. Read the sentences below.

1. The <u>children</u> built a <u>house</u>.   2. <u>They</u> built <u>it</u>.

In sentence 2 the words *they* and *it* are pronouns. The pronoun *they* takes the place of the noun *children*. The pronoun *it* takes the place of the noun *house*.

Singular pronouns take the place of nouns that name one person, place, or thing. Plural pronouns take the place of nouns that name more than one person, place, or thing. Look at the chart below.

Singular Pronouns	Plural Pronouns
I, you, she, he, it me, her, him	we, you, they us, them

Skills Tryout

Name the pronoun in each sentence below.

1. We used tools.
2. Teri gave me a saw.
3. She used a hammer.
4. You bring the nails.
5. I have the wood.
6. The birds watched us.

Practice

A. Write the pronoun in each sentence.

1. Many machines help us work.
2. Craig and I raised the flag at school.
3. We used a pulley on the flagpole.
4. He moved some heavy books with a lever.
5. The wooden board lifted them easily.
6. Nora showed me some new tools.
7. She likes to build things.
8. I would rather paint.
9. You can buy paint at the store.
10. The clerk smiled at her.

B. Choose the pronoun in ( ) to take the place of the underlined noun or nouns. Write each sentence.

EXAMPLE: Kenny watched <u>Rosa</u> and <u>Steve</u>. (her, them)
ANSWER: Kenny watched them.

11. The <u>boy</u> carried a box. (Us, He)
12. The <u>girl</u> pulled a wagon. (She, We)
13. The <u>wagon</u> had four wheels. (Them, It)
14. Rosa had to wait for <u>Steve</u>. (him, them)
15. The <u>wheels</u> made the work easier. (They, She)

Application WRITING SENTENCES

Write five sentences telling how you and your friends made something. Use the pronouns below.

I   he   she   it   we

2 — Subject Pronouns

> ● The words *I, you, she, he, it, we,* and *they* are **subject pronouns**. These pronouns are used in the subject of a sentence.

The subject of a sentence names someone or something. Some pronouns take the place of words in the subject. Look at the underlined subjects.

1. a. <u>Mrs. Lee</u> has a shop.   3. a. <u>Tim and I</u> eat there.
   b. <u>She</u> has a shop.   b. <u>We</u> eat there.
2. a. <u>The shop</u> is small.   4. a. <u>Customers</u> order tea.
   b. <u>It</u> is small.   b. <u>They</u> order tea.

In sentence 1b the pronoun *she* takes the place of *Mrs. Lee.* In sentence 2b the pronoun *it* takes the place of *the shop.* *We* takes the place of *Tim and I* in sentence 3b. What pronoun takes the place of *customers* in sentence 4b?

Skills Tryout

The subject is underlined in each sentence below. Tell if there are pronouns or nouns in the subjects.

1. <u>I</u> walked by the restaurant with Dale.
2. <u>The restaurant</u> is on Front Street.
3. <u>Tamika and Gerald</u> ate lunch there on Saturday.
4. <u>They</u> fix delicious sandwiches.
5. <u>She</u> had a tuna fish sandwich with lettuce.

Practice

A. The subject is underlined in each sentence below.
Write *pronoun* if the subject is a pronoun.
Write *noun* if the subject has a noun in it.

1. The Soup Shop is bright and cheerful.
2. I ate tomato soup with rice yesterday.
3. You should taste the chicken soup.
4. The vegetables are delicious.
5. We like the onion soup best.

B. Change the subject of each sentence to a
pronoun. Write each new sentence.

EXAMPLE: The restaurant is always crowded.
ANSWER: It is always crowded.

6. The customers wait near the door.
7. Mrs. Harris also serves omelets.
8. Ben likes the omelet with cheese.
9. Students eat there often.
10. The meals are tasty and not expensive.
11. Dad always orders the chili.
12. The chili is hot and spicy.
13. Marty and I want beef stew today.
14. Mom ate a bran muffin.
15. The muffin was fresh and warm.

Application WRITING SENTENCES

Write four sentences about your family. Use the
pronouns *he*, *she*, *we*, and *they* as the subjects.

3 — Object Pronouns

> • The words *me, you, him, her, it, us,* and *them* are **object pronouns**. These pronouns are often used in the predicate of a sentence.

Pronouns can take the place of words in the predicate of a sentence. Look at the underlined words.

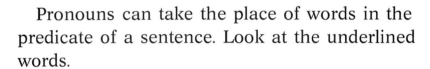

1. a. The stamp is for <u>Pat</u>.
   b. The stamp is for <u>her</u>.
2. a. Lois saves <u>stamps</u>.
   b. Lois saves <u>them</u>.

3. a. Rick has <u>an album</u>.
   b. Rick has <u>it</u>.
4. a. Help <u>Todd and me</u>.
   b. Help <u>us</u>.

In sentence 1b the pronoun *her* takes the place of *Pat.* In sentence 2b the pronoun *them* takes the place of *stamps.* In sentence 3b *it* takes the place of *an album.* What pronoun takes the place of *Todd and me* in sentence 4b?

Skills Tryout

Name the pronoun in each sentence.

1. Mr. Costa gave me some stamps.
2. Emily Costa wrote a letter to him.
3. Emily sent it from Portugal.
4. The teacher wants to see them.
5. Maybe Mr. Costa will save stamps for you.

Practice

A. Write the pronoun in each sentence.

   1. The librarian showed me a special book.
   2. Luís asked him about famous stamp collectors.
   3. Some U.S. Presidents saved them.
   4. Did Mr. Gray tell you about a large collection?
   5. The Queen of England owns it.

B. Use one of the pronouns below for each underlined word or words. Write each new sentence.

her	it	us	them	him

   6. My uncle has collected <u>stamps</u> for years.
   7. He showed <u>Brett and me</u> a strange stamp.
   8. The picture on <u>the stamp</u> was upside down.
   9. I asked <u>Uncle Ray</u> about valuable stamps.
  10. He gave <u>Sally</u> two stamps from Japan.
  11. She studied <u>the watermarks</u> carefully.
  12. Mom gave <u>John</u> a red stamp for his collection.
  13. She could see the silk in <u>the paper</u>.
  14. He will show <u>the album</u> at school.
  15. Give <u>Marla</u> the stamps with pictures of ships.

Application WRITING SENTENCES

Write five sentences about something you or a friend collects. Use each of these pronouns in the predicate of a sentence: *me, us, him, them, her.*

4 — Possessive Pronouns

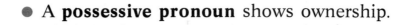

> ● A **possessive pronoun** shows ownership.

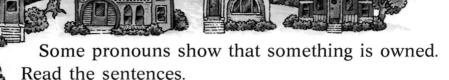

Some pronouns show that something is owned. Read the sentences.

> **Kelly's** house has a bright red roof.
> **Her** house has a bright red roof.

The possessive pronoun *her* shows that the house belongs to Kelly.

The box below shows possessive pronouns. Study the possessive pronouns in the box.

my		your		his		her
	its		our		their	

Skills Tryout

Name the possessive pronoun in each sentence.

1. Barry and his family live in an apartment.
2. There are six floors in our building.
3. Your house is near the school.
4. That is my sister's mobile home.
5. Her kitchen is very tiny.

Practice

A. Write the possessive pronoun in each sentence.

1. There are many old houses in our town.
2. I like my cousins' wind chime.
3. The wind chime hangs from their roof.
4. Your house has a big fireplace.
5. Its bricks are red and black.

B. Copy each sentence pair. Use a possessive pronoun to complete the second sentence in each pair.

EXAMPLE: Ricardo has cousins in California. ____ cousins live in San Francisco.

ANSWER: Ricardo has cousins in California. His cousins live in San Francisco.

6. Claudia and Steve live on Bay Street. ____ street is hilly.
7. I received a postcard from San Francisco. ____ card showed colorful houses.
8. Steve drew a picture of houses in San Francisco. ____ picture showed a house with a tower.
9. Ruth and I will visit San Francisco. ____ plane leaves on Tuesday.
10. Ruth likes bright colors. ____ house is red.

Application WRITING SENTENCES

Write four sentences about your friends' homes. Use a possessive pronoun in each sentence.

5 — Using *I* and *me*

- Use *I* in the subject of a sentence.
- Use a capital letter for the word *I*.
- Use *me* in the predicate of a sentence.

Read the poem that Marie wrote.

<u>I</u> have two sisters.
They are stuck with <u>me</u>.
This trio is special.
We're triplets, you see!

We're three of a kind:
Di, Dee, and Marie!
<u>Di and I</u> look alike,
Just like <u>Dee and me</u>!

Marie used the pronouns *I* and *me* to talk about herself. She used *I* in the subjects of sentences. She used *me* in the predicates of sentences.

When Marie talked about herself and one of her sisters, she named herself last.

<u>I</u> have two sisters.   They are stuck with <u>me</u>.
Di and <u>I</u> look alike, just like Dee and <u>me</u>.

Skills Tryout

Use *I* or *me* to complete each sentence.

1. ＿＿ have a twin brother.
2. Chuck and ＿＿ wear the same size.
3. Aunt Bea sent sweaters to Chuck and ＿＿.
4. Chuck told ＿＿ to choose one.
5. ＿＿ picked the one with blue stripes.

Practice

A. Use *I* or *me* to complete each sentence correctly. Write the pronoun you choose.

1. Last week my cousin Norman called ____.
2. ____ wish my cousins lived closer.
3. ____ would like to visit them in Texas.
4. Uncle Leo would take Norman and ____ to a ranch.
5. My cousin and ____ might ride horses.

B. Choose the correct word or group of words in ( ) to complete each sentence. Write each sentence.

6. Uncle Bob gave ____ a very old book. (Jill and I, I and Jill, Jill and me, me and Jill)
7. ____ read about the Bobbsey twins. (Jill and I, I and Jill, Jill and me, Me and Jill)
8. ____ thought Flossie and Freddie were funny. (Me, I)
9. Jill drew a picture of Nan and Bert for ____. (me, I)
10. Flossie and Freddie Bobbsey look like ____! (me and Jill, Jill and me, I and Jill, Jill and I)

Application WRITING SENTENCES

Pretend that you are telling a new classmate about yourself. Write four sentences. Use *I* or *me* correctly in each sentence.

Homophones

- **Homophones** are words that sound alike. They have different meanings and spellings.

When people write or speak, they may use words that sound alike. Read the sentence below.

We <u>rode</u> along the <u>road</u> to the zoo.

The words *road* and *rode* sound the same. But they are not spelled alike, and they have different meanings. The words *road* and *rode* are homophones.

Look at the homophones in these sentences.

The zoo has <u>four</u> cages <u>for</u> monkeys.
I <u>heard</u> a <u>herd</u> of elephants there.

Spell the homophones in each sentence. Do they have the same meanings?

Skills Tryout

Find the homophones in each sentence. Tell what each homophone means.

1. We waited an hour for our bus to the zoo.
2. Two fathers went to the zoo, too.
3. I hear there is a pond here for ducks.
4. The monkey did not tie a knot in the rope.
5. Did you know that this zoo has no polar bears?

Practice —————————————————————————

A. Write the pair of homophones in each sentence.

    1. Angela read about a red fox.
    2. In the tale the fox had no tail.
    3. The fox ate eight loaves of bread.
    4. The animal wanted to chase two ducks.
    5. But the fat fox had to wait to lose weight.

B. Choose the correct homophone from the words in ( ). Write each complete sentence.

    6. Cal likes to ____ animal stories. (right, write)
    7. He wrote a story about ____ giant whales. (to, two, too)
    8. Those big mammals live in the ____. (see, sea)
    9. A ____ boat landed on one whale's back! (blue, blew)
   10. ____ story was about forest animals. (Won, One)
   11. A ____ named Bo was always afraid. (bear, bare)
   12. Bo became friends with a ____. (hare, hair)
   13. ____ think Cal wants to write a book. (Eye, I)
   14. He will spend a ____ on a ranch. (week, weak)
   15. Maybe he will write about a ____. (hoarse, horse)

Application USING LANGUAGE ————————————————

Use the correct homophone in ( ). Write the story.

Dad told me a (tale, tail) about (two, to) brave sailors. (I, Eye) liked to (hear, here) about their trips on the (see, sea). (Won, One) day I will sail away.

Subject Pronouns *pages 118–121*

A. Change the subject of each sentence to a pronoun. Write each new sentence.

1. The boy climbed a ladder.
2. The paint is still wet.
3. The girls wanted to swim yesterday.
4. My older sister broke her arm last week.
5. Tito and I talked on the phone for an hour.

Object Pronouns *pages 122–123*

B. Choose the correct pronoun in ( ). Write each new sentence.

6. Randy gave (we, us) a drink of lemonade.
7. Suzanne wrote (she, her) a letter.
8. William lent (me, I) money for lunch.
9. Rich told (them, they) how to find the lake.
10. No one at the party knew (he, him).

Possessive Pronouns *pages 124–125*

C. Write the possessive pronoun in each sentence.

11. How was your vacation?
12. My best friend moved away in July.
13. His family went to Alaska.
14. A van is moving their furniture.
15. I hope our friendship continues.

D. Write each pair of sentences. Use *their*, *my*, *its*, or *her* to complete each second sentence.

16. The hat is lovely. ___ color matches your eyes.
17. I went to the store. I bought food for ___ cat.
18. Celia walked to school. ___ bike has a flat tire.
19. Andrea and Russ play soccer. ___ teams practice three times a week.

Using <u>I</u> and <u>me</u> *pages 126–127*

E. Use *I* or *me* to complete each sentence. Write each sentence.

20. Dad asked ___ to go to the store.
21. Frank and ___ walked together.
22. ___ couldn't find the cans of pumpkin.
23. The clerk told ___ where to look.
24. Dad gave Frank and ___ fresh pumpkin bread.

Homophones *pages 128–129*

F. Write the pair of homophones in each sentence.

25. Arthur ate eight sections of grapefruit.
26. We rode on a bumpy road to the cabin.
27. Our plane arrived an hour late.
28. I sent away for a book and four magazines.
29. The flu made me feel weak for a week.
30. What is the correct way to weigh an elephant?

See also Handbook pages 322–325.

Writing with Pronouns

> ● Use pronouns instead of repeating the same nouns too often.

Grammar and Writing Workshop

Read the sentences below.

1. Jerry's mother gave Jerry some money for Jerry's lunch.
2. Jerry's mother gave him some money for his lunch.

Sentence 1 doesn't sound right, does it? The noun *Jerry* is used too often. This makes sentence 1 awkward.

In sentence 2 the noun *Jerry* is used only once. After that, the pronouns *him* and *his* take the place of *Jerry* and *Jerry's*. Sentence 2 is smoother and easier to read.

Look for chances to use pronouns in your writing.

The Pronoun Game Box A below is filled with nouns. Box B is filled with pronouns. Choose a noun from Box A and write it. Then find the pronouns in Box B that could replace the noun you wrote. Write the pronouns.

─────── Box A ───────
Arnold   truth   Sally
ants   Ruth's   cloud
Ted and Angela   Bob's

─────── Box B ───────
it   she   his
he   her   they
hers   him   them

Choose another noun from Box A and start again.

Add-a-Pronoun   Use pronouns to replace the underlined words. Write each new sentence.

EXAMPLE: Diane waited for the clerk to help Diane.
ANSWER: Diane waited for the clerk to help her.

1. The Garcias found an old record player in the Garcias' attic.
2. Joy and Kim think Joy and Kim look like sisters.
3. Lisa can't come out because Lisa has a cold.
4. The library closes the library's doors at six.
5. Will hopes the Drama Club will give Will a part.
6. Alex takes music with Alex wherever Alex goes.
7. The twins promised that the twins would visit us.
8. Laura says Laura left Laura's baton in Laura's locker.
9. The rain fell for hours before the rain stopped.
10. My brother and Sam wonder what Grandfather will give my brother and Sam.

Using the Thesaurus

Find the entry for *end* in the Thesaurus. Then write each sentence. Change the word *end* each time. Use a different synonym for *end* in each sentence.

a. He wore a bandage on the end of his finger.
b. A fence marks the back end of our yard.
c. I heard the end of the story.

Now underline the pronouns in your sentences.

7 Who, What, When, Where, and Why

> ● The five *W* questions are used to gather information.

Five words that start with *W* help you get information. *Who, what, when, where,* and *why* are the five *W* questions. Each one gives you a particular kind of information.

Read the sentences below.

Who **asks for information about people.**
What **asks for information about things.**
When **asks for information about time.**
Where **asks for information about places.**
Why **asks for reasons and explanations.**

You can use the five *W* questions to get information about the jar in the picture.

Who **painted the jar? A Native American painted it.**
What **is the jar made of? It is made of clay.**
When **was the jar made? It was made in the 1890s.**
Where **was the jar made? It was made in New Mexico.**
Why **was the jar made? It was made to hold things.**

Skills Tryout

Read the paragraph at the top of page 135. Use a complete sentence to ask each of the five *W* questions. Then answer the questions.

Margaret Tafoya in Santa Clara often makes polished black pots. She likes to decorate them with a bear paw design. She believes the bear paw brings good luck.

Practice

A. Read the paragraph below. Then answer the questions about the paragraph.

In olden days some Pueblo tribes of New Mexico made beautiful pots. They used the pots to carry water or hold things. These Native Americans painted designs on their pots. They made paints from minerals. They had no brushes. They chewed the yucca plant leaves to make brushes.

1. Who is the paragraph about?
2. What did they do?
3. Why did they do it?
4. Where did they live?
5. When did they live?

B. Write the *W* questions that can be answered by looking at the picture.

Application WRITING A PARAGRAPH

Ask a grown-up five *W* questions about his or her job. Write the answers to your questions. Then use the answers to write a paragraph about that job.

Solving Problems

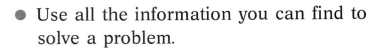

> ● Use all the information you can find to solve a problem.

You can solve problems by gathering clues. Often a clue gives you the information you need to figure something out.

Kim woke up to a well-lighted sky in the early spring. During the night it had rained in great gushes.

She was the first one up. The clock said five. Why did the sky look so bright? Then her dad came out and turned on the radio. After a happy tune the radio announcer said, "At the bell, it will be eight o'clock. Many of you are on your way to work. Drive carefully. That was a bad storm last night."

Think about what happened to Kim.

Skills Tryout

Use all the clues in the story. Then answer the questions below.

1. Where is Kim? Who is with her?
2. What took place during the night?
3. What had happened to the alarm clock? Why did it say *five*, when it was really *eight* o'clock?
4. What clues to the correct time can you find?

Practice

A. Read each group of clues below. Write the answers.

1. There is a smell of gasoline. You hear a rumble. Then a voice says, "Fill it up." Where are you?

2. The flashlight will not go on. You check the batteries. They still work when you try them in a toy. What might be wrong with the flashlight?

3. Beth got home from school early. Mom was usually home by then. Beth called but got no answer. She could hear the water running. Mom was not in the kitchen or in the cellar. No one was taking a bath. Still she heard the sound of water running hard. Where could her mother be?

4. Ted ran to the cellar for a package of sugar. The cellar smelled dank and felt cool and damp. The sugar was on the shelf. But the package was as hard as a rock. Why was the sugar hard and lumpy?

B. Make up a problem like the one in **Practice A1.** Give the clues. Then ask, "Where are you?" Write the answer on the back of your paper.

Application USING THINKING SKILLS

Make up a riddle. Give clues to a special place such as the library or playground. Include clues that use the five senses. Start your riddle with "What has …" or "I am the place…"

9 — Messages Without Words

> ● Messages are not always made up of words. People's faces and body movements can send messages.

Language is the sending and receiving of messages. You speak to others by sending messages. You learn about others by receiving messages. Many messages are made up of words. Often, however, you send messages without words.

In the three pictures above, the children are sending messages. What messages do you receive from their faces and their body movements?

Skills Tryout

Without using words, send each message below.

1. This pie is delicious!
2. I hate spinach!
3. Good-by.
4. I'm afraid.
5. Come on in.
6. No, thank you.

Practice

A. Write a sentence about each picture.

B. Number your paper **1-5**. Write the letter for your answer. The letter should show how you might send each message.

1. surprise
2. sleepiness
3. Shhh!
4. confusion
5. excitement

a. scratch your head
b. look with wide eyes
c. put one finger to your lips
d. jump up and down
e. yawn and stretch

Application USING LIFE SKILLS

Some important messages need to be understood by everyone. Tell what each pictured message means.

10 — Writing a Mystery Story

Writing Project

- A **mystery story** gives clues about something. The mystery is solved at the end of the story.

Do you remember the five *W* questions? They ask *who, what, when, where,* and *why.* In a mystery story the reader must guess the answer to at least one of these questions. You will write a mystery story in this lesson. Your classmates will be detectives, trying to solve your mystery.

1. Prewriting

Suppose you are in your kitchen at home. When you look around, you notice some strange things. Look at this mystery story map. Follow the arrows and read the clues in the circles. Do you know what is hiding under the kitchen table?

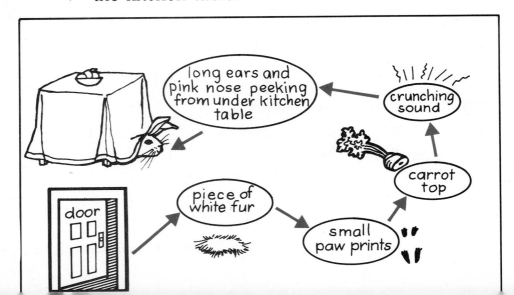

long ears and pink nose peeking from under kitchen table

crunching sound

carrot top

piece of white fur

small paw prints

door

▶ Think of ideas for your own mystery story. Plan the story ending first. List three things that might be hiding. Then list a place where each thing might be hiding. Use your imagination to think of make-believe visitors. Here are some ideas for story endings:

- A friendly space creature is hiding under a bed.
- An elephant is hiding in the bathtub.
- An elf is hiding in the fruit bowl.

Choose your favorite story idea for your mystery.

▶ Think about your story ending. What might you see or hear as a clue from your hidden visitor? Write a list of clues for your story ending.

Now make a story map with your clues. Begin where you notice the first clue. End with the place where something is hiding.

2. Writing

The beginning of a mystery story sets the scene. It may tell *who* is solving the mystery. It may also tell *where* the mystery takes place and *when* it happens. How will you begin your story? Read the example on the next page.

"One day after school I found something hiding under the kitchen table."

▶ Write the beginning of your story. Next write detail sentences that give clues. Use your story map. Write something about each clue.

The ending of your story will solve the mystery. It will tell *what* is hiding. It will also tell *why* it is hiding. Read the example below. Then write the ending for your story.

"I was so surprised when I discovered a rabbit! That rabbit must have been looking for food."

3. Revising

▶ Read your story to someone. Ask your listener how you can improve your story. Use this checklist, too, to think about changes.

Revision Checklist

- Did I begin my story by setting the scene?
- Did I write detail sentences that give clues?
- Does my story ending solve the mystery?
- Did I avoid running sentences together?

Read the sample to see how it was improved. Notice how the story is easier to read when sentences do not run together.

Draft with Editing Marks

  ¶ One day after school I found ∧*something* ~~a rabbit~~ hiding under
the (kichen)*kitchen* table. ~~and~~ I thought it was strange
when I noticed ∧*white* fur on the floor. ~~near me and I~~

Revised Version

    One day after school I found something hiding under the kitchen table. I thought it was strange when I noticed white fur on the floor. I followed some small paw prints and almost slipped on a carrot top. Then I heard a crunching sound. There were two long ears and a pink nose peeking from under the kitchen table. I was so surprised when I discovered a rabbit! That rabbit must have been looking for food.

EDITING MARKS

——	cross out
∧	add
¶	indent
⬯	check spelling

▶ Now use the editing marks to make changes.

4. Publishing

▶ Use the Proofreading Checklist on this page or the one in the Young Writer's Handbook on page 355 to proofread. Use the editing marks to make corrections.

▶ Read your story to the class. Stop just before the ending. Can the class detectives solve your mystery?

PROOFREADING CHECKLIST

1. indent paragraphs ☑
2. capital letters ☑
3. end punctuation ☑
4. spelling ☑
5. handwriting ☑

Writing Project

A Picture Riddle

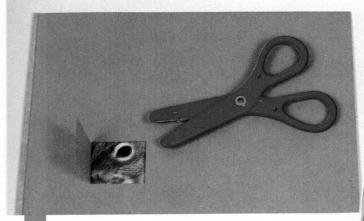

Can you tell what a picture is when you see just one small detail? Reasoning helps you solve picture riddles. Make a picture riddle.

- Choose a large picture from a magazine. Cut it out.
- Paste the picture on construction paper.
- Cover the picture with a sheet of clean paper.
- Choose one interesting detail in the picture.
- Cut a flap in the cover so that it opens to the detail you chose.
- Tape the cover to the picture along one side.
- Ask your friends to look under the flap. See if they can guess what the whole picture is.

Art

Sometimes a painting is like a puzzle. The five *W* questions help you solve the puzzle. When you look at a painting, ask *who, what, when, where,* and *why.*

▶ Try it. Look at this painting called "First Steps," by Picasso. Picasso often painted ordinary objects and people in unusual ways. You might ask questions such as these: *Who* is in the painting? *What* is the child doing? *Why* do you think the mother is holding the baby's hands? *Where* is the child? *Where* is the mother? *When* do you think the child will take its first steps? Talk about the questions and the answers. You will soon understand the painting.

Listeners at Work Artists, architects, building engineers, designers, and potters ask questions before they create a product. They must know *who, what, when, where,* and *why.*

▶ Try it. Use the five *W* questions to gather information. Then design a product for your classmates. Make a sketch. Explain it.

Pronouns   *pages 118–127*

A. Choose the correct pronoun in ( ) to complete each sentence. Write each sentence.

1. (We, Us) rode in a motorboat.
2. Pat told Sam and (I, me) about the party.
3. (She, Her) painted a colorful picture.
4. Carl saw (he, him) marching in the parade.
5. Give (they, them) directions to our house.
6. Don and (I, me) built a tree house.
7. Stella brought (we, us) some peanuts.
8. (They, Them) have two pet turtles.

B. Write the possessive pronoun in each sentence.

9. Your school has a big playground.
10. The boys rode their bicycles to the store.
11. Put the bird back into its cage.
12. Does Niki like her new teacher?
13. Hockey is my favorite sport.
14. Roger was the lion in our class play.

Homophones   *pages 128–129*

C. Write each sentence. Use the correct homophone in ( ).

15. I (sea, see) you.
16. (Right, Write) to me.
17. (Buy, By) some milk.
18. We live (here, hear).

Solving Problems *pages 134–139*

D. Read the paragraph below. Then write the answers to the questions.

The school bell rang at three o'clock. The boys and girls got ready to go home. Karla put on her coat, hat, and scarf. She tried to put on her boots, but they were too small. Karla frowned. She pushed hard, but the boots did not fit. Then Karla heard her friend Peg say, "This morning my boots fit just right. Now they are too big."

19. Where were the boys and girls going?
20. What was the weather like?
21. Why did Karla frown?
22. Who had Karla's boots?

E. For questions **23–26**, write the letter of the group of words that tells how you would send each message.

23. I'm cold.
24. Good luck.
25. Call on me.
26. I'm joking.

    a. wink with one eye
    b. rub hands together
    c. raise your hand
    d. cross your fingers

F. The five *W* questions are *who, what, when, where,* and *why*. Write three *W* questions you might ask a new student in your class.

See also Handbook pages 322–325.

Sentences   *pages 4–17*

A. Write *yes* if the word group is a sentence. Write *no* if the word group is not a sentence.

1. A trip to the beach.
2. The sand was hot.
3. Splashing in the water.
4. Jim saw a sailboat.

B. Write each group of words in sentence order.
5. fixed He my bike.
6. are These ripe pears.
7. game fun was The.
8. can trees Cats climb.

C. Write each sentence correctly. Use a capital letter and put the correct mark at the end.

9. what a fine day it is
10. get me my coat
11. how big that fish is
12. did Dan buy juice
13. we saw a robin
14. is Meg your friend
15. fish live in our pond
16. stir the soup

D. Write *subject* if the subject is underlined. Write *predicate* if the predicate is underlined.

17. These woods are colorful in the fall.
18. Ali sang a song for her grandmother.
19. A brown rabbit hopped across the field.
20. Seth found a box of old post cards.
21. Billy juggled three oranges.
22. The girls made a kite for Peter.

Nouns   *pages 48–57, 86–87*

E. Write the noun in each pair of words.

23. sing, house
24. lawn, read
25. when, lamb

26. now, scarf
27. sister, hot
28. school, write

F. Write *singular* if the underlined noun is singular. Write *plural* if the underlined noun is plural.

29. Sam likes <u>peanuts</u>.
30. Bring your <u>friend</u>.
31. These <u>boots</u> are warm.

32. My <u>desk</u> is neat.
33. Tell me a <u>story</u>.
34. I made my <u>bed</u>.

G. Write the plural form of each noun.

35. lady
36. basket
37. porch
38. face

39. curtain
40. box
41. house
42. foot

H. Write the possessive form of each noun.

43. Ann
44. turtles
45. wheel
46. Mrs. Roy

47. classes
48. men
49. Beth
50. flowers

I. Write the underlined nouns. Then write *common* or *proper* beside each noun.

51. Some <u>farmers</u> raise <u>sheep</u>.
52. <u>Rick</u> washed the <u>dishes</u>.
53. <u>Detroit</u> is a big <u>city</u>.
54. The <u>Blakes</u> sailed to <u>Pearl Island</u>.
55. The <u>goat</u> bumped <u>Mrs. Gray</u>.
56. <u>Mrs. Abramson</u> works in an <u>office</u>.

Capital Letters and Periods   *pages 88–93*

J. Write each name correctly.

57. steven w lewis
58. dr doolittle
59. ms ann l wise
60. robinson crusoe
61. miss g dolan
62. thomas jefferson
63. mr brandon
64. laura ingalls

K. Write each sentence. Use capital letters correctly.

65. In august we visited las vegas, nevada.
66. I went to see a parade on memorial day in may.
67. Tim spent thanksgiving day with friends in iowa.
68. The second monday in october was columbus day.
69. Paul lives on meadow lane in fairfax.
70. We drove to atlantic city on wednesday.

Commas   *pages 94–95*

L. Write each sentence. Use commas correctly.

71. No we cannot take a train to New York City.
72. Joshua is your sister coming to school today?
73. Mario do you want to play football on Saturday?
74. Yes we enjoyed our day at the zoo.

Pronouns   *pages 118–127*

M. Choose the correct pronoun in ( ) to complete each sentence. Write each sentence.

75. Pat told (me, I) about the movie.
76. Show (we, us) how to make a puppet.
77. (She, Her) is a good artist.
78. I will give (they, them) my umbrella.
79. Sharon watched (him, he) swim.
80. Soon (we, us) will be going home.
81. (They, Them) are building a birdhouse.
82. Cal and (I, me) saw a big raccoon.

N. Write the possessive pronoun in each sentence.

83. My aunt writes books for children.
84. Where did Tommy put his shoes?
85. I told Melanie about our trip.
86. Their brother collects old coins.
87. Liz and her friend take dancing lessons.

Grammar
Verbs

Composition
Informing

I Speak, I Say, I Talk

Cats purr.
Lions roar.
Owls hoot.
Bears snore.
Crickets creak.
Mice squeak.
Sheep baa.
But I SPEAK!

Monkeys chatter.
Cows moo.
Ducks quack.
Doves coo.

Pigs squeal.
Horses neigh.
Chickens cluck.
But I SAY!

Flies hum.
Dogs growl.
Bats screech.
Coyotes howl.
Frogs croak.
Parrots squawk.
Bees buzz.
But I TALK!

—Arnold L. Shapiro

What Is a Verb?

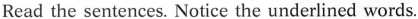

> ● A word that shows action is a **verb**.

Read the sentences. Notice the underlined words.

Heidi <u>skates</u> on the frozen lake.
Two boys <u>build</u> a snow family.
Chad <u>climbs</u> the hill with his sled.

The underlined word in each sentence above tells what someone does. Words like *skates*, *build*, and *climbs* are verbs. They show action.

The verbs are underlined in the sentences below. What action does each verb show? Can you make up another sentence with the same verb?

The dog <u>runs</u> up the hill with Chad.
Katy <u>throws</u> a snowball at the tree.

Skills Tryout

Find the verb in each sentence.

1. Stephanie feeds the birds.
2. The snow falls quietly.
3. The children carry skis.
4. My brother shovels the snow.
5. The baby waves at the squirrel.

A. Write the verb in each sentence.

1. My friends play ice hockey.
2. The team practices every day after school.
3. Pierre carries his new ice skates.
4. Edgar and Jay bring the equipment.
5. Rod scores a goal in almost every game.

B. If the underlined word in the sentence is a verb, write *verb*. If the underlined word is not a verb, write *not a verb*.

6. Peggy and Jack <u>ride</u> in an old-fashioned sleigh.
7. A <u>pony</u> pulls the sleigh around the city park.
8. Peggy <u>holds</u> the pony's reins.
9. The pony <u>trots</u> along in the snow.
10. Two <u>dogs</u> chase after the sleigh.

C. Write the sentences. Use a verb to complete each sentence.

11. Conrad —— his snowshoes.
12. The girls —— new mittens.
13. A squirrel —— up the tree.
14. Wesley —— three deer.
15. A bird —— over the frozen lake.

Application WRITING SENTENCES

Write four sentences about winter activities. In each sentence use a verb that shows action.

2 Verbs in the Present

- A verb in the **present time** shows action that happens now.

A verb in the present time must agree with the noun used in the subject of a sentence. Remember that a singular noun names one person, place, or thing. A plural noun names more than one person, place, or thing. Notice the underlined words in the sentences below.

Lori feeds the gerbils.   The gerbils eat seeds.

The verb *feeds* is used with the singular noun *Lori*. Verbs in the present time that are used with singular nouns end in -*s* or -*es*.

The verb *eat* is used with the plural noun *gerbils*. Verbs in the present time that are used with plural nouns do not add -*s* or -*es*.

Skills Tryout

Choose the correct verb to complete each sentence.

1. This shop (sell, sells) gerbils.
2. The children (look, looks) at different animals.
3. Mia (choose, chooses) two brown gerbils.
4. My friends (buy, buys) a cage for the new pets.
5. Gerbils (need, needs) a metal or plastic cage.

Practice

A. Write the sentences. Choose the correct verb in ( ) to complete each sentence.

1. My friends (raise, raises) gerbils.
2. Gerbils (come, comes) from China.
3. Spot and Dot (exercise, exercises) every day.
4. Cory (clean, cleans) their cage often.
5. Dot (drink, drinks) from a water bottle.

B. Use verbs in the present time in the sentences below. Write each sentence with the correct form of the verb in ( ).

EXAMPLE: Mona ____ pets in the shop. (see)
ANSWER: Mona sees pets in the shop.

6. Glenn ____ with the gerbils. (play)
7. Some gerbils ____ tricks. (know)
8. The boy ____ softly. (whistle)
9. One gerbil ____ on the boy's shoe. (sit)
10. Another gerbil ____ inside the wheel. (climb)
11. Rusty and Dusty ____ in paper bags. (hide)
12. The pets ____ salt from a block. (lick)
13. Their front teeth ____ all the time. (grow)
14. A gerbil ____ on hard foods. (chew)
15. Rusty ____ carrots and sunflower seeds. (like)

Application WRITING SENTENCES

Write four sentences about a pet. Use verbs in the present time.

Making Pronouns and Verbs Agree

> • A verb in the present time must agree with the pronoun used in the subject of a sentence.

Remember that some pronouns are used in the subject of a sentence. Notice the underlined words in the sentences below.

She <u>wears</u> a heavy sweater.
He <u>keeps</u> the heat at a low temperature.
It <u>makes</u> the house cooler.

I <u>save</u> water and electricity in my house.
You <u>turn</u> off extra lights.
We <u>take</u> showers instead of baths.
They <u>fix</u> leaky faucets.

Verbs in the present time used with *she, he,* or *it* end in *-s* or *-es.* Verbs in the present time used with *I, you, we,* or *they* do not add *-s* or *-es.*

Skills Tryout

Choose the correct verb to complete each sentence.

1. We (help, helps) our city stay clean.
2. She (pick, picks) up aluminum cans.
3. You (bring, brings) bottles back to the store.
4. He (throw, throws) litter in containers.
5. They (plant, plants) beautiful flowers.

Practice

A. Write the sentences. Choose the correct verb in ( ) to complete each sentence.

1. They (find, finds) many ways to save materials.
2. We (recycle, recycles) different kinds of things.
3. He (bring, brings) his empty bottles.
4. I (write, writes) on both sides of my paper.
5. We (use, uses) paper bags several times.
6. It (save, saves) trees in the forest.
7. They (replace, replaces) broken windows.
8. She (burn, burns) less coal in the furnace.
9. You (cover, covers) the trash cans carefully.
10. We (want, wants) to keep our town clean.

B. Use verbs in the present time in the sentences below. Write each sentence with the correct form of the verb in ( ).

11. We ____ our car in the garage. (leave)
12. It ____ the air a little cleaner. (keep)
13. They ____ gasoline, too. (conserve)
14. I ____ my bicycle to school. (ride)
15. She ____ the bus to work. (take)

Application WRITING SENTENCES

Tell about ways that people can conserve energy or materials. Write six sentences. Begin each sentence with one of the pronouns below.

You   She   I   They   We   He

4 — Verbs in the Past

> ● A verb in the **past time** shows action that already happened.

Read the sentences. Notice the underlined words.

> **Some dinosaurs <u>walked</u> on land.**
> **Other huge creatures <u>stayed</u> in water.**

The underlined words are verbs in the past time. They tell about actions that already happened. Most verbs in the past time end in *-ed*.

Look at the ending of each verb in the sentences below.

> **Dinah <u>looks</u> at the bones.**
> **Dinah <u>looked</u> at the bones.**

Which verb shows action that is happening now? Which verb shows action that already happened?

Skills Tryout

Find the verb in each sentence below. Tell if it is in the present time or in the past time.

1. My book shows pictures of giant lizards.
2. Cindy asks about dinosaurs.
3. One dinosaur weighed thirty tons.
4. Its long body stretched seventy feet.
5. It filled its mouth with plants.

Practice

A. If the verb is in the present time, write *present*.
If the verb is in the past time, write *past*.

1. Workers in New Jersey discovered large bones.
2. They also uncovered some dinosaur teeth.
3. Dr. Leidy hunted for dinosaur bones in America.
4. Today people look at those bones in museums.
5. Scientists learn about early reptiles from bones.

B. Use verbs in the past time in the sentences below. Write each sentence with the correct form of the verb in ( ).

EXAMPLE: Some dinosaurs ____ on the land. (walk)
ANSWER: Some dinosaurs walked on the land.

6. Dinosaurs ____ warm, moist places to live. (need)
7. Warm seas ____ most of the earth. (flood)
8. The earliest animals ____ in the sea. (remain)
9. Some reptiles ____ to the land. (crawl)
10. These creatures ____ from eggs. (hatch)
11. Some dinosaurs ____ other dinosaurs. (frighten)
12. Flying reptiles ____ from the air. (hunt)
13. Then the earth ____ to change. (start)
14. The air and water temperatures ____. (cool)
15. Dinosaurs ____ from the earth. (disappear)

Application WRITING SENTENCES

Write four sentences. Use the past-time form of each of these verbs: *look, follow, finish, open.*

5 — Spelling Verbs in the Present

- Some verbs in the present time end in -s or -es.
- The spelling of some verbs changes when -es is added.

Verbs in the present time used with singular nouns end in -s or -es. Read the sentences below. What letter has been added to each verb?

The clown dances.   Lou Ann holds the strings.

Sometimes -es is added to verbs in the present time. Add -es to verbs that end in s, x, ch, or sh.

Celia dresses the puppets.   Mom watches the show.
Doug fixes the costumes.   Vic rushes onstage.

If a verb ends in a consonant and *y*, change the *y* to *i* and add -es. Look at the examples below.

carry, carries   spy, spies

Skills Tryout

Use the verb in ( ) to complete each sentence. Spell the correct present-time form of the verb.

1. Gay —— a puppet show for her friends. (prepare)
2. One puppet —— a delicious meal. (fix)
3. He —— eggs for the family. (fry)
4. The boy puppet —— toy dishes. (wash)
5. His sister —— them with a tiny towel. (dry)

Practice

A. Write each verb below. Then write the form that ends in -*s* or -*es*.

1. read
2. wish
3. fly
4. fuss
5. like
6. scratch
7. mix
8. hurry
9. guess
10. try

B. Use verbs in the present time in the sentences below. Write each sentence with the correct form of the verb in ( ).

11. Al ___ up a story about a puppet family. (make)
12. Gert ___ in a swimming pool. (splash)
13. Bernie ___ the water with one toe. (try)
14. Then he ___ the pool on a raft. (cross)
15. The raft ___ near the edge. (float)
16. Polly ___ Bernie into the water. (push)
17. Miss Dimples ___ on a big towel. (relax)
18. Hopper ___ a beach ball to her. (toss)
19. Big Elmer ___ his feathers. (dry)
20. He ___ the beach ball in his beak. (carry)

Application WRITING SENTENCES

Write five sentences. Use a singular noun in the subject of each sentence. Use the present-time form of these verbs: *mix, cry, dress, hatch, smash.*

6 — Spelling Verbs in the Past

- Most verbs in the past time end in -*ed*.
- The spelling of some verbs changes when -*ed* is added.

Verbs in the past time tell about actions that already happened. Many past-time verbs end in -*ed*. Look at the verb in each sentence below.

Our town <u>opened</u> a new park.   We <u>looked</u> at it.

Sometimes the spelling of a verb changes when -*ed* is added. Look at these examples.

try, tr<u>ied</u>   step, step<u>ped</u>

The verb *try* ends in a consonant and *y*. The *y* is changed to *i* before -*ed* is added. The verb *step* ends in one vowel and one consonant. The final consonant is doubled before -*ed* is added.

Skills Tryout

Read each verb below. Spell the form of the verb in the past time.

1. jump
2. carry

3. dry
4. tap

5. slam
6. tug

Practice

A. Write each sentence. Use the form of the verb in ( ) that tells about the past time.

1. We ___ the fitness course. (start)
2. Cathy ___ up and down wooden steps. (skip)
3. I ___ carefully over logs. (hop)
4. Then we ___ to the next exercise. (hurry)
5. Our hearts and other muscles ___ hard. (work)

B. Each underlined verb is in the present time. Change each verb to the past time. Write the new sentence.

6. Fitness courses <u>start</u> in Europe.
7. Our city <u>plans</u> to build a free exercise trail.
8. People of all ages <u>try</u> the exercises.
9. Some folks <u>stop</u> at all the exercise signs.
10. Sometimes they <u>drop</u> out after just a few.
11. At first I <u>worry</u> about not finishing the course.
12. I <u>rest</u> for a little while.
13. I <u>watch</u> a girl in a wheelchair.
14. She <u>pulls</u> herself up a ramp.
15. She <u>explains</u> how muscles and strength improve slowly with regular exercise.

Application WRITING SENTENCES

Change each of the verbs below to tell about the past time. Write five sentences about exercising.

walk   jog   try   stop   carry

7 — Prefixes

> ● A **prefix** is a letter or letters added to the beginning of a word.

A **base word** is the simplest form of a word. *Cover* is a base word. No letters have been added to its beginning or end. The word *uncover* has the prefix *un-* at its beginning. The prefix makes *uncover* mean the opposite of the base word *cover*.

Study the chart below. The prefixes *un-* and *re-* change the meanings of the base words *button* and *heat*.

Prefix	Meaning	Example
un-	the opposite of	unbutton
re-	again	reheat

Read each sentence below. Look at the words with prefixes. Tell how the prefix changes the meaning of the base word.

The magician <u>unties</u> knots in seconds.
The assistant <u>rewraps</u> the chains tightly.

Skills Tryout

Each word has a prefix. Tell what each word means.

1. unsnap
2. rewrite
3. unroll
4. refill
5. unfold
6. replay
7. remake
8. untangle
9. rebuild

Practice

A. Read the meanings below. Then write a word that has the prefix *un-* or *re-* for each meaning.

EXAMPLE: the opposite of load
ANSWER: unload

1. write again
2. place again
3. the opposite of seal
4. the opposite of pack
5. heat again
6. fold again
7. the opposite of hook
8. paint again
9. the opposite of wrap
10. make again

B. Add the prefix in ( ) to the underlined word in each sentence. Write each new sentence.

11. I <u>read</u> a book about a famous magician. (re-)
12. Ehrich Weiss <u>named</u> himself Harry Houdini. (re-)
13. Houdini <u>locked</u> handcuffs easily. (un-)
14. He <u>fastened</u> straps under water. (un-)
15. He <u>tied</u> ropes from inside a box. (un-)
16. People <u>wrapped</u> the box with chains. (re-)
17. Houdini <u>did</u> all the chains quickly. (un-)
18. He <u>opened</u> the box within seconds. (re-)
19. Few people can <u>lock</u> a box from the inside! (un-)
20. Magicians still cannot <u>cover</u> his secrets. (un-)

Application WRITING SENTENCES

Write one sentence for each of the verbs below.

unload   reload   undo   redo

Action Verbs *pages 154–155*

A. Write the verb in each sentence.

1. Mr. Bennett asks for helpers at school.
2. Hazel dusts the shelves and books.
3. Teddy empties the wastebasket.
4. Carrie and Audrey clean the chalkboards.
5. Walter sharpens all the pencils.

Verbs in the Present *pages 156–157, 162–163*

B. Write each sentence. Use the correct present-time form of the verb in ( ).

6. The school band ___ in parades. (march)
7. Colleen ___ a blue and white banner. (carry)
8. Joel and Molly ___ the drums. (play)
9. Once a month Dad ___ the car. (wash)
10. The bus driver ___ at the station. (stop)

Verbs in the Past *pages 160–161, 164–165*

C. Read each sentence. If the verb is in the present time, write *present*. If the verb is in the past time, write *past*.

11. Patricia collects foreign coins.
12. Harold finished his homework before dinner.
13. My sister worked in a hospital last year.
14. Juanita practices the flute every day.
15. Mack watered the plants yesterday.

D. Write each sentence. Use the correct past-time form of the verb in ( ).

16. Edith ____ two miles on Saturday. (jog)
17. My cousins ____ me from Texas. (call)
18. Daniel ____ the gate carefully. (open)
19. The baby ____ for over an hour. (cry)
20. Claudia ____ at the new shoe store. (shop)
21. Ronald ____ the track meet at school. (watch)
22. The students ____ a talent show. (present)

Making Pronouns and Verbs Agree *pages 158–159*

E. Write each sentence. Use the correct verb in ( ).

23. I (sit, sits) near the window.
24. She (brush, brushes) her hair every morning.
25. He (water, waters) the garden twice a week.
26. It (takes, take) three hours to get there.
27. You (writes, write) funny poems.
28. They (carry, carries) their lunch every day.
29. We (sing, sings) along with the radio.

Prefixes *pages 166–167*

F. Read the meanings. For each meaning, write a word that has the prefix *un-* or *re-*.

30. opposite of tangle
31. fill again
32. pack again
33. heat again
34. opposite of button
35. opposite of zip

See also Handbook pages 326–333.

Writing with Verbs

- Use exact verbs to make your writing more interesting.

Read the sentences below.

1. Donald laughed at my joke.
2. Donald roared at my joke.

Both sentences tell us that Donald laughed, but sentence 2 gives more information. Sentence 2 tells _how_ Donald laughed. It tells us that he _roared. Roared_ is a more _exact_ verb than _laughed._ It really tells how much Donald enjoyed the joke!

A different exact verb would give a different picture.

Donald chuckled at my joke.

Try to use exact verbs in your own writing. They help to tell the reader exactly what is happening.

The Verb Game Look at the list of verbs below. Can you think of more exact verbs for each one? Write at least three exact verbs for each word.

walk	fly	talk
play	rain	eat
work	fall	fix

The Verb Switch   Write at least two exact verbs for each underlined word below. Use words from the Verb Bank, or use verbs of your own.

```
┌──────────────── Verb Bank ────────────────┐
│   carried    scrubbed    grabbed    stole  │
│   sniffle    borrowed    washed     sob    │
│   cleaned    dragged     brought    weep   │
└────────────────────────────────────────────┘
```

1. Who <u>took</u> my pen?
2. I <u>did</u> the dishes after the big meal.
3. Do you ever <u>cry</u> at sad movies?
4. Louisa <u>got</u> the ladder back to our house.

Add-a-Verb   Complete the paragraph below. Think of an exact verb to complete each sentence. Then write the paragraph.

Mark ___ the sky every night. He ___ the name of every star. He ___ a map of the sky. The map ___ where the planets can be found. Mark ___ his friends how to find stars.

Using the Thesaurus

Suppose that you want to tell someone about things you like. Find the entry for *like* in the Thesaurus. Then write four sentences about your favorite things. Use a different synonym for *like* in each sentence.

8 — Giving and Following Directions

> ● Directions give information. They *inform*.

How do you do that magic trick?

It's easy. I'll give you directions.

You learn from others. Often you want to know how to do something. Then you ask someone who knows how. You ask for directions. Other people want to learn from you, too. They ask you for directions.

Giving and following directions are skills you use often. Here are some things to think about when you use them.

Giving Directions	1. Keep directions easy, but give *all* the steps.
	2. Give the steps in order. Use words like *first, second, next*, and *last* to show the correct order.
	3. Ask if there are any questions.
Following Directions	1. Listen to remember the directions in order.
	2. Picture yourself doing each step.
	3. Repeat the directions to yourself.
	4. Ask questions if you need to.

Skills Tryout

Listen as your teacher reads these directions. Then answer the questions as they are read to you.

First gather your materials. You will need paper, a thin paintbrush, and lemon juice. Next dip the brush in the juice. Write a message on the paper. Let the paper dry. It will look blank. Finally hold the paper over a light bulb. You will see writing.

1. What did you learn?   3. What will happen?
2. What will you do first?   4. What will you do last?

Practice

A. Listen as your teacher reads directions for making a code. Follow them.

First write the alphabet across your paper. Next number each letter. Write number 1 over *a*, 2 over *b*, and so on. Letter *z* will be 26.

B. Use your code to write each word below.

1. 8, 5, 12, 12, 15   4. 23, 18, 9, 20, 5
2. 19, 13, 9, 12, 5   5. 19, 16, 5, 1, 11
3. 20, 8, 9, 14, 11   6. 12, 9, 19, 20, 5, 14

Application SPEAKING AND LISTENING

Take turns giving and following directions. Start with three directions, such as *stand, yawn,* and *wink.* Then add more. How many can you remember?

Using the Telephone

- When you use the telephone, speak clearly and listen carefully.
- Write all messages correctly and completely.

Pat's family has a bulletin board near the telephone.

Pat wrote this message. Check to see if she wrote all the important information.

Ted,
Coach Roy called on Saturday at 11:15 A.M. Soccer practice is at 4:30 P.M. on Sunday. Bring knee pads and shoes.
Pat

Skills Tryout

Answer these questions about the message above.

1. Who was the call for?
2. Who called?
3. What day was it? What time?
4. What was the message?
5. Who took the message?

Practice

A. Read the information below. Write a message.

> 1. The dentist calls at 3:30 P.M. on Monday. She says Mother has a checkup on Friday morning at 9:15 A.M. Dr. Rose wants Mother to call. The number is 555-1551.
> 2. Joe Allen calls on Tuesday at 7:00 P.M. He wants Dwight to call him at 555-7171.

B. Write *true* or *false* for each statement in this quiz on using the telephone.

> 3. Speak very loudly and quickly on the telephone.
> 4. It is not important to write the time of a call.
> 5. Always write the name of the person who calls.
> 6. Hang up immediately if the call is not for you.
> 7. Don't take a message. They'll call back.
> 8. Listen carefully. Get all of the information.
> 9. Do not write who the message is for.
> 10. The name of the message taker is important.

Application LIFE SKILLS

It is important to know how to report an emergency. In your classroom practice how to report an emergency by telephone. Follow these rules.

> 1. State that this is an emergency.
> 2. Say your name and where you're calling from.
> 3. Be calm and briefly explain the problem.
> 4. Make sure your message was understood.

10 — Writing a Friendly Letter

> ● A **friendly letter** has five parts: the heading, greeting, body, closing, and signature.

Heading

Greeting

Body

Closing
Signature

> 506 Blaine Avenue
> Seattle, Washington 98119
> February 4, 1986
>
> Dear Jerry,
>   On Saturday, February 22, we're having a super sale with three other families. There will be clothes, books, and lots of bargains! The sale will be next door in the Smiths' garage. Please come!
>
>   Your friend,
>   Walt

The heading of Walt's letter tells his address and when he wrote the letter. Notice the comma between the city and state and between the date and the year.

The greeting says "hello" and the closing says "good-by." A comma follows each of these parts. The first word of each begins with a capital letter.

The body is the most important part of a letter. It tells the message. It is a paragraph, so the first word is indented.

What does the signature tell?

Skills Tryout

Tell where commas and capital letters are needed. Then tell which letter part each group of words belongs in.

1. detroit michigan
2. march 1 1986
3. your pal
4. dear lola may
5. 153 pine street
6. mandy

A. Write each part of the letter below correctly. Be sure to write each part in the proper place on your paper. Use the letter on page 176 to help you.

> 2071 green road
> cleveland ohio 44121
> march 14 1986
>
> dear tanya
>
> We went camping on our vacation. We had a lot of fun. I will bring pictures when I come to visit.
>
> sincerely
>
> cheryl

B. Pretend that you received Walt's letter. Answer it. Include the five parts of a friendly letter.

Application WRITING A LETTER

Write a letter to someone you know. You may wish to mail your letter. Turn to page 352 in the Young Writer's Handbook to see how to address an envelope.

11 — Writing Directions

> ● **Directions** give steps to follow for making or doing something. The steps are in order.

Writing Project

Giving directions is an important and useful skill. Every day you follow directions. You give directions, too. In this lesson you will write a set of directions. Your directions will tell your classmates how to make or do something you enjoy.

1. Prewriting

Look at the picture and read what the children said. The children are playing a "Giving Directions" game. If the player follows the directions, she will find a hidden eraser.

"Come into the room," said Maria.

"Turn left," said Ray.

"Walk down the aisle," said Luis.

"Reach on top of the bookcase," said Ann.

▶ Practice giving and following directions. Play the "Giving Directions" game. This is how to do it:

1. <u>Send</u> a classmate into the hallway.
2. <u>Hide</u> an eraser where it cannot be seen easily.
3. <u>Ask</u> your classmate to come into the room.
4. <u>Give</u> one direction that moves your classmate closer to the eraser.
5. <u>Take turns</u> giving directions.

▶ Now think of topics you can write directions for. List things you know how to do or make. Here are some suggestions:

- how to fly a kite
- how to make a bed
- how to play tag
- how to plant a flower
- how to make a mask
- how to do a magic trick

Choose the topic you would like to write about.

2. Writing

Read again the directions for playing the game. Notice these three things:

- Each direction begins with a verb that names the action.
- The directions are numbered. They are given in the order in which they are to be followed.
- Each sentence is short and clear.

▶ Begin your directions by writing the title of your topic. Write "How to ___" or "Directions for ___." Fill in the blank with your topic.

Next write each step of your directions. Pretend someone is doing exactly what you write. Try to picture the person doing each step.

3. Revising

▶ Ask another person to read and follow your directions. Can you improve your directions? Use this checklist for help.

Revision Checklist

- Did I number each step?
- Did I give the steps in the correct order?
- Did I begin each sentence with a verb that names the action?
- Did I leave out any important words?

Read the sample. The directions are clearer when important words are not left out.

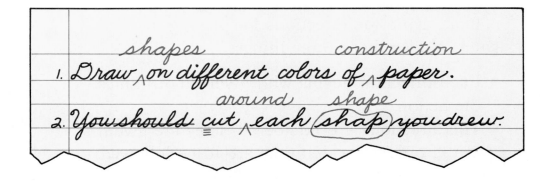

How to Make a Mobile

1. Draw shapes on different colors of construction paper.
2. Cut around each shape.
3. Glue a long piece of string on each shape.
4. Tie the strings to a stick.
5. Hang up your mobile.

▶ Now use the editing marks to make changes.

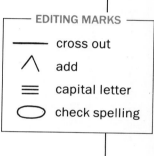

EDITING MARKS

—— cross out

∧ add

≡ capital letter

◯ check spelling

4. Publishing

▶ Proofread your directions. Use the Proofreading Checklist on this page or the one in the Young Writer's Handbook on page 355. Make corrections, using the editing marks.

▶ Make a poster to share your directions with the class. Write your directions on a large piece of paper or cardboard. Draw a picture on your poster, showing what your directions explain. Display your poster in the classroom. Take time to read your classmates' directions. You may find a new project to try.

PROOFREADING CHECKLIST

1. indent paragraphs ☑
2. capital letters ☑
3. end punctuation ☑
4. spelling ☑
5. handwriting ☑

Writing Project

A Puzzle Greeting Card

Make a puzzle greeting card. First, draw a picture, or cut one out of a magazine. Second, paste the picture on cardboard. Next, write your message. Use a crayon or felt-tip marker. Then, cut the picture into twenty pieces for a puzzle.

Finally, put the pieces in an envelope. Mail your card. The person you send it to will enjoy putting together your "puzzling" greeting.

Science

You must follow directions to do experiments in science. Try one of the experiments below.

► Get: a hard-boiled egg, a glass of water, a spoon, a box of salt

1. Drop the egg into the glass of water.
2. Stir some salt into the water. What happens?

► Get: a sheet of newspaper, a piece of wool
Use: the chalkboard

1. Put the sheet of newspaper over the chalkboard.
2. Rub the newspaper with the wool until the newspaper sticks to the chalkboard.
3. Put one hand behind your back. Use the other hand to fold the paper in half. What happens?

► Get: an empty bottle with a narrow neck, a small wad of paper

1. Lay the bottle on its side.
2. Put the small wad of paper in the neck of the bottle. Try to blow the paper into the bottle. What happens?

Speakers at Work Veterinarians are pet doctors. They tell people how to take care of their pets.

► Try it. Choose a pet. Find out how to take care of it. Look in books, or talk to someone who knows about animals. Then give directions to your class. Tell them how to take care of that pet.

Verbs *pages 154–165*

A. Write each sentence. Use the correct present-time form of the verb in (   ).

1. Mr. Parker ___ the school bus. (drive)
2. The ice cubes ___ in the sun. (melt)
3. She ___ for a sled. (wish)
4. They ___ broken clocks and radios. (fix)
5. Alan ___ to the park. (hurry)
6. A bird ___ the sleepy cat. (watch)

B. Write each sentence. Use the correct past-time form of the verb in (   ).

7. We ___ the boat across the lake. (row)
8. Emily ___ into a mud puddle. (step)
9. Our dog ___ a new trick. (try)
10. Last fall the trees ___ many colors. (turn)
11. I ___ two baskets of apples. (pick)
12. Joseph ___ the heavy boxes upstairs. (carry)

Prefixes *pages 166–167*

C. Write a word that has the prefix *un-* or *re-* for each meaning below.

13. the opposite of cover
14. build again
15. the opposite of fasten
16. plant again
17. the opposite of bend
18. load again

Friendly Letter   *pages 176–177*

D. Write each part of a letter correctly. Use commas and capital letters.

19. dear vanessa   **22.** your friend
20. albany new york   **23.** 142 birch lane
21. february 17 1986   **24.** connie

E. Write the answer to each question.

25. Which part of a letter says good-by?
26. What is the important message part of a letter called?
27. Which part of a letter tells the date and the address?
28. Which part of a letter says hello?
29. Which part tells who wrote the letter?

Directions   *pages 172–173*

F. Read the directions for planting a flower. Then write the steps in the right order. Number the steps from **1–5**.

Put the flowerpot in a sunny place.
Fill the flowerpot with soil.
Cover the seed with soil.
Put a seed in the soil.
Get a flowerpot.

See also Handbook pages 326–333, 349.

6

Grammar
Verbs

Composition
Researching

Grownups

They're big,
They're broad,
They're tall,
They're strong.
Their hands are large,
Their legs are long.
And no one tells them
What to do.
I wish I were
A grownup, too.

—*William Wise*

Reviewing Action Verbs

> ● A verb may show action in the present time or in the past time.

You have learned that a verb in the present time shows action that happens now. Present-time verbs that are used with singular nouns end in -*s* or -*es*.

Sometimes the spelling of a verb changes when -*es* is added. Which verb below changes its spelling when -*es* is added? How does the spelling change?

Please <u>address</u> this card.   Then <u>hurry</u> and mail it.
Ida <u>addresses</u> the card.   She <u>hurries</u> to the mailbox.

A verb in the past time shows action that already happened. Most verbs in the past time end in -*ed.*

The pony express <u>delivered</u> mail by horseback.

The spelling of some verbs changes when -*ed* is added. Notice the spelling of the verbs below.

<u>carry</u>: Riders <u>carried</u> sacks of letters.
<u>hop</u>: They often <u>hopped</u> onto fresh horses.

Skills Tryout

Tell if each verb shows past time or present time.

1. worried   3. reads   5. rushes
2. fixes   4. cries   6. stepped

Practice

A. Change each underlined verb to the past time. Write the new sentence.

1. The pony express <u>starts</u> in 1860.
2. Riders <u>hurry</u> from Missouri to California.
3. Each rider <u>stops</u> after riding three horses.
4. Then the next rider <u>carries</u> the mail.
5. Letters <u>cross</u> the country in eight or nine days.

B. Copy the chart below. Fill in the missing form of the verb.

Subject	Present Time	Past Time
6. We	carry	_____
7. A swimmer	_____	splashed
8. Horses	trot	_____
9. Nicole	_____	guessed
10. He	touches	_____
11. The students	_____	watched
12. Mr. Ryan	_____	jogged
13. They	clap	_____
14. She	_____	worried
15. You	look	_____

Application WRITING SENTENCES

Pretend that you have a pony fast enough for the pony express. Write three sentences using verbs in the past time to tell about your pony. Then write three sentences using verbs in the present time.

2 — Verbs with Special Past Forms

- Some verbs in the past time do not end in -ed.

Often -ed is added to verbs that show action that already happened. But some verbs change in other ways to show past time. Look at the chart below.

Verb	Present	Past
come	come, comes	came
do	do, does	did
go	go, goes	went
have	have, has	had
run	run, runs	ran

The sentences below show verbs in the past time. Notice the underlined verbs.

Dave <u>came</u> here often.　　Seth <u>went</u> to the gym.
Tara <u>had</u> new shoes.　　I <u>did</u> push-ups.
We <u>ran</u> on a track.

Skills Tryout

Tell the past-time form of the verb in (　).

1. Many people ___ to the Boston Marathon. (go)
2. They ___ for hours. (run)
3. We ___ to watch. (come)
4. Runners ___ numbers. (have)
5. They ___ their best. (do)

Practice

A. Write each sentence. If the underlined verb is in the past time, write *past*. If the underlined verb is in the present time, write *present*.

1. Our town <u>has</u> a mini-marathon.
2. Runners <u>go</u> from the high school to the park.
3. They <u>do</u> it to raise money for a hospital.
4. Last year everyone <u>ran</u> thirteen miles.
5. People <u>came</u> from many different places.

B. Write each sentence. Use the form of the verb in ( ) that tells about the past time.

6. The name for a long race ____ from Greece. (come)
7. A messenger ____ from a place called Marathon to Athens. (go)
8. He ____ it over two thousand years ago. (do)
9. He ____ with news of a Greek victory. (come)
10. The runner ____ about twenty-five miles. (run)
11. Early Olympic Games ____ marathon races. (have)
12. Those runners also ____ twenty-five miles. (run)
13. Beginning in 1908 the runners ____ more than twenty-six miles. (go)
14. Boston ____ its first marathon in 1897. (have)
15. A woman ____ for the first time in 1967. (run)

Application WRITING SENTENCES

Pretend that you ran in a marathon. Write five sentences about the race. Use the past-time form of each of these verbs: *come, do, go, have, run.*

3 — The Verb *be*

> ● A verb may show being.

Read the sentences. Notice the underlined verbs.

Wendy <u>writes</u> poems.   She <u>finished</u> one today.

Verbs like *writes* and *finished* show action. They tell what something or someone does or did. Some verbs do not show action. Notice the underlined verbs in Wendy's poem.

> **Spring days <u>are</u> now here**
> **With warm sun of gold.**
> **Winter <u>was</u> dreary.**
> **The nights <u>were</u> too cold.**

Wendy wrote more about spring. She used two more verbs that do not show action.

> **I <u>am</u> full of cheer**
> **Now that springtime <u>is</u> here.**

The verbs *am, is, are, was,* and *were* show being instead of action. These verbs tell what something or someone is or was.

Skills Tryout

Find the verb that shows being in each sentence.

1. March days are windy.
2. Yesterday was cloudy.
3. The clouds were puffy.
4. I was in the house.
5. Today is a sunny day.
6. I am glad.

Practice

A. Write the verb that shows being in each sentence.

1. Kites were my friend Paco's favorite toys.
2. Last week his book report was about kites.
3. The book's author is Wyatt Brummit.
4. Kites are very popular.
5. I am a kite builder, too.

B. Copy each sentence. Draw one line under the verb if it shows being. Draw two lines under the verb if it shows action.

6. Early kites were very large leaves.
7. The string was a piece of vine.
8. Most kites are just for fun.
9. Some scientists use kites in their work.
10. Weather kites gather important information.
11. They show wind and air pressure.
12. Once a kite was in the air for seven days.
13. A very large kite weighed over nine tons.
14. Once over a thousand kites were on one line!
15. I am happy with one kite on a windy day.

Application WRITING SENTENCES

Write five sentences about your favorite season. Use each of these verbs in a sentence: *am, is, are, was, were.*

Using the Forms of *be*

> ● The form of *be* that is used must agree with the subject of the sentence.

The verbs *am*, *is*, *are*, *was*, and *were* are forms of the verb *be*. *Am*, *is*, and *are* tell about the present. *Was* and *were* tell about the past.

The form of *be* that is used depends upon the subject of a sentence. When the correct subject and verb are used together, we say that they agree.

Using the Forms of *be*		
Subject	Verb	Example
I	am, was	I am glad. I was cold.
singular nouns and *she, he, it*	is, was	A seal is sleek. It was large.
plural nouns and *we, you, they*	are, were	Seals are mammals. They were on the ice.

Skills Tryout

Choose the correct form of the verb *be* in ( ).

1. I (am, is) interested in dolphins.
2. A dolphin (are, is) a small sea mammal.
3. Two dolphins (am, are) in our city zoo.
4. They (was, were) in a show at the zoo.
5. I (was, were) at the show last week.

Practice

A. Write the correct form of the verb *be* in ( ).

1. The movie (was, were) about sea animals.
2. Dolphins (was, were) in the Pacific Ocean.
3. The water (am, is) warm in parts of the ocean.
4. A dolphin's nose (is, are) pointed.
5. Porpoises (are, is) smaller than dolphins.

B. Write each sentence. Use *am*, *is*, or *are*.

6. A dolphin ____ about six feet long.
7. I ____ smaller than a dolphin.
8. Dolphins and whales ____ mammals.
9. A dolphin's teeth ____ cone-shaped.
10. *Porpoise* ____ another name for *dolphin*.

C. Write each sentence. If the verb shows being in the present time, write *present.* If the verb shows being in the past time, write *past.*

11. I <u>am</u> curious about sea animals.
12. My library book <u>was</u> about dolphins.
13. A school <u>is</u> a group of dolphins.
14. Dolphins <u>are</u> very intelligent.
15. They <u>were</u> always in schools!

Application SPEAKING

Pretend that you are meeting a friendly dolphin. Tell about yourself and your family. Use each of these verbs: *am, was, is, are, were.*

5 — Main Verbs and Helping Verbs

> ● A **helping verb** works with the main verb.

A verb can be more than one word. Look at the underlined verb in the sentence below.

Trains <u>have changed</u> in many ways.

The word *changed* is the main verb. The **main verb** is the most important verb in a sentence. The word *have* is a helping verb. A **helping verb** works with the main verb.

The verbs *have, has,* and *had* are often used as helping verbs. *Have, has,* or *had* helps a main verb show action in the past time. When the helping verb is *have, has,* or *had,* the main verb often ends in *-ed.*

Read the sentence below. The main verb ends in *-ed.* Which helping verb is used?

Mr. Dixon <u>has worked</u> on freight trains.

Skills Tryout

Tell if a helping verb or a main verb is underlined.

1. Trains have <u>carried</u> people and things.
2. Milk has <u>remained</u> cold in a refrigerator car.
3. Flatcars <u>have</u> delivered automobiles.
4. Early trains <u>had</u> used coal for power.
5. Workers had <u>shoveled</u> tons of coal.

Practice

A. Write the helping verb and the main verb in each sentence.

EXAMPLE: Ted and I have started a hobby.
ANSWER: have started

1. The museum has opened a display of trains.
2. Lono and I have returned several times.
3. He has wanted a book about old trains.
4. I had walked through the display before.
5. I have climbed on the engine car three times.
6. Lono has collected model trains for years.
7. His aunt had started the collection.
8. They have added pieces every year.
9. Lono has joined a model train club.
10. Many people have enjoyed this hobby.

B. Write each sentence. Use the correct form of the verb in ( ).

11. One kind of train has ____ underground. (travel)
12. America's first subway had ____ in 1897. (open)
13. Electricity has ____ subways since 1890. (power)
14. Many cities have ____ subway systems. (start)
15. One city has ____ its system the Metro. (call)

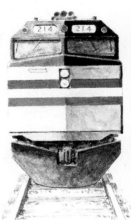

Application WRITING SENTENCES

Write four sentences about a trip that you or someone you know took. Use *have, has,* or *had* with these verbs: *carried, packed, moved, traveled.*

> • Some verbs change their form to show past time.

Not all verbs in the past time end in *-ed*.
Irregular verbs do not add *-ed* to show action in the past. Verbs such as *do, go, eat, give,* and *see* change completely to show action in the past. They change again when they are used with *have, has,* or *had.* Study the chart below.

Verb	Past	Past with *have, has,* or *had*
do	did	done
go	went	gone
eat	ate	eaten
give	gave	given
see	saw	seen

Read the sentences below. The underlined words are irregular verbs. Which form of the irregular verb *eat* is used with a helping verb?

**Johnny Appleseed <u>gave</u> apple seeds to many people.
I <u>have eaten</u> apples from trees he planted.**

Skills Tryout

Tell the correct past-time form of the verb in ( ).

1. I have (go) home.
2. We (see) a play.
3. He had (do) the job.
4. They had (give) up.
5. She (eat) already.
6. You (do) it.

Practice

A. Write the correct past-time form of the verb in ( ).

1. Folks had ____ John Chapman plant seeds. (see)
2. He had ____ west around 1800. (go)
3. They ____ him the name Johnny Appleseed. (give)
4. This pioneer ____ his work without pay. (do)
5. People have ____ apples from his trees. (eat)

B. Change the underlined verb to the form shown in ( ). Write each sentence.

EXAMPLE: I <u>see</u> many apple trees. (past with *have*)
ANSWER: I have seen many apple trees.

6. I <u>do</u> a cookbook of apple recipes. (past with *had*)
7. We <u>eat</u> homemade applesauce last week. (past)
8. I <u>do</u> all the peeling! (past)
9. Lena <u>goes</u> to the store for dried apples. (past)
10. She also <u>sees</u> apple pies for sale. (past)
11. You <u>eat</u> apple butter on toast. (past with *have*)
12. Sheila <u>gives</u> me apple juice. (past with *has*)
13. Rita <u>sees</u> another kind of apple. (past with *has*)
14. She <u>goes</u> to the Big Apple once. (past with *has*)
15. The people of New York <u>give</u> that nickname to their city. (past)

Application WRITING SENTENCES

Write a sentence for each verb form below.

have eaten   saw   has given   did   went

7 — Using Irregular Verbs

- Irregular verbs have special past forms.

You have learned that irregular verbs do not add *-ed* to show action in the past. Study the chart.

Verb	Past	Past with *have*, *has*, or *had*
run	ran	run
come	came	come
grow	grew	grown
know	knew	known
draw	drew	drawn

Read the sentences below. Notice that the underlined words are irregular verbs. Which form of the irregular verb *run* is used without a helping verb?

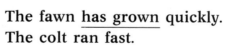

The fawn <u>has grown</u> quickly.
The colt <u>ran</u> fast.
The chicks <u>have come</u> over.

Skills Tryout

Tell the correct past-time form of the verb in ( ).

1. I (run) to the barn.
2. The animals (know) me.
3. I have (come) every day.
4. The pony had (grow).
5. It (come) to me.
6. I (draw) its picture.

Practice

A. Choose the correct past-time form of the verb in ( ). Write each sentence.

1. We (come, came) to my cousin's farm.
2. First I (run, ran) to the pond.
3. The ducklings (knew, known) how to swim.
4. Sean had (drew, drawn) a funny picture of Billy.
5. In the picture Billy the goat had (grew, grown) a long white beard.

B. Write each sentence. Use the correct past-time form of the verb in ( ).

6. I have ＿＿ often to the children's zoo. (come)
7. The zookeeper has ＿＿ me for months. (know)
8. The fawn's wobbly legs have ＿＿ stronger. (grow)
9. It ＿＿ away from me. (run)
10. An artist ＿＿ to watch the animals. (come)
11. She ＿＿ pictures of the spotted fawn. (draw)
12. Last time she had ＿＿ the monkeys. (draw)
13. One shy monkey had ＿＿ to its mother. (run)
14. Then it ＿＿ more brave. (grow)
15. The monkey ＿＿ the artist then. (know)

Application WRITING SENTENCES

Write five sentences about your favorite baby animals. Use each verb form below in a sentence. You may need to use a helping verb.

ran　　drawn　　grown　　came　　known

8 Contractions

> ● A **contraction** is a shortened form of two words.

Look at the underlined words in these sentences.

We are cooking at school. **We're** making chili.

The underlined words in the sentences mean the same thing. In the second sentence the contraction *we're* is a shorter way to say *we are*.

In a contraction an apostrophe (') shows where a letter or letters have been left out. Look at the list of contractions below. Notice that each contraction is made up of a pronoun and a verb.

Pronoun + Verb = Contraction	
I + am = I'm	I + have = I've
he + is = he's	you + have = you've
she + is = she's	I + will = I'll
it + is = it's	you + will = you'll
they + are = they're	we + will = we'll
we + are = we're	

Skills Tryout

Name contractions for the underlined words.

1. She is hungry.
2. Now they are late.
3. I know it is ready.
4. We will help you.
5. I will wait for you.
6. You have done it now.

Practice

A. Write the contraction from each sentence. Then write the two words that make up the contraction.

EXAMPLE: We're learning how to cook.
ANSWER: we're, we are

1. Today we're having tacos for lunch.
2. First we'll buy beef, cheese, and lettuce.
3. I've never tasted a tortilla before.
4. I think you've seen the bread at Elena's house.
5. She says they're made from corn.
6. When it's hot, a tortilla is delicious.
7. I'll help Melissa cook the beef.
8. Then she's going to grate the cheese.
9. Matt says he's cutting the lettuce and tomato.
10. I'm very hungry already!

B. Write each sentence. Use a contraction in place of the underlined words in each sentence.

11. Tomorrow <u>we are</u> making a pot of chili.
12. You know that <u>it is</u> like a hot, spicy soup.
13. Monica, <u>you will</u> have to chop some onions.
14. Then <u>we will</u> serve corn bread, too.
15. <u>I am</u> sure it will taste just like Mom's!

Application WRITING SENTENCES

Plan a lunch for a friend. Write five sentences that tell what you will make. Use a contraction in each sentence.

9 Suffixes

> ● A **suffix** is a letter or letters added to the end of a word.

Remember that the simplest form of a word is a base word. Sometimes a new word is formed by adding a letter or letters to the end of a base word. Look at the pairs of words below.

work	visit	play
work<u>er</u>	visit<u>or</u>	play<u>er</u>

The second word in each pair ends with a suffix. The suffixes *-er* and *-or* may mean "someone who." A *worker* is someone who works. A *visitor* is someone who visits. What is a *player*?

Each underlined word below ends with the suffix *-er*. What does each word mean?

Our <u>teacher</u> talked about famous women. Grandma Moses was a <u>painter</u>.

Skills Tryout

Each word below has a suffix. Tell what each word means.

1. jumper
2. actor
3. singer
4. farmer
5. sailor
6. gardener

Practice

A. Read the meanings below. Then write a word that has the suffix *-er* for each meaning.

1. someone who camps
2. someone who speaks
3. someone who prints
4. someone who travels
5. someone who plays
6. someone who works
7. someone who builds
8. someone who reads
9. someone who walks
10. someone who skis

B. Find the word in each sentence that ends with a suffix that means "someone who." Write the word and its meaning.

EXAMPLE: Amelia Earhart was the first female flyer to cross the ocean alone.

ANSWER: flyer, someone who flies

11. Nelly Bly was a famous newspaper reporter.
12. A teacher named Mary McLeod Bethune helped start a college.
13. Nellie T. Ross was the first woman governor.
14. A photographer named Imogen Cunningham won many prizes.
15. Maria Tallchief is a great ballet dancer.

Application USING LANGUAGE

Use the suffix in ( ) to form a new word for each meaning below. Use each new word in a sentence.

someone who acts (-or)   someone who paints (-er)
someone who sings (-er)   someone who invents (-or)

Action Verbs *pages 188–189*

A. Change each underlined verb from the present time to the past time. Write the new sentences.

1. We <u>carry</u> our books.
2. Leo <u>hops</u> on one foot.
3. They <u>watch</u> the show.
4. Davy <u>tries</u> to help.
5. Jim <u>asks</u> questions.
6. Jo <u>crosses</u> the road.

The Verb <u>be</u> *pages 192–195*

B. Write each sentence. Use the correct form of *be* in (   ).

7. They (were, was) wet.
8. Grapes (is, are) sweet.
9. Stu (was, were) angry.
10. We (was, were) sad.
11. Val (is, are) sick.
12. I (am, is) sleepy.
13. You (is, are) late.
14. Darla (is, are) here.

Main Verbs and Helping Verbs *pages 196–197*

C. Write each sentence. Draw one line under the helping verb. Draw two lines under the main verb.

15. We have visited the new civic center.
16. Jane has scored twenty points.
17. My brothers have entered an art contest.
18. They had cooked breakfast for us.
19. I have ironed all the shirts.
20. He had missed the train.

Irregular Verbs *pages 190–191, 198–201*

D. Write each sentence. Use the form of the verb in ( ) that tells about the past.

21. Ginger ___ the answer yesterday. (know)
22. The teacher has ___ a test. (give)
23. We have ___ in the cafeteria. (eat)
24. Carmen ___ to the movies last week. (go)
25. Milo and Lou had ___ jogging. (go)
26. I have ___ four inches in a year. (grow)
27. My friends ___ over for lunch. (come)
28. Uncle Hank has ___ in many races. (run)
29. The carpenter ___ a good job. (do)
30. You have ___ her many times. (see)

Contractions *pages 202–203*

E. Write the contraction for each pair of words.

31. they are
32. he is
33. I am
34. you will
35. I have
36. we are
37. it is
38. she is
39. you have

Suffixes *pages 204–205*

F. Write a word that has the suffix *-er* for each meaning.

40. someone who sings
41. someone who plays
42. someone who speaks
43. someone who paints
44. someone who works
45. someone who builds

See also Handbook pages 334–341.

Writing with Verbs

> ● Stay in the same time when you write about something.

Grammar and Writing Workshop

Michael asked Marcia for help with his homework. She runs to his house as quickly as she can. She knocked on the door. Michael tells her to come in.

Something is wrong with the paragraph above. The sentences are written in different times. The first and the third sentences tell about past time. The other sentences are part of the same paragraph. But they tell about the present time. Mixing times makes writing hard to read and understand.

In the paragraph below, every sentence tells about the past. See how much better this paragraph sounds!

Michael asked Marcia for help with his homework. She ran to his house as quickly as she could. She knocked on the door. Michael told her to come in.

The Time Game   Look at the verbs below. Write a list of all the past-time verbs. Then write a list of the present-time verbs.

fry	took	melts	danced	hurries	taught
sat	said	close	buried	teaches	spoke
look	hope	heard	wishes	followed	studied

The Time Switch   Make the verbs in each pair of sentences tell about the same time. Change the underlined verbs. Write the sentences.

EXAMPLE: **a.** Dad laughed.   **b.** He <u>smiles</u> and <u>grins</u>.
ANSWER: **a.** Dad laughed.   **b.** He smiled and grinned.

1. **a.** The explosion happened at noon.
   b. I <u>call</u> the fire department and <u>wait</u>.
2. **a.** The stuntman leaps through the ring of fire.
   b. The crowd <u>cheered</u> and <u>whistled</u>.
3. **a.** Lana strolls through the forest.
   b. She <u>looked</u> for birds and <u>listened</u> to them.
4. **a.** I borrowed a pen from Todd.
   b. I <u>thank</u> him and <u>use</u> the pen.

Add-and-Change   Write each sentence below two times. First complete it with a present-time verb. Then complete it with the same verb in the past time.

5. The hikers ____ an elephant the size of a puppy.
6. They ____ a mountain covered with green snow.
7. A huge bat ____ above them.

Using the Thesaurus

Suppose you spent a day moving boxes for a friend. Write five sentences about the day, but don't use the verb *move*. Find five synonyms for *move* in the Thesaurus. Use only present-time verbs.

- Choose a topic that interests you.
- If the topic is too broad, you must narrow the topic.

Suppose that you want to write about a certain topic. Ask yourself some questions about it. Is the topic small enough, or narrow enough, to manage? Or is it too big, or too broad?

Here's how one student narrowed his topic. Len was very interested in music. He wanted to play in a band someday. He knew that *music* was too broad a topic to write about. He thought that *musical instruments* was also too broad a topic. Finally he chose to write about *drums*. That topic was narrow enough.

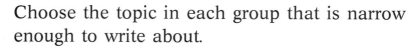

Skills Tryout

Choose the topic in each group that is narrow enough to write about.

1. sailboats, transportation, boats
2. animals, wild animals, baboons
3. planets, Jupiter, the universe
4. roller skating, health, exercise
5. art, watercolors, painting

Practice

A. Write the narrow topic from each group of topics.

EXAMPLE: indoor games, checkers, board games
ANSWER: checkers

1. bodies of water, rivers, Hudson River
2. living things, the brain, the human body
3. Susan B. Anthony, women, famous Americans
4. sports, hockey, winter sports
5. parents, relatives, people

B. For each topic below, write *narrow* or *broad*.

6. American cities
7. San Diego Zoo
8. famous writers
9. oceans of the world
10. sharks

11. food
12. pumpkin plants
13. jobs
14. Mark Twain
15. forest rangers

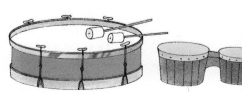
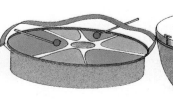

Application USING STUDY SKILLS

For each broad topic below, choose a narrow topic that interests you. For example, for the broad topic *states,* you might choose your own state. Write your narrow topics. Compare them with your classmates' topics.

a. house pets **b.** inventions **c.** outdoor games

11 — Using the Library

> • A library has a section for children's books of all kinds.

What do you want to know? Whatever it is, you can probably find out about it in a library. The library is a treasure house of information. All it takes to unlock this treasure house is a library card!

When you go to a library, look for the children's books. They will be in a special room or a special part of the library.

The library has all kinds of books. Books of the same kind are kept together. This makes them easier to find. Ask the librarian to show you where these kinds of books are kept.

Fiction books
These are storybooks. The stories have been made up.

Nonfiction books
These are books that tell facts. They give information about a subject.

Biographies
These are true stories about the lives of real people.

Reference books
These are books that give information about many subjects. They include dictionaries, encyclopedias, and atlases.

Tell what kind of book each of these is.

1. a mystery story
2. a book telling how to do magic tricks
3. a book telling how to pronounce the word *amphibian* and what it means
4. a book about the life of Daniel Boone
5. a storybook about a friendly dragon

Practice

Read these book titles. After each title write *fiction, nonfiction, biography,* or *reference book.*

1. *All About Whales*
2. *The Tale of Peter Rabbit*
3. *Alice's Adventures in Wonderland*
4. *World Book Encyclopedia*
5. *Abraham Lincoln*
6. *The First Book of Weather*
7. *The True Book of Metric Measurement*
8. *Dictionary of Place Names*
9. *A Mystery for Meg*
10. *The Story of George Washington*

Application USING STUDY SKILLS

Browse through some library books. Choose a fiction book, a nonfiction book, and a biography. Then pick just one book. Tell why you think it might be interesting to read.

12 — Using the Parts of a Book

> ● Books that give information have a **table of contents** and an **index**.

Some books are meant to be read from cover to cover. Others are not. For example, you read an adventure story from beginning to end. You probably do not read a book of information the same way. You may just read the pages that give the information you need.

How can you find out which pages tell what you want to know? Two parts of a book can help you. They are the table of contents and the index. The table of contents is at the front of a book. The index is at the back. Study these examples.

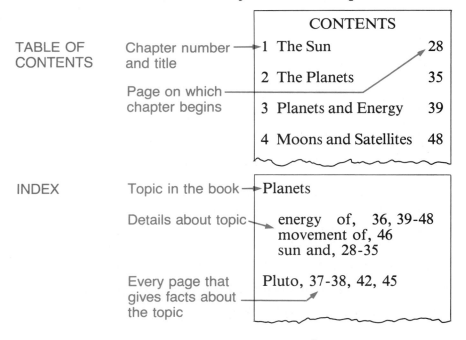

TABLE OF CONTENTS

Chapter number and title
Page on which chapter begins

CONTENTS

1 The Sun   28

2 The Planets   35

3 Planets and Energy   39

4 Moons and Satellites   48

INDEX

Topic in the book
Details about topic
Every page that gives facts about the topic

Planets

   energy   of,   36, 39-48
   movement of, 46
   sun and, 28-35

Pluto, 37-38, 42, 45

Skills Tryout

Use the examples on page 214 to answer **1-4.**

1. Where are topics listed in alphabetical order?
2. Where are chapter titles listed in order?
3. Where are all the pages about one topic listed?
4. On what page does the chapter "The Sun" begin?

Practice

A. Use the table of contents of this book to answer these questions. Write each answer.

    1. How many units are in the book?
    2. Which part of each unit is the Grammar part?
    3. What is the Writing Project for Unit Six?
    4. On what page is Building Bridges in Unit 3?
    5. On what page does the Thesaurus begin?

B. Use the index of this book to answer these questions. Write each answer.

    6. What pages tell about writing letters?
    7. What is the first page on book reports?
    8. Does the book tell anything about adverbs?
    9. Is the word *lion* listed in the index?
    10. What pages tell about homophones?

Application USING STUDY SKILLS

Play an index game. Write five topics from the index of this book. Exchange papers. See who can find the page numbers for each topic first.

13 — Using an Encyclopedia

> • Entries in an encyclopedia are arranged in alphabetical order.

You can find information on a topic in an encyclopedia. An **encyclopedia** is a set of books with facts about people, places, and things.

Each book in an encyclopedia is called a **volume**. On the side of each volume, you will see a volume number and one or more letters. As in a dictionary, the entries are in alphabetical order. Each entry has information on a single topic. The letters on the volumes show what entries are in each volume.

Study this illustration. How many volumes does this encyclopedia contain? In which one would you look for information about *volcanoes*?

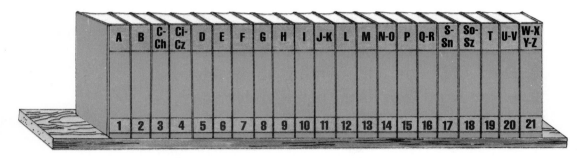

Information about a person is listed by the last name. Ernesto Galarza is a famous Mexican-American writer. Why would you find the entry about him in volume 8?

Skills Tryout

Look at the encyclopedia shown on page 216. Tell which volumes have information about these entries.

1. llama   2. Hawaii   3. Jesse Owens

Practice

A. Write the volume number for each topic below. Use the encyclopedia on page 216.

1. dolls
2. New Zealand
3. Winston Churchill
4. Jane Addams
5. Florida
6. Casey Jones

B. Write each sentence. Fill in the blank with the correct answer. Use the encyclopedia shown.

7. A set of books with facts about people, places, and things is called an ____.
8. Volume 21 contains information about entries beginning with the letters ____.
9. Information about *caves* is in volume ____.
10. Entries beginning with the letter *s* are found in volumes ____ and ____.

Application USING STUDY SKILLS

Go to a library and use an encyclopedia. Choose four topics from **Practice A**, or choose four topics of your own. Write the volume and page number where you found each entry.

Using Your Own Words

> ● To be sure you understand information you read, tell it in your own words.

Darla read about dragons in the encyclopedia. She wanted to tell her friends what she had learned. First she thought about the information to be sure she understood it. Then she told it in her own words.

DRAGON, an imaginary beast in folktales of many countries. In legends, dragons were large, fire-breathing creatures like lizards. They had long scaly tails. In European legends, dragons were fierce and dangerous. But in the legends of China and Japan, dragons were friendly bearers of good luck. In China the traditional New Year's parade includes a large group of people in a dragon costume. The dragon is supposed to prevent bad luck from spoiling the new year.

You can read about dragons in stories from many countries. They were large, make-believe animals that looked like lizards. In legends, dragons breathed fire! In some countries' stories, dragons were bad, but in others they brought good luck. In fact, in a Chinese New Year's parade, a make-believe dragon is there to bring a lucky new year.

Read the encyclopedia entry about dragons again. Close your book. Think about what you just read. Then use your own words to tell about dragons.

Practice

Read each encyclopedia entry below. Then use your own words to write three sentences about each entry.

WRIGHT, FRANK LLOYD, one of the most important American architects. He created architecture that blended in perfectly with its environment. His designs included a home called Fallingwater, built over a waterfall.

SATURN, a large planet, second only to Jupiter in size. Saturn has beautiful rings around it. There are six thin gleaming rings, which cannot be seen with the naked eye. The planet itself can be seen, even though it is very far away. One year on Saturn is about 29½ years in Earth time.

Application USING STUDY SKILLS

Look in an encyclopedia for a topic you are interested in. Read the information. Use your own words to write three sentences about the topic.

15 — Writing a Report

Writing Project

> • A **report** gives facts about a topic.

As you learn about the world, you have many questions. *Why do stars shine? How cold is the South Pole? How big is the moon?* You want to know many things.

In this lesson you will find facts about a topic. You will use the facts to write a report. Then you and your classmates will share your reports in a "Book of Facts."

1. Prewriting

▶ First choose a topic for your report. What do you want to know about? Perhaps you will think of a topic right away. If not, look in your science or social studies book. Check the table of contents and index. You will find many topics. Here are a few from a science book:

- clouds
- glaciers
- machines
- astronauts
- planets
- deserts

Jot down your ideas on what to write about. Then make a choice and circle your topic.

▶ Find your topic in an encyclopedia. Use the first letter of your topic to find the right volume. Then use alphabetical order to find the entry.

The encyclopedia article may be long. If it is, you don't have to read it all. Read the headings in dark print. Choose the one that sounds most interesting and read the information under it.

▶ Now look away from the book. Ask: *What is the main fact I want to tell about?* Write it down in your own words.

Look at the book again. Reread sentences that tell about or explain the main fact you just wrote. Jot down notes, telling about those ideas.

Matt wanted to write a report about Mars. He read each heading under *Mars* in an encyclopedia. He picked *the climate of Mars* for his report. The main fact he wanted to write about was *People could not live on Mars.* His other notes tell more about that fact.

> *People could not live on Mars.*
>
> *too cold*
> *almost no water*
> *no oxygen in air*

2. Writing

▶ You have your information. Now you are ready to write your first draft. Begin with a topic sentence that tells what your report is about: "People could not live on Mars."

Use your notes to write the rest of your report. In the next sentences you write, give more information about the topic sentence. Be sure to use your own words. Then write a title for your report.

3. Revising

▶ Ask someone to listen to your report. Does your listener have questions? How can you improve your report? Use this checklist.

Revision Checklist
- Did I begin with a topic sentence?
- Do my other sentences tell more about the topic sentence?
- Did I use my own words?
- Did I begin my sentences in different ways?

Read the sample. Notice how it was made better by beginning sentences in different ways.

¶ People could not live at all on mars.
    This planet   and   almost
Mars is very cold, Mars has allmost no

       Mars
    People could not live on Mars. This planet is very cold and has almost no water. Also, people could not breathe because Mars does not have oxygen in the air.

▶ Did you think of ways to improve your report? Use the editing marks to make changes.

EDITING MARKS

—— cross out
∧ add
≡ capital letter
¶ indent
◯ check spelling

4. Publishing

▶ The best part of writing can be sharing it with others. First proofread your report. Use the Proofreading Checklist on this page or the one in the Young Writer's Handbook on page 355. Make corrections, using the editing marks.

▶ Make a "Book of Facts" with your classmates.
- Punch three holes in the side of each report.
- List all of the report topics on one page. This will be the table of contents. Place it in the front of the book.
- Make a cover for the book.
- Use yarn to hold all the pages together.

PROOFREADING CHECKLIST

1. indent paragraphs ☑
2. capital letters ☑
3. end punctuation ☑
4. spelling ☑
5. handwriting ☑

Writing Project

"What's the Answer?"

> What is the largest lake in the world?
> The Caspian Sea. It is called a sea, but it is really a lake.
> Robbie
>
> checked by Ana

> Does Saturn have any moons?
> Scientists believe it has at least 21 moons.
> Jennifer M.
>
> checked by Luke Andrews

Make a "What's the Answer?" bulletin board. Find an interesting fact in the encyclopedia. Write a question about it on an index card or a slip of paper. Leave room underneath the question for someone to write the answer. Then attach it to the bulletin board.

Your classmates may use an encyclopedia or any other book to find the answer. The first person to find the answer writes it under the question and signs his or her name.

Check the answer. Then write, "Checked by (your name)."

Social Studies

In social studies you do a lot of reading. Of course, you cannot remember everything you read. You should try to remember the important points, however. A good way to do this is by *summarizing*. When you summarize, you sum up. You tell only the most important points.

▶ Try it. In a few sentences summarize this information from a book about Thomas Jefferson.

Although he had a French chef, Jefferson loved to cook. He wrote favorite recipes into his cookbook and also wrote an essay called "Observations on Soups."

• • •

Jefferson imported plants for study and experiment. He was the first President to grow a tomato; everyone else in America thought they were poisonous.

Listeners at Work News reporters do research by asking questions. They listen, then they write.

▶ Try it. Interview a school worker or a relative or friend. You might ask the person about his or her job. You might ask the person to tell about something exciting he or she has done. Listen carefully. Then write what you learned.

Verbs   *pages 188–201*

A. Write each sentence. Use the correct form of the verb in ( ).

1. Rings (is, are) round.
2. It (went, gone) away.
3. I (known, knew) Pam.
4. Ben (was, were) late.
5. We (ate, eaten) late.
6. Who (done, did) that?
7. A taxi (came, come).
8. We (was, were) busy.

B. Write each sentence. Draw one line under the helping verb and two lines under the main verb.

9. Sara has painted a picture of me.
10. Annie and Tina had missed the bus.
11. Paul, Tim, and Joe have cleaned their desks.
12. Leroy had laughed at the circus clowns.

Contractions   *pages 202–203*

C. Write the contractions for each pair of words.

13. he is   14. we are   15. I have   16. you will

Suffixes   *pages 204–205*

D. Write a word that has the suffix *-er* for each meaning.

17. someone who leads
18. someone who paints
19. someone who climbs
20. someone who helps

Library   *pages 212–213*

E. Write *fiction, nonfiction, biography,* or *reference* for each of these book titles.

21. *Thomas Jefferson*   **23.** *Wildlife Encyclopedia*
22. *You and Your Health*   **24.** *Storybook Hill*

Encyclopedia   *pages 216–217*

F. Where will you find the entry for each topic below? Write the volume number from the encyclopedia.

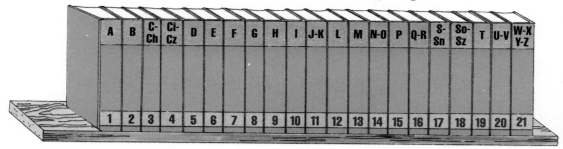

25. clouds   **26.** Amelia Earhart   **27.** New Mexico

Reports   *pages 218–219*

G. Read the encyclopedia entry below. Then use your own words to write three sentences about the entry.

SHREW, a mouse-like animal found in the forests of many parts of the world. The tiny shrew has a huge appetite. It must have food every two or three hours. A shrew may eat ten meals in one day. Its diet includes insects, worms, and seeds.

See also Handbook pages 334–341.

Checkpoint: Unit 6

Sentences   *pages 12–17*

A. Write each sentence. Draw one line under the subject. Draw two lines under the predicate.

1. Danny is asleep.
2. The dog chased us.
3. A ladybug flew by.
4. Our friends live there.

Nouns   *pages 48–57, 86–87*

B. Write the plural form of each noun.

5. tiger   6. lunch   7. hobby   8. wish

C. Write the possessive form of each noun.

9. Annie   10. game   11. men   12. monkeys

D. Write *common* or *proper* for each noun.

13. banana   15. July   17. Ohio   19. ocean
14. Robert   16. train   18. flower   20. Boston

Capital Letters and Commas   *pages 88–95*

E. Write each sentence. Use capital letters and commas correctly.

21. Yes we saw the green mountains in vermont.
22. Sarah is groundhog day in february?
23. The little shop on elm road is closed on friday.
24. No chicago is not in indiana.

Pronouns   *pages 118–127*

F. Change the underlined word or words in each
sentence to a pronoun. Write each new sentence.

25. Mindy drew a picture of <u>Susan and me</u>.
26. <u>Ben's</u> uncle plays soccer.
27. Mark counted <u>the plant's</u> blossoms.
28. <u>Mr. James</u> took care of the puppy.

Verbs   *pages 154–165, 190–191, 196–201*

G. Write the correct present-time form of the verb
in (   ). Then write the correct past-time form.

29. The parrot ___ seeds and crumbs. (eat)
30. Mandy ___ home from school. (hurry)
31. She ___ to the library often. (go)
32. Nick ___ his foot on the floor. (tap)

H. Write each sentence. Draw one line under the
helping verb. Draw two lines under the main verb.

33. Ted has grown tall.   **35.** The rain had stopped.
34. They have come home.   **36.** June has moved away.

Contractions   *pages 202–203*

I. Write the contraction for each pair of words.

37. they are   **38.** he is   **39.** you will   **40.** I have

7

Grammar
Adjectives

Composition
Describing

At the Seaside

When I was down beside the sea,
A wooden spade they gave to me
　To dig the sandy shore.

My holes were empty like a cup.
In every hole the sea came up,
　Till it could come no more.

—*Robert Louis Stevenson*

What Is an Adjective?

> ● A word that describes a noun is an **adjective**.

Remember that a noun is a word that names a person, place, or thing. Some words tell more about nouns. These words are called adjectives. Look at the underlined adjectives below.

We hiked to a small pond.   **I saw a yellow fish.**

The words *pond* and *fish* are nouns. The word *small* is an adjective that describes the size of the pond. The word *yellow* is an adjective that describes the color of the fish.

An adjective may also tell how something looks, feels, tastes, smells, or sounds. What does the underlined adjective below tell about the noun it describes?

Will tossed a stone into the cold water.

Skills Tryout

Tell the adjective that describes each underlined noun.

1. Tiny plants floated in the water.
2. I spotted green frogs.
3. They sat on flat rocks.
4. The frogs jumped over large logs.
5. They blinked at shiny beetles.

Practice

A. Copy each sentence. Draw one line under each adjective. Draw two lines under the noun that the adjective describes.

EXAMPLE: April has warm days.
ANSWER: April has <u>warm</u> <u>days</u>.

1. Kaloma and Ellie walked by little streams.
2. They carried brown bags.
3. Golden butterflies passed near them.
4. Ellie looked for pretty rocks.
5. Kaloma picked up empty shells.
6. Lazy snails had left them behind.
7. Hungry robins flew by.
8. They spied fat worms.
9. Robins landed beside muddy footprints.
10. Everyone enjoys lovely days in spring.

B. Write each sentence. Add an adjective.

11. We saw a ___ tree.
12. It was a ___ day.
13. We sat in ___ grass.
14. A ___ fly buzzed.
15. I smelled ___ roses.
16. Sam ate a ___ pear.
17. I had ___ grapes.
18. A ___ dog ran by.
19. It had a ___ tail.
20. My ___ pal yawned.

Application WRITING SENTENCES

Write four sentences about your favorite spot outdoors. Use adjectives that tell how your special place feels, looks, smells, or sounds.

2 — Adjectives That Tell *How Many*

> ● Some adjectives answer the question "How many?"

Read the sentences below. What do the underlined adjectives tell?

> <u>Two</u> classes had a book fair last Friday.
> <u>Sixty</u> people looked at new and old books.
> <u>Some</u> students exchanged books.

In the sentences above, the number words *two* and *sixty* are adjectives that tell *how many*. The word *some* does not tell an exact number. But this adjective also answers the question "How many?"

The underlined adjectives below tell *how many*. Which are number words? Which do not tell an exact number?

<u>fourteen</u> stories   <u>several</u> tales   <u>three</u> bears
<u>many</u> adventures   <u>eighty</u> pages   <u>few</u> children

Skills Tryout

Name the adjectives that tell *how many*.

1. Hans Christian Andersen wrote many stories.
2. My book has twelve tales by this Danish man.
3. Two brothers from Germany also wrote tales.
4. The Grimm brothers wrote about several animals.
5. Four animals went to Bremen Town.

Practice

A. Write each adjective that tells *how many.*

1. Ed likes the story about three billy goats.
2. Another story is about a tailor and seven flies.
3. You read about Cinderella's two stepsisters.
4. This story has thirty pages.
5. Many children know about the Grimm brothers.
6. I read five tales by Hans Christian Andersen.
7. He was born many years ago in Denmark.
8. One story by Andersen is about a little mermaid.
9. Some people have seen her statue in Denmark.
10. Fifteen people laughed when I said Andersen was a great Dane.

B. Use a different adjective that tells *how many* in each sentence. Write each sentence.

EXAMPLE: Holly can read ⎯⎯ books in a week.
ANSWER: Holly can read several books in a week.

11. Bonnie read ⎯⎯ stories.
12. The first story told about ⎯⎯ children.
13. The children had ⎯⎯ adventures.
14. They traveled for ⎯⎯ days.
15. They met ⎯⎯ animals who helped them.

Application WRITING SENTENCES

Write five sentences about your favorite stories.
Use an adjective that tells *how many* in each sentence.

> • Some adjectives answer the question "What kind?"

Dolores took a bus ride around the city. The paragraph below describes her trip. Notice the underlined adjectives.

First the bus drove through a <u>dark</u> tunnel. Then the bus went on a <u>bumpy</u> road to a <u>wonderful</u> park. The park had a <u>round</u> lake. The <u>friendly</u> driver told <u>funny</u> stories. I want to ride on the <u>blue</u> bus again!

Dolores used many adjectives that tell *what kind* to describe nouns. Adjectives that tell *what kind* may describe size, shape, or color. They tell more about nouns. Dolores wrote about a *dark* tunnel, a *bumpy* road, and a *friendly* driver.

What kind of stories did the driver tell? What kind of bus does Dolores want to ride again?

Skills Tryout

Name the adjectives that tell *what kind.*

1. The bus passed by tall skyscrapers.
2. It crossed over a busy bridge.
3. We heard a loud siren.
4. A red truck hurried by on its way to a fire.
5. I saw a spotted dog on the truck.

Practice

A. Write each adjective that tells *what kind*.

1. Lars rode the tan bus to the library.
2. It was a rainy day.
3. A new neighbor named Pete got on the bus.
4. He wore a shiny slicker.
5. He carried a small backpack.
6. Pete gave Lars a shy smile.
7. He sat in the empty seat beside Lars.
8. The bus stopped near brick steps.
9. Lars shared his green umbrella with Pete.
10. They walked into the square building together.

B. Think of another adjective that tells *what kind* to take the place of each underlined word. Write the new paragraph.

The bus passed many interesting sights. New cars rolled out of a noisy factory. Busy workers were building a skyscraper. They walked on narrow platforms and carried heavy loads. One worker waved a red flag at the traffic. He wore a hard helmet. One funny driver honked a silly horn.

Application LISTENING

Listen to a commercial on television or radio. Make a list of at least five adjectives used to describe something.

4 — Adjectives That Compare

> ● Use the *-er* form of an adjective to compare two persons, places, or things.
>
> ● Use the *-est* form of an adjective to compare three or more persons, places, or things.

Adjectives describe nouns. One way they describe is by comparing persons, places, or things. Notice how the states are compared in these sentences.

1. Connecticut is a <u>small</u> state.
2. Delaware is a <u>smaller</u> state than Connecticut.
3. Rhode Island is the <u>smallest</u> state of all.

When two nouns are compared, the *-er* form of the adjective is used. In sentence 2 two states are compared—Connecticut and Delaware. The letters *-er* have been added to the adjective *small.*

When three or more nouns are compared, the *-est* form of the adjective is used. In sentence 3 Rhode Island is compared with all the other states. The letters *-est* have been added to the adjective *small.*

Skills Tryout

Name the missing form of each adjective.

1. slow, slower, ____
2. steep, ____, steepest
3. ____, newer, newest
4. hard, ____, hardest

A. Write each sentence. Use the correct adjective in ( ).

1. Hawaii is a (smaller, smallest) state than Alaska.
2. The (higher, highest) waterfall in the United States is in Yosemite National Park.
3. The Mississippi River is (longer, longest) than the Ohio River.
4. Maine has (cooler, coolest) summers than Texas.
5. America's (older, oldest) zoo is in Philadelphia.

B. Add -er or -est to each adjective in ( ). Write each sentence.

6. California redwoods are the world's (tall) trees.
7. Georgia has (warm) winters than Indiana.
8. Western Oregon is (green) than eastern Oregon.
9. Death Valley is the (low) spot in the nation.
10. America's (old) city is in Florida.
11. The Grand Canyon is (deep) than Bryce Canyon.
12. Louisiana has the world's (long) railroad bridge.
13. Iowa has a (great) amount of snow than Arizona.
14. The (short) street in the world is in Ohio.
15. Alaska has (cold) winters than Alabama.

Application WRITING SENTENCES

Add -er or -est to each adjective below. Use each adjective in a sentence.

old   warm   dark   hard   soft

5 — Using *a*, *an*, and *the*

> ● The words *a*, *an*, and *the* are a special kind of adjective. They are called **articles.**

Look at the underlined words and the nouns that follow them in these sentences.

1. **The** students went to **the** museum.
2. They watched **an** artist working with clay.
3. He made **a** statue of **a** person.

The underlined words are called articles. Articles are special adjectives that are used with nouns.

The is used before singular and plural nouns. The singular noun *museum* follows *the* in sentence 1 above. What plural noun follows *the* in sentence 1?

A and *an* are used with singular nouns. Use *a* before words that begin with a consonant sound, such as *statue* and *person*. Use *an* before words that begin with a vowel sound.

What singular noun follows *an* in sentence 2? Does it begin with a consonant or a vowel sound?

Skills Tryout

Tell which articles may be used before the nouns.

1. ___ brush   3. ___ leader   5. ___ hands
2. ___ eraser   4. ___ pencils   6. ___ object

Practice

A. Choose the correct article in ( ) to complete each sentence. Write each sentence.

1. Dana goes to (a, an) school in the city.
2. She is studying to be (a, an) engineer.
3. Engineers plan (a, the) bridges people need.
4. Dana works in (a, an) office, too.
5. She is (a, the) assistant to another engineer.

B. Use *a* or *an* to complete each sentence. Write each sentence.

6. Grandfather takes ____ class in oil painting.
7. He uses ____ stand for his paintings.
8. It is called ____ easel.
9. He paints on ____ board of canvas.
10. He can use ____ canvas more than once.
11. Grandpa's paint comes in ____ tube.
12. Each tube contains ____ color.
13. He painted ____ astronaut's picture.
14. He uses ____ brush with thin stiff hairs.
15. I gave Grandpa ____ apron.

Application WRITING SENTENCES

Each noun below names a kind of artist or worker. Write a sentence using each noun. Use *a*, *an*, or *the* before each noun.

actor   painters   engineer   musician

Antonyms

> ● **Antonyms** are words that have opposite meanings.

April was a busy month for Kirk. Here is part of a letter he wrote to his friend.

We had fun in April. On April Fool's Day, I gave Dad cold coffee instead of hot coffee. He gave me an old T-shirt wrapped up as a new present.
We also worked hard in April. We did spring cleaning. Last week the house was dirty. Now it is clean.

In the second sentence Kirk wrote two words that have opposite meanings. The words *hot* and *cold* are antonyms. Then Kirk used another pair of words with opposite meanings. *Old* and *new* are antonyms. What word in the last sentence is the opposite of *dirty*?

Skills Tryout

Name the antonym in ( ) for each word below.

1. happy (glad, sad)
2. hard (easy, difficult)
3. strong (weak, powerful)
4. full (empty, stuffed)
5. open (wide, shut)
6. light (bright, dark)

Practice

A. Write the antonym in ( ) for each underlined word.

1. We did spring cleaning on a <u>cool</u> day. (wet, warm)
2. My <u>older</u> sister washed windows. (bigger, younger)
3. All the floors were <u>dull</u>. (shiny, hard)
4. I pushed the <u>heavy</u> vacuum cleaner. (big, light)
5. Dad vacuumed the <u>narrow</u> staircase. (wide, thin)
6. Mom <u>opened</u> all the closets. (closed, pushed)
7. She cleaned the <u>top</u> shelves. (highest, bottom)
8. Vicky dusted the <u>full</u> bookcases. (crowded, empty)
9. Our house is very <u>small</u>. (large, tiny)
10. It was a <u>short</u> day! (long, happy)

B. Write each sentence below. Use an antonym from the box in place of the underlined word.

dry	laughed	silly	wrong	hello

11. On April Fool's Day people do <u>serious</u> things.
12. My brother wore each shoe on the <u>right</u> foot.
13. I wore my raincoat on a <u>wet</u> day.
14. When we left for school, Dad said <u>good-by</u>.
15. We <u>cried</u> a lot that day!

Application WRITING SENTENCES

Think of an antonym for each word below.
Write a sentence for each word and its antonym.

a. tall **b.** light **c.** slow

Adjectives That Tell <u>How Many</u> *pages 232–235*

A. Write each adjective that tells *how many*.

1. The math test had fifty problems.
2. Several students finished early.
3. The test had fifteen word problems.
4. Some questions had tricky answers.
5. I made two mistakes.

Adjectives That Tell <u>What Kind</u> *pages 236–237*

B. Write each sentence. Underline the adjective that tells *what kind*.

6. The noisy fans cheered at the game.
7. The clowns wore colorful costumes.
8. The hikers climbed the steep trail.
9. Nell took a bite of a juicy peach.
10. My little brother tripped on the curb.

Adjectives That Compare *pages 238–239*

C. Write the missing form of each adjective.

11. clean, cleaner, ____
12. sweet, ____, sweetest
13. ____, louder, loudest
14. green, ____, greenest
15. long, longer, ____

D. Add *-er* or *-est* to each adjective in ( ). Write each sentence.

16. The steak knife is (sharp) than the bread knife.
17. Wally is the (young) boy in our class.
18. Katrina ate dinner (fast) than I did.
19. This green pear is (firm) than that ripe one.
20. The Central Bank is the (tall) building in town.

Using <u>a</u>, <u>an</u>, and <u>the</u> *pages 240–241*

E. Choose the correct article in ( ). Write each sentence.

21. We heard (a, the) sirens coming.
22. First (a, an) ambulance raced by.
23. Then (the, an) engines hurried to the fire.
24. One fire fighter saved (a, an) puppy.
25. She chopped through the roof with (a, an) ax.

Antonyms *pages 242–243*

F. Write the antonym in ( ) for each underlined word.

26. Nancy wrote me a <u>long</u> letter. (short, angry)
27. Grandma arrived on the <u>first</u> day of March. (busiest, last)
28. The news made her <u>happy</u>. (glad, sad)
29. Greg carried two <u>heavy</u> packages. (light, large)
30. Sylvia likes <u>fancy</u> cakes. (plain, good)

See also Handbook pages 342–345.

Writing with Adjectives

> ● Use adjectives to add detail to your writing.

Read the sentences below.

1. **I dreamed about a monster.**
2. **I dreamed about a tall purple monster.**

Both sentences tell about a dream, but sentence 2 gives more details about the dream. It tells us that the monster was tall and purple. The adjectives *tall* and *purple* help us to picture the monster in our mind.

Different adjectives would give a different picture. They might tell us that the monster was *round* and *hairy*. Other adjectives might describe a *long* and *shiny* monster.

Adjectives add important details to sentences.

The Adjective Game   Look at the list of nouns below. Think of at least three adjectives to describe each noun. Try naming adjectives that are very different from each other.

day	sandwich	goat
hair	clown	forest
radio	house	medicine
birthday	dream	sweater

Add-an-Adjective Write each underlined noun below. Then write at least two adjectives that describe the noun. Use words from the Adjective Bank, or use adjectives of your own.

EXAMPLE: Norma has a <u>voice</u>.
ANSWER: voice—sweet, loud

Adjective Bank

dark   thick   round   orange   loud   constant
scary   funny   lonely   small   wonderful
terrible   quick   hot   true   good   dull
exciting   wise   brave   dangerous   sharp

---

1. The <u>clouds</u> showed that it would be raining soon.
2. The <u>moon</u> rose over the trees.
3. The <u>sound</u> of the machines kept me awake.
4. The man told us many <u>stories</u>.
5. The <u>dog</u> followed me around town all day.
6. There was a <u>smell</u> coming from the kitchen.
7. I took a <u>shower</u> after our kickball game.
8. Nicky told Clark some <u>things</u> about me.
9. Checkers is a <u>game</u>.
10. The <u>captain</u> steered away from the <u>rocks</u>.

Using the Thesaurus

Write five sentences about a scary night, but don't use the word *scary*. Find five synonyms for *scary* in the Thesaurus. Use a different synonym in each sentence.

7 — Using Details to Describe

> ● Writers use details to describe.

Read this paragraph. It is a description from the book *Little House on the Prairie*. Let the words paint a picture for you.

Spring had come. The warm winds smelled exciting, and all outdoors was large and bright and sweet. Big white shining clouds floated high up in clear space. Their shadows floated over the prairie.

—*Laura Ingalls Wilder*

Writers use details to paint word pictures. You can, too. Here are some guides to help you.

Think of a main idea.
MAIN IDEA: Jenny's room was messy.

Give details that explain the main idea.
DETAIL: Clothes lay heaped on the floor.

Give details that help the reader see, hear, smell, taste, or touch.
DETAIL: The smell of dust tickled my nose.

Read the description on the opposite page again.
Then answer these questions.

1. What does the paragraph describe?
2. Which sentence tells about a smell?
3. What adjectives describe the clouds?

Practice

A. Write each main idea sentence below. Then
write three details that tell about each sentence.

EXAMPLE: The ocean is rough.
ANSWER: The ocean is rough. (waves, mist,
strong winds)

1. Spring is here!
2. The park is noisy.
3. Bakeries smell good!
4. My bike is beautiful.

B. Write a sentence to describe each of these.

5. smells in a cafeteria
6. the feel of mud
7. a classroom sound
8. a rainbow
9. the sound of rain
10. a wet mitten

Application WRITING SENTENCES

No two things in the world are exactly alike.
Take your shoe, for example. Look at it carefully.
Does it have scuff marks or worn parts?

Write at least four sentences about your shoe.
Use details to describe how it looks and feels.

8 — Describing What You See and Hear

> ● Writers often describe what they see and hear.

How can you describe what you see and hear? Use the chart below as a guide.

What You See	Use words that describe color, size, or shape. pink, gold, tan, pale-blue, lobster-red tiny, large, medium-sized, small, thin square, round, oval, pointed, curved
What You Hear	Use words that describe softness or loudness. quiet, low, faint, noisy, loud Use words that sound like the sounds they name. bang, crash, meow, hiss, drip, splat, buzz If a sound is hard to describe, just name the sound and tell what is making it. screech of tires, wolf's howl, train's whistle

Skills Tryout

Name words to describe each thing listed below. You may use words from the chart if you wish.

1. the sound of a balloon bursting
2. the size, shape, and color of a balloon
3. a sound heard in the city
4. a sound made by a timid kitten
5. the size, shape, and color of a robin's egg

Practice

A. Write the sentences. Complete each one with words that describe color, size, or shape.

1. The ___ guinea pig nibbled a ___ carrot.
2. The hamster blinked its ___ ___ eyes.
3. The snake flicked its ___ ___ tongue in and out.
4. We made a ___ ___ birdhouse from wood scraps.
5. The fox's ___ ___ ears stood up.

B. Write the sentences. Complete each one with words that describe sounds or loudness.

6. The angry cat began to ___.
7. Andy tiptoed ___ into the room.
8. The frightened puppy began to ___ very ___.
9. A mosquito ___ around Rover's ears.

C. Write five sentences to describe Basil the Bloodhound. Follow the directions below.

10. Describe Basil's color.
11. Describe his expression.
12. Describe his ears.
13. Describe his nose.
14. Describe his voice.
15. Describe his coat.

Application USING WRITING SKILLS

Pretend that you have lost Basil—or any other pet. Write an ad for your missing pet. The ad is for a newspaper's Lost and Found column. Give a clear description of your missing pet. You may want to offer a reward for his or her return.

9 — Describing What You Taste, Smell, and Touch

> ● Writers often describe what they taste, smell, and touch.

In Lesson 8 you practiced describing what you see and hear. Now you will practice describing what you taste, smell, and touch. Use the chart below as a guide.

Use words that tell how something tastes, smells, or feels.
Tastes: salty, sweet, sour, spicy, bitter
Smells: smoky, sweet, musty, rotten
Feels: hot, sticky, sharp, icy, rough, smooth

If a taste or smell is hard to describe, just name the taste or smell.
the taste of vanilla, the taste of garlic
the smell of mothballs, the smell of damp leaves

Skills Tryout

Describe each of these things. You may use words from the chart if you wish.

1. the way peanut butter feels in your mouth
2. the taste of lemonade
3. the smell of shampoo
4. the way ice cubes feel
5. the taste of pumpkin pie

Practice

A. Make three columns on your paper. Label them like this: <u>Taste</u> <u>Smell</u> <u>Touch</u>. Then read each word below. Decide if it describes a taste, a smell, or the way something feels. Write each word in the correct column. Some words can go in more than one column.

1. bumpy
2. stale
3. bitter
4. delicious
5. refreshing
6. damp
7. warm
8. scratchy
9. gooey
10. slimy
11. sugary
12. fluffy

B. Write a sentence to describe each of these.

13. the way sandpaper feels
14. the smells of autumn
15. how your favorite fruit tastes
16. what you think an elephant's skin feels like
17. what walking barefoot through mud feels like
18. your favorite picnic smells
19. how clay feels when you work with it
20. the smells in a bakery

Application WRITING A PARAGRAPH

Think of a place that would have interesting smells or interesting things to taste or touch. Write a paragraph describing the place. Only tell about one sense—what you smell or taste or touch. Use the chart on the opposite page to help you.

You may want to begin with a main idea such as:
I love the smells of Hank's gas station.

10 — Writing a Description

Writing Project

> • A **description** may tell what the writer sees, hears, feels, smells, and tastes.

Would you like to take your classmates to your favorite place? That's what you can do in this lesson, without leaving your classroom. You will share your favorite place by writing a description of it. Then you and your classmates will play a game that "takes" you to many special places.

1. Prewriting

What is a favorite place? It is a place where you like to be. A favorite place is special to you. Talk about favorite places with your classmates.

▶ Now list three of your favorite places.

- Name one favorite place at home.
- Name one favorite place at school.
- Name one favorite place outdoors.

Choose one favorite place for your topic.

▶ Draw a picture of your favorite place. Show what is in it. Show who goes there. Make notes on your drawing, too. List things you do in your favorite place. List what you see, hear, touch, smell, and taste.

2. Writing

▶ Use the ideas in your drawing and notes to write your description. How will you begin? Write a topic sentence about your favorite place. Here are some examples:

- My favorite place is ＿＿ because ... .
- My favorite place is a noisy place.
- This is why ＿＿ is my favorite place.

Next add detail sentences to your description. Describe what you see, hear, feel, smell, and taste. Tell why your favorite place is special and what you like to do there.

3. Revising

▶ Read your description to yourself. Is there anything you would like to tell more about? Did you leave anything out? This checklist will help you improve your description.

Revision Checklist

- Did I begin with **a topic sentence about my** favorite place?
- Do my detail sentences tell more about my favorite place?
- Did I tell what I see, hear, feel, smell, and taste?
- Did I avoid repeating the same words?

Read the sample. Notice how it was changed to avoid repeating the same words.

My ~~favrite~~ *favorite* place is my basement because~~,~~ *that's where* my friends and i play there. ~~There are lots of~~ *It has* great hiding places there for hide-and-seek. ~~There~~ I see *in my favorite place* a gray floor

> My favorite place is my basement because that's where my friends and I play. It has lots of great hiding places for hide-and-seek. In my favorite place I see a gray floor and white walls. Silver and black pipes are above me. I hear the chugging of the washing machine and smell soap. My favorite place makes me feel happy. I could play in my basement all day.

EDITING MARKS

——	cross out
∧	add
♂	move
≡	capital letter
¶	indent
⬭	check spelling

▶ How can you improve your description? Use the editing marks to make your changes.

4. Publishing

▶ Carefully check your description. Use the Proofreading Checklist on this page or the one in the Young Writer's Handbook on page 355. Use the editing marks to make corrections.

▶ Play a game that will take your classmates to your favorite place. Ask everyone to close their eyes. Say, "I am taking you to my favorite place." Then give clues about it. For example, "I see ..., I hear ... ." Ask the class to guess where you have taken them. Then read your description.

PROOFREADING CHECKLIST

1. indent paragraphs ✓
2. capital letters ✓
3. end punctuation ✓
4. spelling ✓
5. handwriting ✓

Writing Project

A Collage

Create a cut-and-paste description of a favorite person. A description like this is called a collage.

Look through newspapers and magazines. Cut out words and pictures that remind you of your special person. Cut out the person's name if you find it. Or make the name from single letters.

Place the words and pictures on a sheet of colored paper. Place small objects on it, too, if you wish. Make an arrangement you like. Then paste everything in place. You have created something special for someone who is special!

Science

How many kinds of insects are there? Some scientists say more than a million! New ones are still being discovered. When a new one is found, scientists describe it. They must describe it exactly for other scientists.

▶ Try it! Choose one of the insects shown on this page. Describe it, but do not name it. Make your description exact. See if your classmates can name the insect with just one guess.

grasshopper

beetle

ant

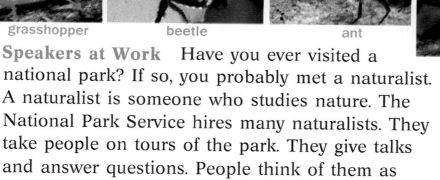
moth

Speakers at Work   Have you ever visited a national park? If so, you probably met a naturalist. A naturalist is someone who studies nature. The National Park Service hires many naturalists. They take people on tours of the park. They give talks and answer questions. People think of them as "walking encyclopedias."

▶ Pretend you are a naturalist. Prepare a short talk to give to park visitors. Pick a nature topic that interests you. Here are a few topics: bears, eagles, camping, snakes, a national park.

Adjectives   *pages 232–241*

A. Write each sentence. Underline the adjective.

1. Mandy found three nickels.
2. Brown horses pranced by.
3. Joshua makes clay bowls.
4. We saw several puppies.

B. Add *-er* or *-est* to each adjective in ( ). Write the sentences.

5. Oranges are ___ than lemons. (sweet)
6. A horse can run ___ than a cow. (fast)
7. Eric is the ___ child in the class. (tall)
8. Pat swam in the ___ part of the pool. (deep)

C. Write the correct article in ( ).

9. Sid mailed (a, the) letters today.
10. Maria gave (a, an) apple to Betsy.
11. Take (a, the) umbrella with you today.
12. Where can I buy (a, an) balloon?

Antonyms   *pages 242–243*

D. Write the antonym in ( ) for each word below.

13. near (close, far)
14. begin (finish, start)
15. shout (yell, whisper)
16. under (beneath, over)

Describing   *pages 248–253*

E. Read the paragraph below. Then write the answer to each question.

Fall had arrived. A cool breeze was blowing. Gold and red leaves drifted slowly to the ground. They made soft, rustling sounds as I walked through them. Gray smoke curled from the chimney of my neighbor's house.

17. What does the paragraph describe?
18. Which adjective helps you feel temperature?
19. Which sentence tells how the leaves look?
20. Which adjective describes the smoke?

F. Complete each sentence with the type of adjective shown in (   ). Write each sentence.

21. My uncle always wears ＿＿ socks. (color)
22. Did you hear that ＿＿ clap of thunder? (sound)
23. This lemonade is too ＿＿ to drink. (taste)
24. Albert wants to paint this ＿＿ box. (size)
25. Henry's rabbit has ＿＿ white fur. (touch)
26. These pink flowers have a ＿＿ scent. (smell)

G. Write three sentences about your favorite kind of fruit. Use adjectives describing the shape, color, and taste of the fruit.

See also Handbook pages 342–345.

Grandmother's Brook

Grandmother tells me about a brook
   She used to pass on her way to school;
A quick, brown brook with a rushing sound,
   And moss green edges, thick and cool.
When she was the age that I am now
   She would cross over it, stone by stone,
I like to think how she must have looked
   Under the greenery, all alone.

Sometimes I ask her:—"Is it there,
   That brook you played by,—the same, to-day?"
And she says she hasn't a doubt it is—
   It's children who change and go away.

—Rachel Field

Nouns in Sentences

- The main word in the subject of a sentence is often a noun.

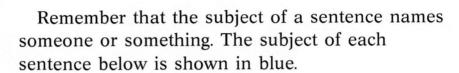

Remember that the subject of a sentence names someone or something. The subject of each sentence below is shown in blue.

1. **The children watched an old movie.**
2. **A friendly robot knew how to drive.**
3. **His planet was far away.**

The main word in each subject above is underlined. Notice that each underlined word is a noun. In sentences 1 and 2, what person or thing does each noun name? In sentence 3 what noun names a place?

Skills Tryout

Each subject is underlined. Name the main word.

1. A smart robot appeared on television.
2. Robby helped a lost family.
3. Their spaceship crashed on a strange planet.
4. The show ended after several years.
5. Many people can see Robby in a museum.

Practice

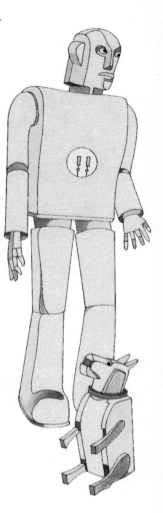

A. The subject is underlined in each sentence. Write the main word in each subject.

1. A large <u>company</u> made two robots in 1939.
2. The electrical <u>robots</u> appeared at a World's Fair.
3. The mechanical <u>man</u> weighed 260 pounds.
4. <u>Elektro</u> counted on his fingers.
5. The electrical <u>dog</u> was named Sparko.
6. A <u>scientist</u> built a mechanical woman in 1940.
7. That <u>inventor</u> lived in California.
8. <u>Isis</u> played a musical instrument.
9. The <u>robot</u> rested on a sofa.
10. Her <u>machinery</u> contained many wheels.

B. Write each sentence. Underline the main word in each subject.

11. My sister dreamed about robots.
12. A huge spaceship came from Mars.
13. A short creature carried a suitcase.
14. Strange sounds came from its stomach.
15. The mysterious robot had three eyes.

Application WRITING SENTENCES

Imagine that you met a robot. Write five sentences about your meeting. Use a different noun in each subject. Underline the main word in each subject.

2 — Verbs in Sentences

> ● The main word in the predicate of a sentence is a verb.

The predicate of a sentence tells what the subject is or does. The predicate of each sentence below is shown in green.

> Ira and Edna <u>unfold</u> the flag.
> They <u>raise</u> the flag on the flagpole.

The main word in each predicate above is underlined. Notice that each underlined word is a verb. Verbs are always found in the predicate of a sentence. Many verbs show action. What actions do Ira and Edna do?

Skills Tryout

Name the verb in the predicate of each sentence.

1. Derek makes flags for his friends.
2. He cuts a big rectangle of white paper.
3. Derek pastes seven red stripes on it.
4. He adds a blue square to the upper left corner.
5. He draws fifty white stars.

Practice

A. Write the verb in each predicate.

1. Everyone marches in a parade on June 14.
2. Connie wanted an American flag for Flag Day.
3. She walked to a new store.
4. The store sells flags from different countries.
5. Connie saw many flags with stars.
6. She looked at red, white, and blue flags from England and France.
7. Connie waved Italy's red, green, and white flag.
8. The salesperson told her about the U.S. flag.
9. The American flag has thirteen stripes.
10. Connie carried her new flag proudly.

B. Write each sentence. Underline the verb.

11. Roger collects flags from other countries.
12. Aunt Lily gave him a Mexican flag.
13. The flag shows an eagle on it.
14. The eagle stands on a rock.
15. It holds a snake in its mouth.

Application WRITING SENTENCES

Tell what it would be like to carry a flag in a parade. Write four sentences about the parade. Underline the verb in each sentence. You may draw a picture to go with your sentences.

3 — Adverbs

> ● A word that describes a verb is an **adverb.**

T.J. went to see William. He wrote about his trip. Look at the underlined words in his sentences.

I went there on the bus.   **The bus left early.**

Each underlined word is an adverb. Adverbs describe verbs. The adverb <u>there</u> tells *where* T.J. went. The adverb <u>early</u> tells *when* the bus left.

Study the adverbs in the chart below.

Adverbs That Tell *When*		Adverbs That Tell *Where*	
early	once	here	someplace
late	yesterday	there	up
now	today	everywhere	down
soon	tomorrow	inside	in
then	always	outside	out

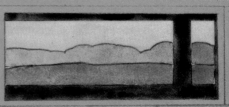

Skills Tryout

Tell whether each adverb tells *where* or *when.*

1. always   3. in   5. then   7. inside
2. inside   4. once   6. down   8. yesterday

Practice

A. Write each underlined adverb. Then write if the adverb tells *where* or *when*.

EXAMPLE: We went <u>down</u> to the bus station.
ANSWER: down, where

1. My family travels <u>everywhere</u> by bus.
2. We <u>always</u> look at the schedule.
3. <u>Once</u> I forgot to check the timetable.
4. I was going <u>someplace</u> by myself.
5. The bus was leaving <u>here</u> at seven o'clock.
6. I arrived <u>late</u> at the terminal.
7. I ran <u>outside</u> to look for the bus.
8. <u>Then</u> I went to the ticket agent.
9. She pointed <u>up</u> at a schedule on the wall.
10. <u>Now</u> I remember to read the timetable!

B. Write each sentence. Underline the adverb.

11. Roberta arrived today.
12. She put her suitcase inside.
13. We played out in the yard.
14. She will leave tomorrow.
15. I will visit Roberta soon.

Application WRITING SENTENCES

Write six sentences about a day in your classroom. In three sentences use adverbs that tell *when*. In three sentences use adverbs that tell *where*. Underline each adverb.

4 — Adverbs That End in -ly

> ● Some adverbs answer the question "How?"

Adverbs are words that describe verbs. Look at the underlined adverbs below. How does each adverb end?

The telephone rang <u>loudly</u>.
Floyd answered it <u>quickly</u>.

The adverb <u>loudly</u> tells *how* the telephone rang. The adverb <u>quickly</u> tells *how* Floyd answered. Many adverbs that answer the question "How?" end in *-ly*.

Read the sentence below. What adverb tells how Floyd spoke?

Floyd spoke to Ms. Yamamoto politely.

Skills Tryout

Name the adverb in each sentence.

1. Charles answers the telephone calmly.
2. He takes messages correctly.
3. He writes messages neatly on a pad.

Practice

A. Write the adverb in each sentence.

    1. Darren uses the telephone nicely.
    2. He answers its ring quickly.
    3. He listens patiently to the other person.
    4. Darren speaks clearly.
    5. Then he politely asks the caller to wait.

B. Add *-ly* to each word in ( ) to form an adverb. Then write each sentence.

    6. Kiki waited (impatient) by the telephone.
    7. Her sister watched her (curious).
    8. The phone rang (sudden).
    9. (Nervous) Kiki answered it.
    10. She listened (quiet) for a moment.
    11. She hung up the telephone (silent).
    12. Then she (slow) turned around.
    13. She clapped her hands (loud).
    14. (Proud) she announced that she had won first prize in the Space Age Science Fair.
    15. Kiki's sister hugged her (tight).

Application WRITING SENTENCES

Write three rules about telephone manners. Use each adverb below.

    kindly   clearly   nicely

5 — Using Commas in a Series

> ● Use a comma to separate words in a series.

The underlined words in the sentences below are items in a series. Notice the commas in the sentences.

1. The children <u>cut</u>, <u>paste</u>, and <u>color</u> their map.
2. The map shows <u>buildings</u>, <u>streets</u>, and <u>parks</u>.

In sentence 1 commas separate the words *cut, paste,* and *color.* Which words are separated by commas in sentence 2?

Commas are used in a series of three or more words. The last comma is placed just before the word *and.*

Commas help to make the meaning of a sentence clearer. Which sentence below describes the picture? Why?

> Bobbie Jo and Fred are making a map.
> Bobbie, Jo, and Fred are making a map.

Skills Tryout

Tell where commas are needed in each sentence.

1. Jane Cassie and Yolanda borrowed a map.
2. They looked for rivers lakes bays and oceans.
3. People fish swim and play in rivers.
4. Wayne Dennis and Ramon like to draw maps.
5. I would rather draw robins wrens and sparrows.

Practice

A. Write each sentence. Use commas correctly.

1. We made maps last Monday Tuesday and Friday.
2. We looked at communities counties and states.
3. People live work and play in communities.
4. Communities are near rivers ponds or lakes.
5. Toya Curt May and Jim live in my community.
6. They pointed to hospitals factories and banks.
7. One map showed states borders and capitals.
8. Maps show islands mountains and oceans.
9. Stars circles and dots stand for cities.
10. I drew painted and hung my own map.

B. Add three words to each sentence. Use commas.

EXAMPLE: ___ ___ and ___ ran. (girls' names)
ANSWER: Sherry, Rose, and April ran.

11. ___ ___ and ___ walked home. (boys' names)
12. I cook ___ ___ and ___. (foods)
13. We bought ___ ___ and ___. (clothing)
14. The zoo has ___ ___ and ___. (animals)
15. I play ___ ___ and ___. (games or sports)

Application SPEAKING

Say each sentence below, naming two things.
Say each sentence again, naming three things.

a. We have paper cups and spoons.
b. They bought ice cream and bread.

6 — Contractions

> ● Some contractions are formed from a verb and *not*.

Remember that a contraction is a shortened form of two words. An apostrophe (') shows where a letter or letters have been left out. Each underlined contraction below is made up of a verb and *not*.

Dawn <u>isn't</u> careless.   **She <u>doesn't</u> take chances.**

The contraction *isn't* is a shorter way to write *is not*. The apostrophe replaces the letter *o* in *not*. What contraction is a shorter way to write *does not*?

Study the contractions in the chart below.

Verb + not = Contraction	
is + not = isn't	have + not = haven't
are + not = aren't	has + not = hasn't
was + not = wasn't	had + not = hadn't
were + not = weren't	can + not = can't
do + not = don't	could + not = couldn't
does + not = doesn't	would + not = wouldn't
did + not = didn't	should + not = shouldn't

The contraction *won't* is unusual. It is a shorter way to write *will not*.

Skills Tryout

Tell the contractions you can make with these words.

1. did + not **2.** was + not **3.** are + not **4.** do + not

Practice

A. Find the contraction in each sentence. Write the two words that make up each contraction.

1. Bicycle riders shouldn't forget safety rules.
2. Some people don't always stop at corners.
3. Reggie didn't stay close to the curb.
4. Margie and Arnold aren't riding safe bicycles.
5. Pat couldn't remember hand signals for turns.
6. Ben and Cam hadn't stopped at every stop sign.
7. They weren't watching for other traffic.
8. Sheldon wasn't wearing bright clothing at night.
9. It isn't difficult to remember these rules.
10. Then you won't have an accident.

B. Write each sentence. Use a contraction in place of the underlined words.

11. I <u>could not</u> wait for the safety poster contest!
12. Tom <u>has not</u> followed the contest rules.
13. I <u>have not</u> finished my large poster.
14. I hope the paint on my poster <u>does not</u> streak.
15. My poster <u>would not</u> fit in my desk.

Application WRITING SENTENCES

Pedestrians are people who walk. Write four safety rules for pedestrians. Use these contractions.

don't   can't   aren't   shouldn't

7 — Homographs

> ● **Homographs** are words that are spelled alike but that have different meanings. Some homographs sound alike.

Kim wrote these sentences for a spelling lesson.

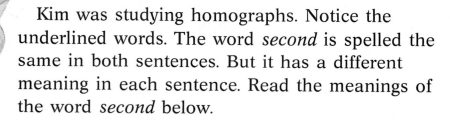

> I lost the race by one <u>second</u>.
> I won <u>second</u> prize.

Kim was studying homographs. Notice the underlined words. The word *second* is spelled the same in both sentences. But it has a different meaning in each sentence. Read the meanings of the word *second* below.

second   the next after the first
second   one of sixty very short periods of equal time that make up a minute

Find the homographs below. What does each homograph mean?

I bit into an apple.   A bit of my tooth broke!

Skills Tryout

Tell what each underlined homograph means.

1. I <u>saw</u> him cut logs with a <u>saw</u>.
2. I <u>can</u> open this <u>can</u> of fruit cocktail.
3. When she <u>left</u>, I waved with my <u>left</u> hand.

Practice

A. Write each sentence. Use the homographs below.

| light | seal | bark | tag | match |

1. The card showed a ___ with large flippers.
   I will ___ the envelope.
2. It is a new ___ for my desk.
   I can carry this ___ package with one hand.
3. My dog will ___ at strangers.
   Some animals eat the ___ from trees.
4. The buttons on your jacket don't ___.
   Never throw away a lit ___.
5. My cousins like to play ___.
   The package had a bright red ___ on it.

B. Write a new sentence for each underlined word. Use the meaning in ( ).

EXAMPLE: I <u>duck</u> when he bats. (a swimming bird)
ANSWER: The duck quacked.

6. I heard the phone <u>ring</u>. (jewelry for a finger)
7. Soldiers stood in a <u>row</u>. (to paddle a boat)
8. I bought a new spinning <u>top</u>. (the highest part)
9. Please do the <u>rest</u> of your work. (to relax)
10. Dad will <u>rock</u> the baby's cradle. (a large stone)

Application USING LANGUAGE

Read each sentence. Write a new sentence using another meaning for the underlined homograph.

a. Don't <u>jar</u> the table!   **b.** They will <u>lie</u> down.

Nouns and Verbs in Sentences *pages 264–267*

A. Write the main word in each underlined subject.

1. The <u>frog</u> leaped to a rock.
2. <u>Two robins</u> built a nest.
3. <u>A yellow duck</u> swam across the pond.
4. <u>Joanna</u> listened to the orchestra.
5. <u>The new library</u> shows free movies.
6. <u>Our teacher</u> picked three volunteers.

B. Write each sentence. Underline the verb.

7. The taxi stopped in front of her house.
8. A cricket chirped during the night.
9. The baby threw the bottle on the floor.
10. We found the lost kitten.
11. My sister bought a new sweater.
12. The baseball shattered the window.
13. Our family cooks hamburgers on the grill.

Adverbs *pages 268–271*

C. Write each underlined adverb. Then write *how* if the adverb tells how. If it tells when, write *when.* If it tells where, write *where.*

14. Mark laughed <u>quietly</u>.
15. She will visit <u>soon</u>.
16. The dog sleeps <u>outside</u>.
17. The ice melted <u>slowly</u>.
18. We talked <u>once</u>.
19. Bells rang <u>loudly</u>.
20. We drove <u>there</u>.
21. I can see you <u>now</u>.

Using Commas in a Series *pages 272–273*

D. Write each sentence. Use commas correctly.

22. Healthy people work rest and play.
23. The salad has lettuce peppers and celery.
24. She has traveled by boat train plane and car.
25. Letters came from Tulsa Seattle and Albany.
26. They sold dishes clothing and games.
27. Alice Helen and Tracy are my sisters.

Contractions *pages 274–275*

E. Write the contraction for each pair of words.

28. are not	31. was not	34. do not
29. could not	32. has not	35. were not
30. will not	33. did not	36. have not

Homographs *pages 276–277*

F. Each sentence in group **A** has a homograph. Find the sentence in group **B** with the matching homograph. Then write each pair of sentences.

Group A	Group B
37. Ellie swung the bat.	**a.** Make a right turn.
38. His answer was right.	**b.** The bear growled.
39. We played cricket.	**c.** A bat eats fruit.
40. I can't bear noise.	**d.** A cricket chirped.

See also Handbook pages 346–347, 359, 361.

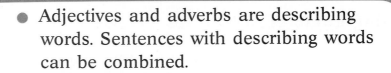

Sentence Combining

> ● Adjectives and adverbs are describing words. Sentences with describing words can be combined.

Read the sentences below.

    A. Monica listened to her radio.
    B. The radio was <u>new</u>.
A + B. Monica listened to her new radio.

Sentence A tells about Monica and her radio. Sentence B tells that the radio was new. The adjective *new* can be placed in sentence A. Sentence A + B tells as much as both sentences A and B. This new sentence is written in a shorter, better way.

Read the example below. The adverb *carefully* tells the only new fact in sentence D. Adding *carefully* to sentence C combines the two sentences. Sentence C + D is a better sentence. It gives all the facts, and it is easier to read.

    C. Monica placed the radio in her book bag.
    D. The radio was placed <u>carefully</u>.
C + D. Monica carefully placed the radio in her book bag.

Sentence C and sentence D can also be combined as shown below.

C + D. Monica placed the radio in her book bag carefully.
C + D. Monica placed the radio carefully in her book bag.

Combine-a-Pair Combine each pair of sentences below. The underlining clues will help you. Write each new sentence.

1. The radio was invented by a scientist.
   The scientist was <u>Italian</u>.
2. Sam follows the news on his radio.
   The news is the <u>latest</u>.
3. I never play music on the bus.
   The music is <u>loud</u>.
4. The mayor spoke on the radio show.
   She spoke <u>angrily</u>.
5. The radio commercial was repeated.
   It was repeated <u>endlessly</u>.

No-Clue Time Combine each pair of sentences without clues. Find the new fact in the second sentence of each pair. Write each new sentence.

6. I called up a talk show.
   The talk show is weekly.
7. I asked the guest a question.
   The guest is famous.
8. A friend heard my voice on the radio.
   The friend is close.
9. He turned on his tape recorder.
   The tape recorder was turned on quickly.
10. He gave me a copy of the recording.
    He gave me the copy generously.

8 — Listening for Facts and Opinions

> ● A **fact** is true information about something.
> ● An **opinion** is what a person *thinks* about something.

Look for facts and opinions in this commercial.

ADULT VOICE: Let's face it, kids. Alphabet soup is boring. Those soggy little letters are blahs-ville. But cheer up! There's a new soup in town. It's called Number Facts, the soup that helps you learn at lunch. You'll love its crunchy little numbers! You'll flip when you taste its pluses, its minuses! It's made from vitamin-packed vegetables.

FIRST CHILD: Zowie! The number 5 tastes great!

SECOND CHILD: The 3's are made from carrots. The plus signs are pure eggplant! Quick, what's 4 + 8? I just ate it.

FIRST CHILD: That's easy. Stringbeans + corn = 12. These 12's are pretty tasty!

ADULT VOICE: Don't settle for second best. Get the soup that's number one—Number Facts!

How can you tell a fact from an opinion? A fact can be checked. You can check it in these ways.

1. **Remember:** You already know this fact is true.
2. **Experiment:** Test the fact yourself.
3. **Investigate:** Ask an expert or read about the fact.

Skills Tryout

These sentences are from the commercial on page 282. Tell whether each is a fact or an opinion.

1. Alphabet soup is boring.
2. The 3's are made from carrots.
3. There's a new soup in town.

Practice

A. Write *fact* or *opinion* for each sentence below.

1. The letters in alphabet soup can be eaten.
2. Some soups are made with meat.
3. Number Facts is the best soup money can buy.
4. Lunch is a good time to learn number facts.
5. Tomato soup is much too salty.

B. Number your paper **6–10**. Then close your book and listen as your teacher reads each sentence. Write *fact* or *opinion* for each sentence.

6. Nothing tastes as good as Presto Pizza!
7. Oranges are rich in vitamin C.
8. Vinegar makes French fries taste better.
9. The price of bananas goes up and down.
10. Milk used to come in glass bottles.

Application LISTENING

Write three facts and three opinions that you hear on TV commercials. After each, write *fact* or *opinion*.

9 — Sharing Opinions

> ● Share opinions in a helpful way.

MARIE: Alphabet Chase is a great video game!
MATT: Are you kidding? It's a silly game!
       How could anyone like Alphabet Chase?
MARIE: Well, *I* do, and it's *not* silly!

Marie and Matt have different opinions. But they are not really sharing their ideas. Instead, they are beginning to argue. How can you share opinions in a helpful way? Here are some pointers.

Speaking	
	1. Give a clear opinion. Do not be undecided. THIS: Alphabet Chase is an exciting game! NOT THIS: That game's okay, I guess.
	2. Back up your opinion. Give facts or reasons. THIS: You race to put the alphabet in order. Meanwhile, Letter Eater gobbles up letters. NOT THIS: It's exciting. Do you know what I mean?
	3. Believe what you say. At the same time give the other person a chance. Do not be a know-it-all. THIS: I've told you what I think. Do you agree? NOT THIS: That's how it is. And that's final!
Listening	
	1. Respect the opinions of others. THIS: Could you give me an example? NOT THIS: That's a dumb idea.
	2. Look for points you both agree on. THIS: I agree that chase games are fun. NOT THIS: Everything you've said is wrong!

Discuss the conversation on the opposite page.

1. Tell Marie's opinion.   3. Was Matt a good listener?
2. Tell Matt's opinion.   4. What could he have asked?

Practice

A. Read each sentence. If it follows the guides for speaking, write *yes*. If it does not, write *no*.

1. Playing outside is healthier than watching TV.
2. Watching cartoons may be a waste of time. Then again, it may not be.
3. Cartoons are a waste of time, and that's that!
4. I think you can learn a lot from TV, don't you?

B. Read each sentence. If it follows the guides for listening, write *yes*. If it does not, write *no*.

5. How could you say such a thing and mean it?
6. I may not agree, but you do have a good point.
7. I don't think all cartoons are bad, but I do agree that some are too violent.
8. I never heard such a ridiculous idea in my life!

Application SPEAKING AND LISTENING

Practice sharing opinions with a friend. Try to give different opinions without arguing.

10 — Writing a Book Report

> ● A **book report** is a way to give information and share opinions about a book.

Read Lauren's book report.

> <u>Ramona Quimby, Age 8</u>
> by Beverly Cleary
>
> Many things are different for Ramona in third grade. Now she rides the school bus. She gives herself the nickname Superfoot. Ramona's father goes back to college, so she helps more at home.
>
> <u>Ramona Quimby, Age 8</u> is a very funny book. My favorite part is Ramona's book report. She gives her report like a TV commercial to the class!

The report begins with the title of the book and the author's name. The title is underlined. Notice that the words in the title begin with capital letters. Where else did Lauren write the title? How can you tell it is the title?

In the first paragraph of her report, Lauren told some facts about the book. In the second, she gave her opinion. How did she feel about this book? Does her report make you want to read about Ramona? Why or why not?

Skills Tryout

Answer each question about Lauren's book report.

1. What is the title of the book?
2. What is the author's name?
3. Who is the most important person in the book?
4. What are two things she does?

Practice

A. Write the answers to these questions about a book you have read.

1. What is the title?
2. What is the author's name?
3. Who is the most important person in the book?
4. What are two things he or she does?

B. Use your answers to **Practice A** to write a report about your book. Follow the form shown on the opposite page.

▶ Write the title and the author's name.
▶ Write a paragraph about some of the most interesting facts or events in the book.
▶ Share your opinions in a new paragraph.

Application SPEAKING

Tell your classmates about a book. Your report should keep the listeners' attention. Tell the most interesting part, but do not give the story away.

11 — Writing an Advertisement —

> ● An **advertisement** persuades readers to buy a product.

Writing Project

How are advertisements persuasive? They get your attention with catchy words. They tell why a product is great. They tell why you should buy the product. The writer wants you to remember the product when you see it in a store.

In this lesson you will write an advertisement for any product you choose. Then you will make a poster for your advertisement. See if you can persuade your classmates to try your product.

1. Prewriting

▶ What product do you want to advertise? It should be something you really like. That will make it easy for you to think why others would enjoy it, too. Make a list of products. Here are a few ideas to start you thinking:

- your favorite record
- a game or a toy
- something to wear
- a book or a magazine
- something to eat

Talk over your ideas with your classmates. Choose the product you like best or use most.

► Have your classmates help you think of ideas for your advertisement. Say the name of your product. Ask your classmates to say the first word that comes into their mind. Write down their ideas quickly. Add ideas of your own to your list. Try to list as many ideas as quickly as you can.

Peanuts
great snack
crunchy
natural
tasty
no sugar
delicious

2. Writing

► Read the list of words you made about your product. What if you could say only one thing about your product? What would it be? Circle that idea. Use that idea in a sentence. This will be the first line of your advertisement. Read these beginnings and then write yours:

- (a game) Spin and Win is full of surprises!
- (a book) How to Catch an Elephant is so funny!
- (a snack) The taste of peanuts can't be beat!

Add more ideas from your list to your advertisement. Give reasons why someone should try your product. Choose your words carefully, and keep your advertisement short. You can write single words, groups of words, or sentences. Draw a picture of your product on your advertisement, too.

3. Revising

▶ Show your advertisement to someone. Ask the person for suggestions to improve your advertisement. This checklist will help you, too.

Revision Checklist
- Did I begin by telling the best thing about my product?
- Did I choose my words carefully?
- Did I give good reasons for using my product?
- Did I give the reasons in the best order?

Read the sample. Notice how it was improved by giving reasons in the best order.

the taste of peanuts can't be ~~beet~~ beat!

~~They are good for you, too~~

You will love to ~~eat~~ munch on crunchy ~~crunshy~~ peanuts.

The taste of peanuts can't be beat!
You will love to munch on crunchy peanuts.

They are good for you, too.
✗ natural
✗ no sugar
✗ great snack

peanuts

Try some peanuts today!

▶ Now use the editing marks to make changes.

—— EDITING MARKS ——
—— cross out
∧ add
♂ move
≡ capital letter
◯ check spelling

4. Publishing

▶ Proofread your advertisement before you display your work. Use the Proofreading Checklist on this page or the one in the Young Writer's Handbook on page 355. Use the editing marks to make corrections.

▶ Pretend you are really selling your product. Make a poster for your advertisement and display it in your classroom. Next to your poster, hang a blank piece of paper. Ask your classmates to read your advertisement. Those who would like to try your product can write their name on the paper.

PROOFREADING
CHECKLIST

1. indent
   paragraphs ✔
2. capital letters ✔
3. end punctuation ✔
4. spelling ✔
5. handwriting ✔

Writing Project

A Safety Poster

Make a safety poster. Try to persuade people to be careful.

First decide on a safety topic. Look at the posters on this page. What safety rule do you want others to remember? Write that message on your poster. Use as few words as possible, but be persuasive.

Then illustrate your poster using bold bright colors. Hang it where others will see it!

Health

In this unit you gave your opinion. You wrote an advertisement. You used speaking and writing to persuade others. Persuading is important to those who work in the field of health. Doctors, nurses, dentists, and health teachers are all persuaders. They convince people to practice good health habits.

► Can you persuade a younger child to practice a good health habit? Test yourself. Think of a good habit. One example is: *Brush your teeth after meals.* Now think of the child. How could you persuade him or her? Remember, children usually want to know "Why?" What would you say? Look in a health book for facts and reasons.

First plan what you want to say. Choose one way to say it. Record it, write it out, or give your talk to a child.

Speakers at Work Some people in exercise classes do not really try. The leader must persuade them. He or she says, "Come on! ... You can do it! ... Go for it!"

► If you were the leader, what would you say? Ask some friends to pretend to be a lazy exercise class. Push them with words. Encourage them. Scold them. Convince them. Find out what it takes to persuade them to move.

Nouns, Verbs, and Adverbs   *pages 264–271*

A. Write the main word in each underlined subject.

1. My <u>cat</u> likes yarn.   3. This <u>movie</u> ends soon.
2. The <u>new snow</u> fell.   4. A <u>tiny ant</u> hid.

B. Write the verb in the predicate of each sentence.

5. Nan made a paper hat.   7. Seth washes his hair.
6. Rob ate lunch.   8. Kim flew her kite.

C. Write whether each adverb tells *how, when,* or *where.*

9. later   10. inside   11. softly   12. today

Commas   *pages 272–273*

D. Write each sentence. Use commas correctly.

13. Tim Juan Al and Amy drew pictures of animals.
14. We need napkins cups and plates for our picnic.
15. The children played danced and laughed together.
16. Dan packed shirts socks and pants for his trip.

Contractions   *pages 274–275*

E. Write the contraction for each pair of words.

17. had + not   19. are + not   21. does + not
18. can + not   20. should + not   22. will + not

Homographs   *pages 276–277*

F. Match each underlined homograph with the correct meaning. Then write the letter of the meaning.

23. I wear a gold <u>ring</u>.
24. Did the bell <u>ring</u>?
25. <u>Fall</u> follows summer.
26. The apples <u>fall</u>.

a. to drop down
b. jewelry for a finger
c. a season
d. to sound loudly

Fact and Opinion   *pages 282–285*

G. Write *fact* or *opinion* for each sentence.

27. Nothing smells sweeter than Rosebud Soap.
28. Calico Cat Food comes in three flavors.
29. *Pirate Ship* is the most exciting movie ever!
30. The word *softly* is an adverb.
31. Rhonda has a beautiful smile.

H. Read each sentence. If the sentence follows the guides for speaking and listening on page 284, write *yes*. If it does not, write *no*.

32. I think seat belts are important, don't you?
33. That's the silliest opinion I've ever heard!
34. Could you explain your idea to me?
35. Seat belts can save lives.

See also Handbook pages 346-347, 359-361.

Sentences   *pages 8–17*

A. Write each sentence correctly. Use a capital letter and put the correct mark at the end.

1. what a beautiful shirt Gerald is wearing
2. tell me your telephone number
3. when does the train leave
4. the snow fell softly during the night

B. Write each sentence. Draw one line under the subject. Draw two lines under the predicate.

5. I collect stamps.   7. Peanuts grow in Georgia.
6. Our teacher laughed.   8. The boy made some toast.

Nouns   *pages 48–57*

C. Write the plural form of each noun.

9. paper   10. family   11. man   12. inch

D. Write the possessive form of each noun.

13. nieces   14. ship   15. bee   16. factories

Capital Letters and Periods   *pages 86–93*

E. Write each proper noun correctly.

17. saturday   19. valentine's day   21. gold street
18. m g bates   20. dr susan ming   22. new jersey

Pronouns   *pages 118–127*

F. Change the underlined word or words in each sentence to a pronoun. Write each new sentence.

23. Bob thanked Jen and me.
24. The candle burned.
25. Use Ernie's pencil.
26. Find Jeff and Rita.
27. Ann fixed the vase.
28. Read Mary's letter.

Verbs   *pages 154–165, 190–191, 196–201*

G. Write the correct present-time form of the verb in ( ). Then write the correct past-time form.

29. Tommy ____ his lunch in a paper bag. (carry)
30. We ____ to the dentist once a year. (go)
31. She ____ the street carefully. (cross)
32. The scouts ____ the camp flag. (raise)
33. Tracy ____ me a box of crayons. (give)
34. Ben ____ the puppy with a towel. (dry)
35. They ____ about our surprise party. (know)
36. Mrs. Cortez ____ four miles every day. (jog)

H. Write each sentence. Draw one line under the helping verb. Draw two lines under the main verb.

37. Joe has won the race.
38. We have traveled far.
39. The plants had grown.
40. My watch has stopped.

Cumulative Review

Adjectives   *pages 232–241*

I. Write the adjective that describes each underlined noun.

41. The loud <u>thunder</u> frightened the horses.
42. Many <u>people</u> came to the class play.
43. My sister sang a funny <u>song</u>.
44. I ate two <u>apples</u> this afternoon.

J. Write each pair of words. Underline each adjective.

45. six weeks
46. fancy hat
47. old car
48. some books
49. smooth fur
50. few shells

K. Add *-er* or *-est* to each adjective in ( ). Write each sentence.

51. This is the (steep) hill in town.
52. One sock is (long) than the other.
53. Is Mike (old) than Elizabeth?
54. Nancy is the (tall) player on our team.

L. Choose the correct article in ( ). Write each sentence.

55. I need (a, the) apron.
56. We saw (a, an) eagle.
57. Sit in (a, an) chair.
58. Al has (a, an) pen.
59. Lock (a, the) doors.
60. Take (a, an) apple.

Nouns, Verbs, and Adverbs   *pages 264–271*

M. Write the main word in each underlined subject.

61. The big <u>fish</u> swam away.   63. A <u>bell</u> rang.
62. <u>My new shirt</u> ripped.   64. <u>Many bees</u> buzzed.

N. Write the verb in the predicate of each sentence.

65. Kenny waved to me.   67. Tina won the prize.
66. I found a clue.   68. We planted a garden.

O. Write whether each adverb tells *when, where,* or *how*.

69. loudly   70. always   71. inside   72. tomorrow

Commas   *pages 94–95, 272–273*

P. Write each sentence. Use commas correctly.

73. Craig Ruth and Mary explored the cave.
74. Yes the clown did some magic tricks.
75. Mr. Murphy would you tell us a story?
76. We visited Montana Idaho Iowa and Utah.
77. Jeff picked washed and ate the berries.

Contractions   *pages 202–203, 274–275*

Q. Write the two words that make up each contraction.

78. wouldn't   79. hasn't   80. it's

Acknowledgments continued from page ii

PERMISSIONS: We wish to thank the following authors, publishers, agents, corporations, and individuals for their permission to reprint copyrighted materials. Page 2: Poem "Buried Treasure" by Aileen Fisher, from *My Weekly Reader*, October 30, 1968. Reprinted by permission of the author. Page 46: Poem "Moon" excerpted from *Laughing Time* by William Jay Smith. Copyright © 1953, 1955, 1956, 1957, 1959, 1968, 1974, 1977, 1980 by William Jay Smith. Reprinted by permission of Delacorte Press/Seymour Lawrence. Page 64: "The Practical Princess" from *The Practical Princess and Other Liberating Fairy Tales* by Jay Williams. Copyright © 1978 by Jay Williams. Reprinted by permission of Four Winds Press, a division of Scholastic Inc. Page 84: Poem "George Washington" by Winifred Catherine Marshall. Reprinted from *Instructor*, February 1938. Copyright © 1938 by The Instructor Publications, Inc. Used by permission. Page 102: Poem "How to Eat a Poem" from *It Doesn't Always Have to Rhyme* by Eve Merriam. Copyright © 1964 by Eve Merriam. Reprinted by permission of the author. Poem "April Rain Song" from *The Dream Keeper and Other Poems* by Langston Hughes. Copyright © 1932 by Alfred A. Knopf, Inc., and renewed 1960 by Langston Hughes. Reprinted by permission of Alfred A. Knopf, Inc. Page 103: Poem "Knitted Things" (text only) in *Dogs and Dragons, Trees and Dreams* by Karla Kuskin. Copyright © 1962 by Karla Kuskin. Reprinted by permission of Harper & Row, Publishers, Inc. Page 104: Poem "A Modern Dragon" from *Songs from Around a Toadstool Table* by Rowena Bastin Bennett. Copyright © 1967 by Rowena B. Bennett. Used by permission of Modern Curriculum Press. Poem "Frog" from *Small Poems* by Valerie Worth. Copyright © 1972 by Valerie Worth. Reprinted by permission of Farrar, Straus and Giroux, Inc. Poem "The Rains of Spring" by Lady Ise from *Little Pictures of Japan* by Olive Beaupré Miller. Reprinted by permission of the Book House for Children. Page 105: "In spring the chirping..." from *Cricket Songs: Japanese Haiku*, translated and copyright © 1964 by Harry Behn. Reprinted by permission of Harcourt Brace Jovanovich, Inc. "Central Park Tourney" by Mildred Weston; © 1953, 1981 by The New Yorker Magazine, Inc. Page 106: Poem "Whispers" from *Whispers and Other Poems* by Myra Cohn Livingston. Copyright © 1958 by Myra Cohn Livingston. Reprinted by permission of Marian Reiner for the author. Page 113: Poem "I See a Thousand Roofs" from *I Live in a City* by James S. Tippett. Copyright © 1927 by Harper & Row, Publishers, Inc. Renewed 1955 by James S. Tippett. Reprinted by permission of Harper & Row, Publishers, Inc. Page 116: Poem "Little" from *Everything and Anything* by Dorothy Aldis. Copyright © 1925–1927, copyright © renewed 1953–1955 by Dorothy Aldis. Reprinted by permission of G.P. Putnam's Sons. Page 152: Poem "I Speak, I Say, I Talk" by Arnold Shapiro. From *Childcraft — The How and Why Library*. Copyright © 1982 World Book-Childcraft International, Inc. Page 186: The first stanza of the poem "Grownups" from *Jonathan Blake: The Life and Times of a Very Young Man* By William Wise. Copyright © William Wise, 1956. Reprinted by permission of Curtis Brown, Ltd. Page 225: Excerpts from *The Last Cow on the White House Lawn & Other Little Known Facts About the Presidency* by Barbara Seuling. Copyright © 1978 by Barbara Seuling. Reprinted by permission of Doubleday & Company, Inc. Page 230: Poem "At the Seaside" from *A Child's Garden of Verses* by Robert Louis Stevenson. Page 248: Excerpt from *Little House on the Prairie* by Laura Ingalls Wilder. Copyright © 1935, as to text, by Laura Ingalls Wilder. Renewed, 1963, by Roger L. MacBride. Reprinted by permission of Harper & Row, Publishers, Inc. and Methuen Children's Books. Page 262: Poem "Grandmother's Brook" from *Branches Green* by Rachel Field. Copyright © 1934 by Macmillan Publishing Co., Inc., renewed 1962 by Arthur S. Pederson. Reprinted by permission of Macmillan Publishing Co.

Contributors to the Teacher's Edition: James J. Alvino, gifted notes; Nancy S. Bley, learning disabled notes; Claudia Campbell, translation of Parent Letters into Spanish; Contemporary Perspectives, Inc., marginal notes, Reinforcement Masters, and Practice Masters; Rita M. Deyoe-Chiullán, English as a Second Language notes; Anthony D. Fredericks, Parent Letters; National Evaluation Systems, Inc., tests; Rita Steinglass, Unit Sparkler language games.

SCHOOL ADVISORY PANEL

CLASSROOM TEACHERS

Levels 3 and 4

Kathie Feldman, List School, Frankenmuth, Michigan; Nancy R. Keefer, Sunset Elementary School, Issaquah, Washington; Janet Nelson, Jordan Elementary School, Chandler, Arizona; Barbara Pavlic, St. Gabriel School, Washington, D.C.; Diane Rushing, Audubon Elementary School, Baton Rouge, Louisiana; Deborah Sturtevant, Assumption of The BVM School, Morristown, New Jersey; Carolyn Tolleson, The Meadows School, College Park, Georgia

SPECIAL CONSULTANTS

Betty Gould, Patchogue, New York; Barbara Todd, Los Angeles, California

Teacher Focus Group, New Jersey Public and Parochial Schools: Marie Antieri, Phyllis Mordente Farese, Constance B. Fenner, Maureen Fulop, Carole Guild, Linda Larner, Eileen C. Molloy, Annette Rauscher, Eileen St. André, Barbara M. Silvernale, Barbara Verian *Thesaurus Lessons Consultant:* Rosemary Cooke, Southern Boulevard School, Chatham Township, New Jersey

Review and Practice Handbooks

Grammar Handbook

Sentences	302
Four Kinds of Sentences	306
Subjects and Predicates	310
Nouns	314
Singular and Plural Nouns	316
Possessive Nouns	318
Common and Proper Nouns	320
Pronouns	322
Verbs	326
Verbs in the Present and Past	330
Verb Forms	334
Irregular Verbs	338
Adjectives	342
Adverbs	346

Young Writer's Handbook

Paragraphs	348
Writing Forms: Friendly Letters	349
Writing Forms: Thank-You Notes and Invitations	350
Writing Forms: Book Reports	351
Addressing Letters: Envelopes	352
Addressing Letters: State Abbreviations	353
Editing Marks	354
Proofreading Checklist	355
Capitalization	356
Punctuation	359
5 Helpful Spelling Rules	362
50 Words Often Misspelled	363
Handwriting Models	364
6 Tips for Taking Tests	366

Sentences

sentence
- A **sentence** is a group of words that tells a complete thought. *page 4*

The bus stops here.

word order
- The words in a sentence must be in an order that makes sense. *page 6*

library from the got I book the.
I got the book from the library.

restaurant ate We a at dinner.
We ate dinner at a restaurant.

MORE PRACTICE 1 Sentences ─────────────

Read each word group. For each pair, write the word group that is a sentence.

1. **a.** Fell in the valley.
   b. The rain beat on the roof.
2. **a.** We visited Puerto Rico last year.
   b. A beautiful island.
3. **a.** Sue plays the flute.
   b. Sounds something like a whistle.
4. **a.** Jerry and his best friend Billy Joe.
   b. The boys live near each other.
5. **a.** In some countries long ago.
   b. Many people lived in huge castles.
6. **a.** A gift for Mom.
   b. We went shopping on Saturday.

GRAMMAR HANDBOOK

MORE PRACTICE 2 Sentences

A. Read each word group. For each pair, write the word group that is a sentence.

    1. a. We walk in the park every day.
      b. The grass and lovely flowers.
    2. a. The fire fighter climbed up the ladder.
      b. A kitten in a tree.
    3. a. Waved my hand at it.
      b. A fly buzzed around my head.
    4. a. Wearing a cast.
      b. Samantha broke her right arm.

B. Use each group of words to make a sentence. Write each sentence.

    5. a bike new has He.
    6. crisp Fresh are apples.
    7. weather Bo cold likes.
    8. cold caught bad a Sally.
    9. long have Giraffes necks.
    10. red a Kevin bought cap.
    11. two The carrots ate pony.
    12. park to Ella walked the.
    13. away floated His balloon.
    14. drove states three to They.

C. Change the order of the underlined words in each sentence. Write the new sentence.

    15. The <u>children</u> smiled at the <u>clown</u>.
    16. The <u>fox</u> stared at the <u>chicken</u>.
    17. The <u>car</u> ran into the <u>ambulance</u>.
    18. <u>Carlos</u> waved at <u>Sheila</u>.
    19. This <u>game</u> costs more than that <u>book</u>.
    20. <u>Stephen</u> is taller than <u>Amanda</u>.

MORE PRACTICE 3   Sentences

GRAMMAR HANDBOOK

A. Read each word group. For each pair, write the word group that is a sentence.

   1. **a.** Games and funny songs.
      b. Suzanne went to a party last week.
   2. **a.** My cat naps near the window.
      b. Sleeping in the warm sun.
   3. **a.** Joe's house has a big basement.
      b. Fun on rainy days.
   4. **a.** No electricity for hours.
      b. The storm lasted for two days.

B. Use each group of words to make a sentence. Write each sentence.

   5. friend is My best Juan.
   6. The Saturday is party on.
   7. banana ate a monkey A.
   8. salty is soup This.
   9. blowing The is wind.
  10. hours Kim eleven slept.
  11. oranges These sweet are.
  12. funny I movie saw a.
  13. watch work not This does.
  14. scored Jackie points ten.
  15. raced Engines to fire a.
  16. I pencil my broke.

C. Change the order of the underlined words in each sentence. Write the new sentence.

  17. The skunk ran away from the puppy.
  18. Our telephone is louder than our clock.
  19. We ate our salad before our dessert.
  20. The officer did not see the driver.

MORE PRACTICE 4 Sentences

A. Read each word group. For each pair, write the word group that is a sentence.

1. **a.** Dad's bicycle has a flat tire.
   b. Walked to his office building.
2. **a.** Luisa dropped a plate.
   b. A very loud crash.
3. **a.** Many beautiful colors.
   b. We raked the autumn leaves into a big pile.
4. **a.** Traveling to a rodeo.
   b. The trailer carried two horses.

B. Use each group of words to make a sentence. Write each sentence.

5. swung the Bruce bat.
6. nest in eggs Two blue the were.
7. under The bed kitten the hid.
8. buried Fido the in bone yard the.
9. baked pies three for We party the.

C. Change the order of the underlined words in each sentence. Write the new sentence.

10. The <u>duck</u> followed the <u>child</u> to the lake.
11. The <u>frog</u> jumped over the <u>grasshopper</u>.
12. The <u>band</u> followed the <u>floats</u> in the parade.
13. <u>Joan</u> showed the pictures to <u>Terry</u>.
14. I <u>read</u> faster than I <u>write</u>.
15. These <u>potatoes</u> weigh more than those <u>apples</u>.

Four Kinds of Sentences

- The first word of a sentence begins with a capital letter.

statement
- A **statement** is a sentence that tells something. It ends with a period (.).   *page 8*

> **Many birds fly south in the winter.**

question
- A **question** is a sentence that asks something. It ends with a question mark (**?**).   *page 8*

> **What color is your jacket?**

command
- A **command** is a sentence that gives an order. It ends with a period (.).   *page 10*

> **Give me the yellow pencil.**

exclamation
- An **exclamation** is a sentence that shows strong feeling. It ends with an exclamation mark (**!**).   *page 10*

> **I just love to play the piano!**

MORE PRACTICE 1   Four Kinds of Sentences——————

Write each sentence. Then write *statement, question, command,* or *exclamation* to tell the kind of sentence.

1. We got there at six o'clock.
2. Does she live near the school?
3. Tell me about your trip.
4. What a happy baby he is!

MORE PRACTICE 2 Four Kinds of Sentences

A. Write each sentence. Write *statement, question, command,* or *exclamation* to tell the kind of sentence.

   1. Why did you choose that book?
   2. That was an exciting movie!
   3. Raul is building a birdhouse.
   4. Bring your favorite story to school.
   5. We peeled potatoes for the stew.

B. Write each statement or question correctly. Begin with a capital letter. End with a period or a question mark.

   6. many people visit the state of Hawaii
   7. did you remember to bring your ticket
   8. why do the stars seem to twinkle
   9. the Scout troop had a car wash last Saturday
  10. where is the nearest grocery store
  11. the zoo keeper threw fish to the seals
  12. would you like some more lemonade

C. Write each command or exclamation correctly. Begin with a capital letter. End with a period or an exclamation mark.

  13. close the door
  14. i am so tired
  15. look at the deer
  16. take off your hat
  17. what a great party you had
  18. that is a terrific idea
  19. answer the question
  20. i won first prize

A. Write each sentence. Write *statement, question, command,* or *exclamation* to tell the kind of sentence.

1. I love to eat avocados!
2. Did you hear the owl?
3. Fold your paper in half.
4. George was late today.
5. Wait for me after school.
6. Do you like mysteries?
7. What was that noise?
8. The flowers are beautiful!
9. Alana did some homework.
10. Have you been to Ohio?
11. Pat the lamb gently.
12. The parade is beginning!

B. Write each statement or question correctly. Begin with a capital letter. End with a period or a question mark.

13. have you read this magazine yet
14. richard pulled the sled to the top of the hill
15. we are not buying lunch today
16. when did you mail the letter to Aunt Elizabeth
17. the hikers stopped for a short rest
18. has anyone seen my new box of pens

C. Write each command or exclamation correctly. Begin with a capital letter. End with a period or an exclamation mark.

19. lock the door when you leave the house
20. that is the biggest pumpkin I have ever seen
21. choose your favorite flavor for dessert
22. this fresh fruit salad is delicious
23. jane won first prize in the poster contest
24. put that sign on the bulletin board
25. save me a piece of pie

MORE PRACTICE 4 Four Kinds of Sentences

A. Write each sentence. Write *statement, question, command,* or *exclamation* to tell the kind of sentence.

1. How much does a bag of peanuts cost?
2. Today is the coldest day in five years!
3. The magician made a rabbit disappear.
4. Send in the coupon for a free box of cereal.
5. Have you met the new music teacher yet?
6. I smell something burning!
7. Set the alarm for seven o'clock.
8. Brush your teeth at least twice a day.

B. Write each statement or question correctly. Begin with a capital letter. End with a period or question mark.

9. she went skating
10. how soon will he arrive
11. do you speak Spanish
12. she broke a mirror
13. where did Edna go
14. they live on a big farm
15. which poem did you read
16. my stomach hurts
17. we eat dinner at six
18. did I miss the bus
19. do you like to jog
20. my cousin has the measles

C. Write each command or exclamation correctly. Begin with a capital letter. End with a period or an exclamation mark.

21. he ran more than eight miles yesterday
22. return these books to the library before Friday
23. come to my house for supper tonight
24. your haircut looks great
25. bring an extra sweater in case it gets cold

Subjects and Predicates

subject ● The **subject** of a sentence names someone or something. *pages 12 and 14*

The <u>small bird</u> flew to its nest.

predicate ● The **predicate** of a sentence tells what the subject is or does. *pages 12 and 16*

The small bird <u>flew to its nest.</u>

MORE PRACTICE 1 Subjects and Predicates

A. Read each sentence. Write *subject* if the subject is underlined. Write *predicate* if the predicate is underlined.

1. Strawberries <u>taste good on cereal.</u>
2. <u>The Scouts</u> are camping here this weekend.
3. <u>Many trees</u> were planted near my school.
4. The airplane <u>had four propellers.</u>
5. <u>Kevin</u> sewed a button on his shirt.

B. Write each sentence. Draw a line between the subject and the predicate.

6. The tallest flowers grow along the fence.
7. Megan swims at the lake every summer.
8. A skunk is a very shy animal.
9. My best friend went horseback riding at Mr. Wharton's farm.
10. The twins wore matching jackets.

MORE PRACTICE 2   Subjects and Predicates

A. The subject is underlined in each sentence. Think of a different subject. Write each new sentence. Then underline the new subject.

EXAMPLE: The dog ran across the yard.
ANSWER: A child ran across the yard.

1. The car has four wheels.
2. Two friends went to the movie together.
3. The teacher walked to the front of the room.
4. Many runners entered the marathon.
5. The team practiced for an hour.
6. The dish broke with a loud crash.
7. Mrs. Winters has a new pair of glasses.
8. The green frog hopped off the log.

B. The predicate is underlined in each sentence. Think of a different predicate. Write each new sentence. Underline the new predicate.

EXAMPLE: Many children like to sing.
ANSWER: Many children are in my class.

9. The people watched the animals at the zoo.
10. I like books about sports.
11. Her hobby is collecting old coins.
12. The pony jumped over the fence.
13. Bob ate some fresh figs.
14. The secretary wrote down the telephone message.
15. The glass was filled with apple cider.

MORE PRACTICE 3 Subjects and Predicates

A. Add a subject to each word group below. Write each complete sentence.

1. ____ laughed at my joke.
2. ____ is in my class.
3. ____ plays soccer.
4. ____ likes broccoli.
5. ____ builds model cars.
6. ____ wrote a play.
7. ____ was lost last week.
8. ____ moved away.
9. ____ baked corn bread.
10. ____ is too hot.
11. ____ took a trip.
12. ____ climbed a tree.
13. ____ wants to leave now.
14. ____ wore a sweater.
15. ____ rode on a horse.
16. ____ floated in the sky.
17. ____ has two sisters.
18. ____ loves to ski.
19. ____ fell off the table.
20. ____ chased a cat.
21. ____ slammed the door.
22. ____ brought presents.

B. Add a predicate to each word group below. Write each complete sentence.

23. Some friends ____.
24. A large animal ____.
25. The terrible storm ____.
26. A scary movie ____.
27. A striped tiger ____.
28. These juicy oranges ____.
29. The art teacher ____.
30. The spider ____.
31. The football team ____.
32. His toy robot ____.
33. My home computer ____.
34. The heavy box ____.
35. Uncle Lou ____.
36. The hot iron ____.
37. A police officer ____.
38. The moving van ____.
39. Two sleepy bears ____.
40. Some lovely roses ____.
41. A rainbow ____.
42. Dr. Ortiz ____.
43. A prickly cactus ____.
44. Joey's bicycle ____.

MORE PRACTICE 2 Nouns

A. One of the words in each pair is a noun. Write the nouns.

1. mittens, fuzzy
2. friendly, lawyer
3. eagle, golden
4. jumped, avenue
5. angry, pizza
6. Patricia, helpful
7. pretty, carrot
8. walked, sneaker
9. how, sunset
10. Alaska, carried
11. room, smoky

12. painted, pencil
13. donkeys, tired
14. thirsty, water
15. globe, slowly
16. pulled, foot
17. horse, gray
18. father, cheerful
19. salty, ocean
20. airplane, noisy
21. sad, Roger
22. elevator, empty

B. Write each sentence below. Underline the nouns.

23. A turtle crawled on the sandy beach.
24. Rita works in a bank.
25. The acrobat did a stunt on the trapeze.
26. Our city has many busy streets.
27. A bird built a nest on our roof.
28. My cousin goes to a big school.
29. The farmer milked the brown cow.
30. The smog hurts my eyes.
31. Carolyn brought a toy for the baby.
32. This rose has many sharp thorns.
33. The teacher wrote on the chalkboard.
34. Paul read a funny story to the class.
35. The children played in the snow.

Singular and Plural Nouns

singular noun
- A **singular noun** names one person, place, or thing.   *page 50*

  She ate a juicy <u>pear</u>.

plural noun
- A **plural noun** names more than one person, place, or thing.   *page 50*

- Add *-s* to form the plural of most nouns.   *page 50*

  Greg ate two <u>bananas</u>.

spelling plural nouns
- Add *-es* to form the plural of nouns that end in *s, x, ch,* or *sh*.   *page 52*

  glasses   boxes   lunches   wishes

- If a noun ends in a consonant and *y*, change the *y* to *i* and add *-es* to form the plural.   *page 52*

  party–parties   blueberry–blueberries

MORE PRACTICE 1   Singular and Plural Nouns

Read each sentence. Write *singular* if the underlined word is a singular noun. Write *plural* if the underlined word is a plural noun.

1. The <u>cabin</u> was in the woods.
2. I need two airmail <u>stamps</u>.
3. The jar was full of <u>pennies</u>.
4. He ate two <u>dishes</u> of pudding.
5. The <u>boy</u> was very thirsty.
6. Turn out both <u>lights</u>.
7. She ate some <u>grapes</u>.
8. Three <u>men</u> held a ladder.
9. A <u>branch</u> fell down.
10. The <u>lion</u> roared loudly.

MORE PRACTICE 2   Singular and Plural Nouns

A. Write each sentence. Use the correct form of the noun in (   ).

1. Laura made a ___. (sandwich, sandwiches)
2. Ten ___ live in my building. (family, families)
3. Mrs. Sykes is our ___. (neighbor, neighbors)
4. That ___ works at the bank. (man, men)
5. Many ___ marched in the parade. (band, bands)
6. Two elephants have eight ___. (foot, feet)
7. A shy ___ hid beneath the log. (fox, foxes)
8. Sam drank two ___ of milk. (glass, glasses)

B. Write the plural of each singular noun.

9. crash	13. box	17. cloud
10. foot	14. flower	18. branch
11. dress	15. pony	19. wish
12. plate	16. woman	20. baby

C. Write each sentence. Use the plural form of the noun in (   ).

21. Texas has many ___. (ranch)
22. Ginny has new running ___. (shoe)
23. Two ___ were in the nest. (egg)
24. The movers carried heavy ___. (box)
25. They heard strange ___ outside. (noise)
26. They have painted all the ___ at the park. (bench)
27. We saw some pretty ___ in the forest. (butterfly)
28. He blew out all the ___. (candle)
29. I drank three ___ of water. (glass)
30. My uncle tells funny ___. (story)

Possessive Nouns

possessive
noun

● A **possessive noun** shows ownership. *page 54*

singular
possessive
noun

● To form the possessive of a singular noun, add an apostrophe and *s* ('**s**). *page 54*

Stephen's dog ran away.   The <u>dog's</u> name is Rusty.

plural
possessive
noun

● To form the possessive of a plural noun that ends in *s*, add an apostrophe ('). *page 56*

The <u>students'</u> desks are empty in the summer.
The <u>puppies'</u> eyes are not open yet.

MORE PRACTICE 1   Possessive Nouns

A. Write the possessive form of each singular noun.

1. Jennifer	6. baby	11. Rafael
2. girl	7. Mrs. Clay	12. goat
3. cat	8. zebra	13. father
4. nurse	9. teacher	14. person
5. Dr. Kimura	10. family	15. Susan

B. Write the possessive form of each plural noun.

16. players	21. tigers	26. coaches
17. animals	22. students	27. doctors
18. kings	23. mothers	28. relatives
19. joggers	24. chickens	29. giraffes
20. aunts	25. writers	30. painters

MORE PRACTICE 2   Possessive Nouns

A. Write each sentence below. Use the possessive form of the noun in (   ).

EXAMPLE: My ____ favorite food is chili. (sister)
ANSWER: My sister's favorite food is chili.

1. We had fun at ____ party. (Helen)
2. The ____ hat blew away. (man)
3. The ____ office is next door. (principal)
4. ____ house is being painted. (Mr. Gold)
5. An ____ feathers are very soft. (ostrich)
6. The ____ gloves were white. (officer)
7. This ____ paper was late. (student)
8. Her ____ picture was in the newspaper. (uncle)
9. ____ bicycle has a flat tire. (Ron)
10. My ____ collar is lost. (pet)

B. Write each sentence below. Use the possessive form of the plural noun in (   ).

11. My ____ suitcases were on the wrong plane. (cousins)
12. Our ____ yards all have orange trees. (neighbors)
13. Goldilocks sat in the ____ chairs. (bears)
14. My ____ letters arrived yesterday. (grandparents)
15. The ____ uniforms are blue and white. (players)
16. Those ____ radios are very noisy. (boys)
17. The ____ rooms were just cleaned. (guests)
18. Her ____ tickets are for the show on Sunday. (friends)
19. The ____ hooves sounded like thunder. (horses)
20. Two ____ bicycles had bright flags. (girls)

Common and Proper Nouns

common noun
- A **common noun** names any person, place, or thing. *page 86*

> The <u>girl</u> went to the <u>park</u>.

proper noun
- A **proper noun** names a particular person, place, or thing. *page 86*

> <u>Walter Mayo</u> lives in <u>Dallas</u>.

MORE PRACTICE 1 Common and Proper Nouns

Copy the underlined nouns from the sentences below. Write *common* beside each common noun. Write *proper* beside each proper noun.

1. <u>Lorenzo</u> studied at the <u>library</u>.
2. My <u>cousin</u> goes to <u>Arizona State University</u>.
3. The <u>lambs</u> were born in <u>March</u>.
4. <u>Josie</u> washed the <u>windows</u> for <u>Mrs. Bates</u>.
5. Their <u>family</u> camped near <u>Lake Tahoe</u> in <u>California</u>.
6. The <u>musician</u> from <u>Austria</u> played the <u>viola</u>.
7. We had a <u>picnic</u> at <u>Emerald Island</u>.
8. The <u>eagle</u> soared high in the <u>sky</u>.
9. <u>Dr. Williams</u> works at <u>Greeley Medical Center</u>.
10. My <u>brother</u> fished in the <u>Pacific Ocean</u> for <u>salmon</u>.
11. The <u>Kansas City Royals</u> won both <u>games</u>.
12. A <u>sunset</u> over the <u>Mohave Desert</u> is beautiful.
13. <u>Mr. Casey</u> and his <u>daughter</u> ran down <u>Hodges Street</u>.
14. We ate a delicious <u>dinner</u> at <u>Lotus Blossom Restaurant</u>.
15. I practiced the <u>piano</u> for an <u>hour</u> on <u>Saturday</u>.

MORE PRACTICE 2 Common and Proper Nouns

A. Copy the underlined nouns from the sentences below. Write *common* beside each common noun. Write *proper* beside each proper noun.

1. During our <u>vacation</u> we will go to <u>Tennessee</u>.
2. The <u>Statue of Liberty</u> is on an <u>island</u> in <u>New York</u>.
3. <u>Mary Lou Costa</u> will read at the <u>assembly</u> on <u>Thursday</u>.
4. They bought a <u>computer</u> at a <u>store</u> downtown.
5. The <u>parachute</u> came down near <u>Elmville</u>.
6. <u>Marie Curie</u> and her <u>husband</u> were <u>scientists</u>.
7. We saw a <u>movie</u> about a <u>magician</u> named <u>Harry Houdini</u>.
8. <u>Bugs Bunny</u> has a very famous <u>voice</u>.
9. <u>Mount Vesuvius</u> is an active <u>volcano</u> in <u>Italy</u>.
10. The <u>game</u> will be held at <u>Washington High School</u>.

B. Each sentence below has two nouns. Write them. Then write *common* or *proper* beside each noun.

11. The <u>hikers</u> camped near <u>Carson Creek</u>.
12. <u>Richard Adams</u> works at <u>First City Bank</u>.
13. The <u>airplane</u> disappeared behind the <u>clouds</u>.
14. The big <u>race</u> was held on <u>Saturday</u>.
15. The <u>tunnel</u> goes under the <u>Hudson River</u>.
16. <u>Joanna</u> wants to visit <u>Norway</u>.
17. <u>Frank</u> attends <u>Lincoln Elementary School</u>.
18. <u>Christopher Columbus</u> sailed with three tiny <u>ships</u>.
19. <u>Emily Dickinson</u> was a famous <u>poet</u>.
20. This pink <u>grapefruit</u> came from <u>Florida</u>.

Pronouns

pronoun ● A **pronoun** takes the place of a noun or nouns. *page 118*

> The <u>students</u> read a <u>play</u>. <u>They</u> read <u>it</u>.

subject pronoun ● The words *I, you, she, he, it, we,* and *they* are **subject pronouns**. These pronouns are used in the subject of a sentence. *page 120*

> <u>Lee</u> fixed lunch. <u>He</u> fixed lunch.

object pronoun ● The words *me, you, him, her, it, us,* and *them* are **object pronouns**. These pronouns are often used in the predicate of a sentence. *page 122*

> Tim talked to <u>Sue</u>. Tim talked to <u>her</u>.

possessive pronoun ● A **possessive pronoun** shows ownership. *page 124*

> <u>Gail's</u> shoes are muddy. <u>Her</u> shoes are muddy.

using <u>I</u> and <u>me</u> ● Use *I* in the subject of a sentence. *page 126*

● Use *me* in the predicate of a sentence. *page 126*

> <u>I</u> like to sing. The teacher taught <u>me</u> a song.

MORE PRACTICE 1   Pronouns

Write the pronoun in each sentence.

1. Rick and I played tennis.
2. Mr. Bay gave us a test.
3. Aunt Ellen called them.
4. You can wait for Henry here.

MORE PRACTICE 2 Pronouns

A. Write the pronoun in each sentence.

1. The cat stared at me.
2. We rode on a crowded bus.
3. Marty gave him a book.
4. She borrowed a pencil.
5. Dad wants you to help.
6. Grandpa sent us a card.
7. I am Sue's best friend.
8. Oscar found it at home.
9. They are always late.
10. She opened the window.

B. The subject is underlined in each sentence below. Write *pronoun* if the subject is a pronoun. Write *noun* if the subject has a noun in it.

11. The dentist pulled two of Roy's teeth.
12. She planted tomatoes in the garden.
13. Some acrobats did stunts at the circus.
14. Grandma is taking a typing class at the city college.
15. You ought to try this spicy soup.
16. We must hurry before the rain starts.

C. Change the underlined subject of each sentence to a pronoun. Write each new sentence.

EXAMPLE: The students waited on the playground.
ANSWER: They waited on the playground.

17. Mom rides a bicycle to work every day.
18. Selma and I are taking a walk.
19. The clock is broken.
20. Mr. Richards makes wooden furniture.

MORE PRACTICE 3   Pronouns

GRAMMAR HANDBOOK

A. Use one of the pronouns below for each underlined word or words. Write each new sentence.

her	it	us	them	him

1. Lucy fed <u>the ducks</u> at the lake.
2. The thunder warned <u>Donna and me</u> of the storm.
3. I gave my seat on the bus to <u>Mr. Davis</u>.
4. Please put <u>the plate</u> on the table.
5. The fire fighter showed <u>Erika</u> the engine.

B. Write the possessive pronoun in each sentence.

6. Our house is large.
7. My stomach hurts.
8. Gary is their brother.
9. Is this your apple?
10. Jim lost his socks.

11. Your haircut looks nice.
12. Her sister plays tennis.
13. The cat licked its paw.
14. Tim rang our bell.
15. Their dog is brown.

C. Copy each sentence pair. Use a possessive pronoun to complete the second sentence in each pair.

EXAMPLE: Giraffes have long necks. ____ necks are long.

ANSWER: Giraffes have long necks. Their necks are long.

16. The bicycle has a flat tire. ____ tire needs air.
17. Pedro has a broken arm. ____ arm is in a cast.
18. Nora and I play basketball. ____ team has won ten games.
19. Judith works on Saturdays. ____ job is at the library.
20. I have twin brothers. ____ brothers share a room.

MORE PRACTICE 4   Pronouns

A. Use *I* or *me* to complete each sentence correctly. Write the pronoun you choose.

1. ___ jumped when the telephone rang.
2. The coach chose ___ for the team.
3. A kite sailed over ___.
4. Hank and ___ arrived at the same time.
5. The monkey made faces at Natalie and ___.

B. Choose the correct word or group of words in ( ) to complete each sentence. Write each sentence.

6. Tamara invited ___ to a party. (Pat and I, I and Pat, Pat and me, me and Pat)
7. ___ swam twelve laps without stopping. (I, Me)
8. ___ chose books about space travelers. (Ed and I, I and Ed, Ed and me, Me and Ed)
9. The bus driver waited for ___ at the corner. (I, me)

C. Choose the pronoun in ( ) to take the place of the underlined word or words. Write each sentence.

EXAMPLE: Cynthia called <u>Uncle Robert</u>. (him, them)
ANSWER: Cynthia called him.

10. The <u>penguin</u> jumped into the icy water. (It, Us)
11. The audience laughed at <u>the clowns</u>. (they, them)
12. <u>Noriko</u> rode the elevator to the top floor. (Her, She)
13. <u>Lisa and Ned</u> delivered the newspapers. (They, Them)
14. The scared kitten scratched <u>Jeff</u>. (him, he)
15. George rode by <u>Kay and me</u> on a bicycle. (we, us)

Verbs

verb ● A word that shows action is a verb. *page 154*

The pony <u>pulls</u> the red cart.

present-time verb ● A verb in the **present time** shows action that happens now. *page 156*

The students <u>visit</u> the airport.
Milton <u>rides</u> in a helicopter.

pronoun-verb agreement ● A verb in the present time must agree with the pronoun used in the subject of a sentence. *page 158*

<u>I</u> <u>like</u> broccoli.   <u>She</u> <u>likes</u> cabbage.

MORE PRACTICE 1   Verbs

If the underlined word in the sentence is a verb, write *verb*. If the underlined word is not a verb, write *not a verb*.

1. The kitten <u>plays</u> with the piece of string.
2. Carlene <u>skates</u> at the park every afternoon.
3. Two <u>spiders</u> crawl up the tree.
4. A moth <u>flutters</u> near the light.
5. My parents <u>pull</u> weeds from the garden.
6. <u>Celeste</u> reads the newspaper every day.
7. Our <u>dog</u> barks at strangers.
8. The owl <u>blinks</u> at me.
9. The <u>child</u> holds three bright balloons.
10. The students <u>wash</u> the chalkboards.

MORE PRACTICE 2 Verbs

A. Write the verb in each sentence.

1. The school nurse talks about good health.
2. Water drips from the faucet.
3. The cows wander in the meadow.
4. My turtle moves very slowly.
5. The baby listens to the music box.
6. Rockets travel in space at high speeds.
7. Robins hatch from blue eggs.
8. Suzanne collects flags from different countries all over the world.
9. That truck carries heavy sacks of grain.
10. Nancy brushes her teeth after every meal.
11. James exercises four times a week.
12. The chef adds many spices to the food.
13. Strong winds blow in March.
14. My alarm clock rings at six in the morning.

B. Write the sentences below. Use a verb to complete each sentence.

15. The bus ＿＿ on the road.
16. A duck ＿＿ in the pond.
17. Andy ＿＿ after school.
18. My brother ＿＿ pizza.
19. Don ＿＿ two skunks.
20. Ms. Wong ＿＿ my name.
21. Flowers ＿＿ in our yard.
22. The officer ＿＿ the car.
23. Birds ＿＿ nests in trees.
24. The cashier ＿＿ money.
25. Rudy ＿＿ television.
26. A kite ＿＿ in the sky.
27. The ball ＿＿ in a hole.
28. Cars ＿＿ near the curb.
29. The coach ＿＿ to us.
30. Mollie ＿＿ a red hat.

A. Write the sentences. Choose the correct verb in (   ) to complete each sentence.

1. Don ___ groceries on his bicycle. (deliver, delivers)
2. We ___ aluminum cans for recycling. (save, saves)
3. Mona ___ cinnamon in hot cocoa. (sprinkle, sprinkles)
4. The teachers ___ classrooms. (share, shares)
5. My canary ___ all day long. (whistle, whistles)
6. They always ___ to school together. (walk, walks)
7. This plant ___ a lot of sunlight. (need, needs)
8. She ___ to become a doctor. (want, wants)
9. Snakes ___ their skins once a year. (shed, sheds)
10. The elevator ___ on every floor. (stop, stops)

B. Use verbs in the present time in the sentences below. Write each sentence with the correct form of the verb in (   ).

EXAMPLE: Mickey ___ the goldfish. (feed)
ANSWER: Mickey feeds the goldfish.

11. The dentist ___ my teeth twice a year. (clean)
12. You ___ like my oldest cousin. (look)
13. Sheila ___ a telescope. (own)
14. Some dogs ___ blind people. (help)
15. My grandfather ___ two miles a day. (jog)
16. We ___ in the library at school. (whisper)
17. The earth ___ around the sun. (revolve)
18. This map ___ our city streets. (show)
19. The wolves ___ at the moon. (howl)
20. Some kangaroos ___ more than twenty feet. (leap)

MORE PRACTICE 4 Verbs

A. Write the sentences. Choose the correct verb in ( ) to complete each sentence.

1. Babies ____ most of the day. (sleep, sleeps)
2. We ____ vegetables at a farm stand. (buy, buys)
3. She ____ her notebook to school. (bring, brings)
4. Magicians ____ magic tricks. (perform, performs)
5. Some players ____ the rules. (change, changes)
6. He ____ many funny jokes. (tell, tells)
7. Our kitten ____ its tail. (chase, chases)
8. I ____ the words to that song. (remember, remembers)
9. You ____ the last piece of pie. (take, takes)
10. They ____ apples in Washington. (grow, grows)

B. Use verbs in the present time in the sentences below. Write each sentence with the correct form of the verb in ( ).

11. Loud noises ____ my puppy. (frighten)
12. We ____ clothes once a week. (wash)
13. Mr. Brim ____ the clarinet. (play)
14. Crickets ____ all night long. (chirp)
15. She ____ the lawn every Saturday. (mow)
16. You ____ near my best friend. (live)
17. He ____ a green baseball cap. (wear)
18. My brother ____ in the shower. (sing)
19. The artist ____ beautiful mountain scenes. (paint)
20. Gloria and Bob ____ Mr. Grant at school. (help)

Verbs in the Present and the Past

past-time verb

● A verb in the **past time** shows action that already happened. *page 160*

Mr. Harris <u>mailed</u> a package.

spelling present-time verbs

● Some verbs in the present time end in *-s* or *-es*. *page 162*

| run, run<u>s</u> | use, use<u>s</u> | pass, pass<u>es</u> |
| mix, mix<u>es</u> | wash, wash<u>es</u> | catch, catch<u>es</u> |

● The spelling of some verbs changes when *-es* is added. *page 162*

try, tr<u>ies</u>   hurry, hurr<u>ies</u>

spelling past-time verbs

● Most verbs in the past time end in *-ed*. *page 164*

We <u>waited</u> nearly five hours.

● The spelling of some verbs changes when *-ed* is added. *page 164*

worry, worr<u>ied</u>   plan, plan<u>ned</u>

MORE PRACTICE 1   Verbs in the Present and Past

If the verb is in the present time, write *present*. If the verb is in the past time, write *past*.

1. begins   3. grin   5. cried   7. jump
2. stopped   4. wishes 6. stayed   8. prepared

GRAMMAR HANDBOOK

MORE PRACTICE 2 Verbs in the Present and Past

A. If the underlined verb is in the present time, write *present.* If the verb is in the past time, write *past.*

1. Kelly sneezed six times.
2. Our cat teases the neighbors' dog.
3. The snake hissed at us.
4. Everyone hurried home before the storm.
5. Kim's uncle fixes old clocks.
6. The little child scratched the mosquito bite.
7. She speaks three different languages.
8. Eduardo wrapped the present in bright paper.
9. I like to roller-skate on sunny days.
10. Vicky and Jim raise guppies.

B. Use verbs in the past time in the sentences below. Write each sentence with the correct form of the verb in (   ).

EXAMPLE: Pioneers ____ by horse and wagon. (travel)
ANSWER: Pioneers traveled by horse and wagon.

11. Caroline ____ all her homework. (finish)
12. The chicks ____ the hen around the barnyard. (follow)
13. We ____ fresh trout for dinner. (fry)
14. Mrs. Evans ____ her car. (wax)
15. Eleanor ____ at my silly costume. (giggle)
16. Carlos ____ the birthday gift. (unwrap)
17. The hiker ____ a heavy knapsack. (carry)
18. The canoe ____ over into the river. (tip)
19. He ____ the envelope with tape. (seal)
20. The eggs in the nest ____ yesterday. (hatch)

GRAMMAR HANDBOOK

A. Write each verb below. Then write the form that ends in -s or -es.

1. pitch	**7.** fuss	**13.** spy
2. kiss	**8.** write	**14.** watch
3. send	**9.** burn	**15.** insist
4. occupy	**10.** scare	**16.** push
5. smash	**11.** cry	**17.** express
6. catch	**12.** dress	**18.** dry

B. Use verbs in the present time in the sentences below. Write each sentence with the correct form of the verb in ( ).

19. Sandy ____ of running in a marathon. (dream)

20. They ____ coffee and chocolate to make mocha. (mix)

21. Aunt Lil ____ to my letters quickly. (reply)

22. Coach Green ____ the ball to Arthur. (toss)

23. Some birds ____ over oceans. (fly)

24. My uncle ____ all his own bread. (make)

25. Many athletes ____ ropes for exercise. (climb)

26. A safety guard ____ the street with us. (cross)

27. We ____ the silver vase twice a year. (polish)

28. The clothesline ____ across our backyard. (stretch)

29. I ____ when I don't know the right answer. (guess)

30. She ____ potatoes for dinner. (mash)

31. The players often ____ positions. (switch)

32. I ____ the floor with a mop. (wax)

33. We ____ the windows tightly in winter. (close)

34. Maggie ____ all the broken toys. (repair)

35. We ____ breakfast on Sunday. (cook)

MORE PRACTICE 4   Verbs in the Present and Past

A. Write the form of the verb in the past time.

1. knock   **3.** deny   **5.** crash   **7.** hurry
2. slip   **4.** scream   **6.** slam   **8.** match

B. Write each sentence. Use the form of the verb in ( ) to tell about the past time.

9. The musicians ___ many hours for the concert. (practice)
10. Gregory ___ the tire with a piece of rubber. (patch)
11. Everyone ___ for the spelling test. (study)
12. The weeds in the garden ___ quickly. (multiply)
13. I ___ my fingers to the music. (snap)
14. We ___ the bakery's delicious smells. (sniff)
15. He ___ the slippery fish into the net. (drop)
16. She ___ the papers to the folder. (attach)

C. Each underlined verb is in the present time. Change each verb to the past time. Write the new sentence.

17. Fay <u>grabs</u> the last sandwich on the plate.
18. Betty <u>dries</u> the dishes after dinner.
19. The officer <u>arrests</u> the bank robber.
20. My parents <u>rely</u> on me to rake the leaves.
21. He <u>grips</u> the bat very tightly.
22. The children <u>splash</u> each other in the pool.
23. The bus driver <u>stops</u> at railroad crossings.
24. The diver <u>flips</u> twice in the air.
25. We <u>relax</u> during our summer vacation.

Verb Forms

special
verb forms ● Some verbs in the past time do not end in
-ed. *page 190*

Present	Past
come, comes	came
do, does	did
go, goes	went
have, has	had
run, runs	ran

the verb be ● A verb may show being. *page 192*

● The form of *be* that is used must agree with the
subject of the sentence. *page 194*

I <u>am</u> a student.   I <u>was</u> late.
(He, She, It, The dog) <u>is</u> in the house.
(You, They, We, My parents) <u>are</u> late.
(I, He, She, It, The child) <u>was</u> happy.
(You, They, We, The twins) <u>were</u> at the store.

helping verb ● A **helping verb** works with the main verb. *page 196*

I <u>have tasted</u> the salad.   Leo <u>has worked</u> hard.
They <u>have moved</u> away.   Our friend <u>had called</u> us.

MORE PRACTICE 1   Verb Forms ─────────────

Write the past-time form of the verb in (   ).

1. My pet ___ away. (run)   3. They ___ to a picnic. (go)
2. Katy ___ over. (come)   4. Jacob ___ homework. (do)

MORE PRACTICE 2 Verb Forms

A. Write each sentence. If the underlined verb is in the past time, write *past*. If the underlined verb is in the present time, write *present*.

1. Our cat <u>had</u> kittens.
2. Joe and Cary <u>are</u> absent.
3. Dr. Osawa <u>came</u> to help.
4. A llama <u>was</u> at the zoo.
5. Olga <u>goes</u> on the early bus.
6. You <u>did</u> that job quickly.
7. Dad <u>has</u> a bad cold.
8. I <u>am</u> an only child.
9. They <u>ran</u> out of mustard.
10. The skiers <u>were</u> cold.
11. Helen <u>is</u> a fine singer.
12. He <u>went</u> home.
13. A path <u>runs</u> near the lake.
14. We <u>do</u> the dishes together.

B. Write each sentence. Use the form of the verb in ( ) that tells about the past time.

15. The letter ___ from Portland. (come)
16. Our family ___ an extra load of wash yesterday. (do)
17. The class ___ to the aquarium last week. (go)
18. We ___ a surprise birthday party for Grandma. (have)
19. Water ___ over the edge of the bathtub. (run)
20. Many people ___ to watch our basketball team. (come)

C. Write the verb that shows being in each sentence.

21. This milk is sour.
22. Wanda was angry at me.
23. They were asleep.
24. I am eight years old.
25. The windows are dirty.
26. July was a hot month.
27. You are in Joyce's class.
28. Ron is a photographer.
29. The muffins were fresh.
30. I am very sorry.

MORE PRACTICE 3 Verb Forms

A. Write each sentence. Draw one line under the verb if it shows being. Draw two lines under the verb if it shows action.

1. No one was hurt in the accident.
2. Glen heard a knock on the door at midnight.
3. We were dizzy from the roller coaster.
4. Aunt Esther and Uncle Jack are in New York.
5. I am not hungry right now.
6. Fresh snow covered all the cars.
7. The chimney is black with soot.
8. Lonnie knows my whole family.

B. Write the correct form of the verb *be* in (   ).

9. The light switch (is, are) beside the door.
10. My boots (is, are) too small.
11. Yvonne (was, were) at the movies on Saturday.
12. Laura and Ed (is, are) the best spellers in our class.
13. I (is, am) excited about the game tonight.
14. His notebook (was, were) on the desk.
15. The boxes (was, were) full of valuable jewels.

C. Write each sentence. Use *am, is,* or *are.*

16. Word problems ___ easy.
17. He ___ the youngest.
18. The gravy ___ lumpy.
19. I ___ ready to leave.
20. We ___ on the wrong bus.
21. The circus ___ exciting.
22. Dolphins ___ mammals.
23. They ___ too noisy.
24. Ms. Lopez ___ a lawyer.
25. You ___ in my chair.

MORE PRACTICE 4 Verb Forms

A. Write *helping verb* or *main verb* to tell which is underlined.

1. The rice <u>has</u> cooked too long.
2. Mr. Gray had <u>locked</u> his keys in the car.
3. I <u>have</u> sprained my ankle.
4. Everyone has <u>complained</u> about the food there.
5. The builders have <u>finished</u> the new parking garage.
6. The players <u>had</u> started the game late because of rain.

B. Write the helping verb and the main verb in each sentence.

EXAMPLE: Darlene has played badminton before.
ANSWER: has played

7. The heavy rains had caused a flood.
8. My cousins have moved to Lincoln, Nebraska.
9. The school chorus has appeared on local television.
10. I have waited for the bus for over an hour.
11. Karen had dropped a jar full of strawberry jam.
12. Charles and Bert have prepared a report about Mars.

C. Write each sentence. Use the correct form of the verb in ( ).

13. The ice cream had ___. (melt)
14. School has ___ for summer vacation. (close)
15. They have ___ all around the state. (travel)
16. She has ___ five birthday presents. (receive)
17. The police officer had ___ the speeding driver. (stop)
18. The plumber has ___ the leaky faucet. (fix)
19. We have ___ everywhere for our lost cat. (search)
20. The campers had ___ their supplies in knapsacks. (carry)

Irregular Verbs

- Some verbs change their form to show past time. *page 198*

irregular verbs
- Irregular verbs have special past forms. *page 200*

Verb	Past	Past with Helping Verb
do	did	done
go	went	gone
eat	ate	eaten
give	gave	given
see	saw	seen
run	ran	run
come	came	come
grow	grew	grown
know	knew	known
draw	drew	drawn

MORE PRACTICE 1 Irregular Verbs

Write the correct past form of the verb in ( ).

1. They ____ to the movies yesterday. (go)
2. Elliot has ____ me part of his sandwich. (give)
3. Liza had ____ in a race last summer. (run)
4. Mr. Banks ____ the combination to the safe. (know)
5. We have ____ at that restaurant many times. (eat)
6. The artist ____ some funny cartoons. (draw)
7. This rubber tree plant has ____ six inches. (grow)
8. I have ____ my homework. (do)
9. Nobody ____ the dog sneak away with the steak. (see)
10. Warm weather has ____ early this year. (come)

MORE PRACTICE 2   Irregular Verbs

A. Write the correct past form of the verb in (   ).

1. Joanie has ___ taller than Mother. (grow)
2. Brian and Edith have ___ each other for years. (know)
3. The cashier ___ me too much change. (give)
4. The art teacher has ___ out of red paper. (run)
5. She had ___ the last blueberry muffin. (eat)
6. Dad has ___ to the dentist. (go)
7. In school we have ___ pictures of ourselves. (draw)
8. Richard had ___ the fire engine race by. (see)
9. The carpenter ___ with boards and tools. (come)
10. A TV station has ___ a program about fire safety. (do)

B. Change the underlined verb to the form shown in (   ). Write each sentence.

EXAMPLE: We <u>do</u> book reports in school. (past with have)
ANSWER: We have done book reports in school.

11. I <u>see</u> my best friend at the fair. (past with have)
12. The children <u>go</u> on a camping trip. (past with have)
13. The farmer <u>grew</u> many pumpkins. (past with has)
14. Arthur <u>drew</u> a picture of a zebra. (past with had)
15. Two creeks <u>run</u> through the forest. (past)
16. The mayor <u>gave</u> her the key to the city. (past with has)
17. Rae and Stan <u>do</u> all the math problems. (past with have)
18. Mrs. Morgan <u>knew</u> who borrowed the broom. (past with had)
19. Our cousins <u>come</u> over for lunch often. (past with have)
20. Gilberto <u>ate</u> with chopsticks before. (past with had)

MORE PRACTICE 3   Irregular Verbs

A. Write the correct past form of the verb in (   ).

1. We (run) a mile three times last week.
2. By September the nights have (grow) cooler.
3. The chimpanzee had (eat) twelve bananas.
4. Sean has (draw) a beautiful rainbow.
5. I have (give) the frisky puppy a bath.
6. That airmail letter has (come) back.
7. Nobody had (do) the last assignment.
8. The pilot (see) the map.
9. Mrs. Nelson (know) the shortest way to get there.
10. Michael has (go) back to look for his sweater.

B. Choose the correct form of the verb in (   ). Write each sentence.

11. The corn stalks have (grew, grown) over five feet this summer.
12. Everyone had (went, gone) to watch the big parade.
13. We have (did, done) our shopping.
14. The shopper (come, came) to buy a jacket.
15. The cafeteria has (run, ran) out of straws again.
16. Joan (eaten, ate) some raw carrots.
17. Kenneth (drew, drawn) the winning number at the raffle.
18. The children had (saw, seen) the puppet show.
19. Norma (known, knew) the words to all the songs.
20. The army officer has (gave, given) an order to the soldiers.

MORE PRACTICE 4 Irregular Verbs

A. Write each sentence. Use the correct past form of the verb in ( ).

1. She had ____ a large salad for lunch. (eat)
2. Our car ____ out of gas on the main road. (run)
3. Mrs. Leonard ____ how to tie a square knot. (know)
4. Sonia had ____ the wrong page of problems. (do)
5. His sore throat has ____ much worse. (grow)
6. Gerald ____ a movie about astronauts. (see)
7. The electrician had ____ to fix the lights. (come)
8. This artist has ____ pictures with chalk. (draw)
9. They ____ to the beach for the day. (go)
10. The school orchestra ____ a concert last week. (give)

B. Choose the correct form of the verb in ( ). Write each sentence.

11. Crystal had (knew, known) about the surprise party.
12. The football team has (run, ran) across the playing field.
13. Nelda (went, gone) to Terry's house for dinner.
14. Mr. Cleveland has (drew, drawn) my name for the top prize.
15. Juanita (come, came) to help me wash the windows.
16. Seth (knew, known) the name of each state capital.
17. The kittens have (ran, run) out the back door.
18. His boss has (given, gave) my brother a raise.
19. We have (ate, eaten) all our salad.
20. I have (saw, seen) three jets in the sky today.

Adjectives

adjective ● A word that describes a noun is an
adjective. *page 232*

> The <u>funny</u> poem was about an <u>old</u> house.

● Some adjectives answer the question "How many?" *page 234*

> <u>two</u> ducks   <u>some</u> trees   <u>fifty</u> eggs

● Some adjectives answer the question "What kind?" *page 236*

> a <u>white</u> cloud   the <u>round</u> table   <u>small</u> birds

adjectives that compare ● Use the *-er* form of an adjective to compare two persons, places, or things. *page 238*

● Use the *-est* form of an adjective to compare three or more persons, places, or things. *page 238*

> Noel is <u>taller</u> than Jo.   Mark is the <u>tallest</u> of all.

article ● The words *a, an,* and *the* are a special kind of adjective. They are called **articles.** *page 240*

> <u>a</u> cap   <u>an</u> owl   <u>the</u> baby   <u>the</u> papers

MORE PRACTICE 1 Adjectives

Write the adjective that describes each underlined noun.

1. Young <u>babies</u> cry often.
2. Did three <u>roosters</u> crow?
3. We ate juicy <u>peaches</u>.
4. I saw brown <u>dogs</u>.

MORE PRACTICE 2 Adjectives

A. Copy each sentence. Draw one line under each adjective. Draw two lines under the noun that the adjective describes.

EXAMPLE: Aunt Lillian found a beautiful shell.
ANSWER: Aunt Lillian found a <u>beautiful</u> <u>shell</u>.

1. They live on busy streets.
2. I used sticky glue.
3. Alan wore red socks.
4. He lost three dimes.
5. Large crows flew by.
6. Linda has new shoes.
7. We drank hot cocoa.
8. Ana loves rainy days.
9. Green frogs hopped by.
10. He read fourteen pages.

B. Write each adjective that tells *how many*.

11. The farm has twenty cows.
12. Three letters arrived.
13. He sold many tickets.
14. Several people called.
15. They bought some apples.
16. It rained for nine days.
17. I lost one glove.
18. Few people knew him.

C. Write each adjective that tells *what kind*.

19. Wild geese were flying.
20. We blew tiny bubbles.
21. Sam carried heavy boxes.
22. We swam in shallow water.
23. I have a blue notebook.
24. Mary has curly hair.
25. The narrow path ended.
26. The noisy crowd cheered.

D. Write the missing form of each adjective.

27. cold, colder, ____
28. ____, deeper, deepest
29. long, ____, longest
30. high, higher, ____

MORE PRACTICE 3 Adjectives

A. Write each sentence. Add an adjective.

1. I bought ___ boots.
2. We watched a ___ show.
3. Gail writes ___ poems.
4. Sunday was a ___ day.
5. She is a ___ teacher.
6. I ate ___ plums.
7. Pat found a ___ coin.
8. He spoke in a ___ voice.
9. I saw your ___ bicycle.
10. We own a ___ jeep.
11. I washed ___ dishes.
12. He has ___ eyes.
13. The ___ cat stretched.
14. I like ___ weather.

B. Choose the correct adjective in ( ). Write each sentence.

15. Wool is a (warmer, warmest) fabric than cotton.
16. February is the (shorter, shortest) month of the year.
17. The (faster, fastest) runner on the team is Heather.
18. This string is (weaker, weakest) than that rope.
19. My brother is (older, oldest) than my sister.
20. Grant Street is the (straighter, straightest) road in our city.

C. Choose the correct article in ( ) to complete each sentence. Write each sentence.

21. We heard (a, an) car drive by.
22. The carpenter hammered (a, the) nails into boards for a new house.
23. The sailor threw (a, an) anchor into the water.
24. They fed (a, the) ducks at Crystal Lake.
25. I brought (a, an) umbrella in case of rain.

MORE PRACTICE 4 Adjectives

A. Add *-er* or *-est* to each adjective in ( ). Write each sentence.

1. Cedar Mountain is (steep) than Holloway Hill.
2. A pencil is (sharp) than a crayon.
3. Baker Beach must be the (clean) beach in the world.
4. The (deep) lake in the county is Mirror Lake.
5. This muffin is (fresh) than that roll.
6. That person has the (long) fingernails I have ever seen.

B. Write the articles that may be correctly used before the nouns.

7. ____ carrot
8. ____ alligator
9. ____ pianos

10. ____ operator
11. ____ zipper
12. ____ elevator

13. ____ campers
14. ____ igloo
15. ____ nurse

C. Write each sentence. Add an adjective that tells *how many.*

16. ____ inches of snow fell during the last storm.
17. Susan invited ____ people to the party.
18. ____ puppets danced across the stage.
19. I read ____ books during the month of March.

D. Write each sentence. Add an adjective that tells *what kind.*

20. The ____ gorilla made faces at us.
21. The train passed through ____ tunnels.
22. I drank a pitcher of ____ lemonade.
23. Sharon lives near a ____ park.
24. We rode our bicycles by ____ buildings.
25. The ____ dog chased every car that passed.

Adverbs

adverb ● A word that describes a verb is an **adverb.** *page 268*

We arrived <u>late</u>.   I walked <u>inside</u>.

● Some adverbs answer the question "How?" *page 270*

The children whispered <u>softly</u> in the library.

MORE PRACTICE 1   Adverbs ─────────────

A. Write each underlined adverb. Then write if the adverb tells *where* or *when*.

1. The grocery store opens <u>early</u> in the morning.
2. Mary Ellen is leaving <u>now</u>.
3. The vase fell <u>down</u> with a crash.
4. The children searched <u>everywhere</u> for the missing watch.
5. Summer vacation begins <u>tomorrow</u>.
6. Herb rode his bicycle <u>someplace</u> with Eddie.
7. <u>Yesterday</u> I received two letters in the mail.
8. We eat our lunches <u>outside</u> in nice weather.

B. Write the adverb in each sentence.

9. The dog waits patiently for its owner.
10. That scratch is healing nicely.
11. The store manager spoke kindly to the lost child.
12. Penny held her mother's hand tightly.
13. I sipped the mug of hot cocoa slowly.
14. The alarm clock rang loudly.
15. The fox watched the chickens slyly.

MORE PRACTICE 2 Adverbs

A. Write each sentence. Underline the adverb.

1. The lion roared loudly.
2. He beat the drum evenly.
3. The ice melted quickly.
4. I will go skating soon.
5. She talked to him politely.
6. We will wait here.
7. Beth looked up at the sky.
8. I raised my hand nervously.
9. The phone rang suddenly.
10. She walks everywhere.
11. The bus stops there.
12. He always wears a hat.
13. I folded the shirt neatly.
14. The cat hid outside.
15. Once I ate a mango.
16. The plane landed safely.

B. Add *-ly* to each word in ( ) to form an adverb. Then write each sentence.

17. Everyone listened (quiet) to the teacher.
18. Jan spelled every word (perfect).
19. (Proud) the captain accepted the trophy for the team.
20. I answered the last question (correct).
21. We waited (eager) for the show to start.
22. He tapped his foot (impatient).
23. The science test will begin (immediate).
24. Martin spoke (clear) into the microphone.
25. I (sad) told my best friend that I was moving away.
26. The driver turned (sharp) to the left.
27. The officer smiled (pleasant) as we waited on the corner.
28. (Swift) the deer leaped across the meadow.
29. The artist (light) added some lines to the drawing.
30. The mother duck waited (anxious) for the ducklings to swim across the pond.

Paragraphs

paragraph

- A **paragraph** is a group of sentences about one main idea.   *page 32*

topic
sentence

- The **topic sentence** tells the main idea of the paragraph.   *page 32*

- The first word of a paragraph is indented.

Indent → The prairie dog builds a safe home underground. It digs a long tunnel and many rooms. Here it sleeps, stores food, and hides from its enemies. Both ends of the tunnel lead to the prairie. This gives the prairie dog two ways to escape. Around each opening are piles of dirt. The prairie dog sits on these to watch for enemies.

Topic
sentence

The other
sentences
tell about
the topic
sentence.

PRACTICE

Write a paragraph about something special—something you really like. Here are some ideas for a topic:

a cute pet   a favorite toy
a funny TV show   a tasty snack
a special place   a school subject

Ask yourself, "What is the main thing I want to say about my topic?" Then begin your paragraph with a topic sentence that tells your main idea. Remember to indent the first word of your paragraph.

Writing Forms: Friendly Letters

- A **friendly letter** has five parts: the heading, greeting, body, closing, and signature. *page 176*

friendly letter

- Write your address and the date in the **heading.** Put a comma between the city and state and between the date and the year.

heading

- Begin the **greeting** with a capital letter. Put a comma after the greeting.

greeting

- Indent each paragraph in the **body** of the letter.

body

- Begin the **closing** with a capital letter. Put a comma after the closing.

closing

- Write your name clearly for the **signature.**

signature

Heading	18 Green Street Akron, Ohio 44309 May 4, 1986
Greeting	Dear Amy,
Body	Today Daisy had six puppies. They are so adorable! When can you come to see them?
Closing Signature	Your friend, Marie

PRACTICE

Write a friendly letter to mail to a friend or relative. Tell some news about yourself.

Writing Forms: Thank-You Notes and Invitations

thank-you note

- A **thank-you note** is a short letter of thanks for a gift or favor.

> 20 Maple Avenue
> Clinton, Utah 84015
> March 3, 1986
>
> Dear Uncle Jim,
>   Thanks so much for the soccer ball! I really wanted one! Now my friends and I can play every day.
>
>   Love,
>   Chris

invitation

- An **invitation** is a note or short letter that invites someone to an event. It should answer these questions: *What is happening? Where? When? Who sent the invitation?*

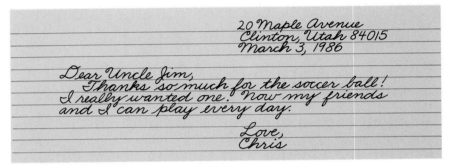

What?   **Please come to** my birthday party

Where?   **Place** 3 Lenox Avenue

When?   **Date and time** June 4, 2:00–4:00 P.M.

Who?   **From** Your friend, Dan Stein

PRACTICE

Pretend you are having a birthday party. Write an invitation. Then write a thank-you note for a birthday gift.

Writing Forms: Book Reports

- A **book report** is a way to give information and share opinions about a book.   *page 286*

  book report

- When you write the title of a book, underline it.

  book title

Study this book report form. It shows what you should tell about a book when you write a book report.

Title *A Bear Called Paddington*

Author *Michael Bond*

What the book is about *The Brown family met Paddington on a railroad platform. He had a sign around his neck. It said, "Please look after this bear. Thank you." So that's what they did. The Browns took Paddington home. They had all kinds of adventures.*

Your opinion *This book is so funny! I loved the part about Paddington's first bath.*

PRACTICE

Copy the book report form. On the form, write a book report to share with your class.

Addressing Letters: Envelopes

return address

receiver's address

state abbreviations

- When you address an envelope, you write the return address and the receiver's address.

- Write your name and address in the upper left-hand corner. This is the **return address.** It shows where to return the letter if it cannot be delivered.

- In the center of the envelope, write the **receiver's address.** This is the address of the person who will receive the letter.

- You may use an abbreviation for the name of a state. See the chart on the next page. It lists the abbreviations that the Postal Service would like people to use.

Return address

Amy Kito
128 Grove Street
Anchorage, AK 99502

Receiver's address

Miss Melissa Sheehy
348 Sunrise Avenue
Silver City, NM 88061

State abbreviation

PRACTICE

Use a ruler. Draw an envelope like the sample above. Then write this information where it belongs.

Return address: Jeff Gray   42 Pine Street   Ada, OH 45810
Receiver's address: Mr. I. Taft   5 Oak Way   Rye, NY 10580

Addressing Letters: State Abbreviations

- When you address a letter, use the following abbreviations of state names.

Alabama	**AL**	Maine	**ME**	Oregon	**OR**
Alaska	**AK**	Maryland	**MD**	Pennsylvania	**PA**
Arizona	**AZ**	Massachusetts	**MA**	Rhode Island	**RI**
Arkansas	**AR**	Michigan	**MI**	South Carolina	**SC**
California	**CA**	Minnesota	**MN**	South Dakota	**SD**
Colorado	**CO**	Mississippi	**MS**	Tennessee	**TN**
Connecticut	**CT**	Missouri	**MO**	Texas	**TX**
Delaware	**DE**	Montana	**MT**	Utah	**UT**
Florida	**FL**	Nebraska	**NE**	Vermont	**VT**
Georgia	**GA**	Nevada	**NV**	Virginia	**VA**
Hawaii	**HI**	New Hampshire	**NH**	Washington	**WA**
Idaho	**ID**	New Jersey	**NJ**	West Virginia	**WV**
Illinois	**IL**	New Mexico	**NM**	Wisconsin	**WI**
Indiana	**IN**	New York	**NY**	Wyoming	**WY**
Iowa	**IA**	North Carolina	**NC**	* * *	
Kansas	**KS**	North Dakota	**ND**	District of	
Kentucky	**KY**	Ohio	**OH**	Columbia	**DC**
Louisiana	**LA**	Oklahoma	**OK**		

PRACTICE

Write the names of ten states you would like to visit. On the other side of your paper, write their abbreviations. Exchange papers. Read the abbreviations your partner wrote. Try to name the states. Turn the paper over to see if you were right.

Editing Marks

● Use editing marks to make changes when you revise and proofread.

Mark	Meaning	Example
——	cross out	I ~~also~~ have a dog, too. I have a dog, too.
∧	add	I have a *white*∧horse. I have a white horse.
⬭↗	move	I rode my bike ⟨yesterday⟩ to school. I rode my bike to school yesterday.
≡	capital letter	joe is on my softball team. Joe is on my softball team.
¶	indent	¶Ana is my best friend. We are are in the same class. Our teacher is Mr. Ortega. Ana is my best friend. We are in the same class. Our teacher is Mr. Ortega.
⬭	check spelling	My cat is black and ⟨fury⟩. *furry* My cat is black and furry.

Proofreading Checklist

When you proofread, you check your writing for errors. To do this, read slowly and carefully. Look at each word. If you find a mistake, correct it neatly. Use the editing marks on page 354 to make changes.

Below is a proofreading checklist. It will help you to find errors when you proofread. You may copy the form if you wish. Notice that the writer has checked *No* for questions **4** and **6**. That writer needs to be more careful about spelling and handwriting.

Questions	YES	NO
1. Did I indent the first word of each paragraph?	✔	
2. Did I begin each sentence with a capital letter?	✔	
3. Did I use the correct mark at the end of each sentence?	✔	
4. Did I spell each word correctly?		✔
5. Did I use capital letters correctly?	✔	
6. Did I use my best handwriting?		✔

Capitalization

persons or pets
- Each word in the name of a person or pet begins with a capital letter. *page 88*

James   Mary Ann   Diane T. Jones
Snoopy   Thomas Alva Edison

titles
- A title, such as *Miss* or *Mr.*, begins with a capital letter.

Miss Deanna Ferro   Mr. Fred A. Rogers
Ms. Lee Yamaha   Dr. Dolores Perez

place names
- Each word in the name of a street, town, city, or state begins with a capital letter. *page 90*

Main Street   River Road   Boyertown
New York City   Maine   North Dakota

- Each important word in the name of a country, a school, or a building begins with a capital letter.

United States of America   Mexico
Franklin School   Northeast High School
Empire State Building   City Hall

calendar words
- The name of a day or month begins with a capital letter. *page 92*

Monday   December   Friday   May

- The name of a holiday or special day begins with a capital letter. *page 92*

Thanksgiving   Mother's Day   Halloween

Capitalization

- The pronoun *I* is always written as a capital letter.   *page 126*

  pronoun I

    If I don't hurry, I'm going to be late!

- A capital letter is used to begin the first word, the last word, and all important words in a book title.

  titles of books

    Little House in the Big Woods
    The Case of the Cat's Meow

- A capital letter is used to begin the first word, the last word, and all important words in the title of a story or a poem.

  titles of stories and poems

    "Two of Everything" (story)
    "The Path on the Sea" (poem)

PRACTICE 1   Capitalization

Write each sentence. Use capital letters correctly.

1. My friend billy joe has a cat named marmalade.
2. Have you read any books by laura ingalls wilder?
3. Did mary invite kim and kristen to her party?
4. My dog max likes fluffy, our new kitten.
5. Did harry name his hamster sammy?
6. Has elizabeth ann cummings signed her letter?
7. Only michael smith and sue ellen jackson are absent today.
8. The winner of the spelling bee is reggie m. jones.
9. Why is lassie barking at rover?
10. Did e. b. white write <u>Charlotte's Web?</u>

A. Write each address. Use capital letters correctly.

1. miss sue ann shea
   42 east broad street
   westfield, new jersey 07090

2. mr. ralph fox
   3 north plainfield avenue
   dover, new hampshire 03820

3. dr. joyce stonebach
   48 galloway drive
   cedar falls, iowa 50613

4. mrs. christine iverson
   411 la salle street
   quay, new mexico 88433

B. Write each sentence. Use capital letters correctly.

5. Mark's party is on saturday, july 22.
6. Jenny makes her own valentine's day cards.
7. Is thanksgiving always on a thursday?
8. The third sunday in june is father's day.
9. We celebrate washington's birthday on a monday.
10. The first monday in september is labor day.
11. The library is closed every saturday in july.

C. Write each sentence. Use capital letters correctly.

12. Yes, i enjoyed the book <u>the carp in the bathtub</u>.
13. When i went to the library, i took out <u>the moffats</u>.
14. One of my favorite books is <u>a toad for tuesday</u>.
15. For my book report i will write about <u>no room for a dog</u>.

D. Write each sentence. Use capital letters correctly.

16. Mike wrote a story called "a wonderful surprise."
17. Our class learned the poem "the swing."
18. Do you know the poem "there once was a puffin"?

YOUNG WRITER'S HANDBOOK

Punctuation

- Use a **comma** after *yes* or *no* at the beginning of a sentence.   *page 94*

> Yes, that is the right answer.
> No, Ann hasn't come home yet.

- Use a **comma** after the name of a person spoken to.   *page 94*

> Carol, please pass the salt.
> Pedro, have you seen my glasses?

- Use a **comma** to separate words in a series.   *page 272*

> Amy bought milk, cheese, apples, and eggs at the store.

- Use an **apostrophe** to show where a letter or letters have been left out of a contraction.

he	+	is	= he's	we	+ are = we're
I	+	have	= I've	you	+ will = you'll
had	+	not	= hadn't	do	+ not = don't

- **Underline** the title of a book.

> Danny and the Dinosaur (book)

- Use **quotation marks** (" ") before and after the title of a story or a poem.

> "The Little Match Girl" (story)
> "Little Jack Horner" (poem)

comma

apostrophe

underlining

quotation marks

Punctuation

- Most **abbreviations** end with a period.

  Below are common abbreviations. Each begins with a capital letter and ends with a period.

Mr. = Mister (a man)			St. = Street			
Ms. = a woman			Ave. = Avenue			
Mrs. = a married woman			Rd. = Road			
Dr. = Doctor			Blvd. = Boulevard			
A.M. = before noon			P.M. = after noon			
Mon.	Tues.	Wed.	Thurs.	Fri.	Sat.	Sun.
Jan. = January			Sept. = September			
Feb. = February			Oct. = October			
Mar. = March			Nov. = November			
Apr. = April			Dec. = December			
Aug. = August						

PRACTICE 1 Punctuation

Write each sentence. Use commas correctly.

1. Yes I do know how to swim.
2. No I have never flown in an airplane.
3. Chico is this your glove?
4. Yes we're going to the zoo this afternoon.
5. Ryan let's play baseball after school.

PRACTICE 2 Punctuation

A. Write each sentence. Use commas correctly.

1. Only Anita Bob and Carla are absent today.
2. I had soup milk eggs and an apple for lunch.
3. Yes we need to buy bananas strawberries and peaches.
4. No I haven't been to Texas Oklahoma or Arkansas.
5. Susan be sure to wear your boots scarf hat and mittens.

B. Write the contraction for each pair of words.

6. have + not	**8.** she + is	**10.** I + have
7. they + have	**9.** he + will	**11.** will + not

C. Write each title. Use underlining and quotation marks correctly.

12. Spring Rain (poem)	**14.** The Borrowers (book)
13. Born Free (book)	**15.** Kite Days (poem)

D. Write the abbreviation for each word or meaning.

16. November	**19.** Friday
17. a married woman	**20.** before noon
18. Road	**21.** Tuesday

E. Write the sentences. Replace the underlined words with their abbreviations.

22. Mister Zonda lives at 221 Beacon Boulevard.
23. Doctor Kim can see you on Thursday, March 8.
24. Meet me this Sunday at 3:00 after noon.
25. The bank is on the corner of Maple Avenue and Green Road.

5 Helpful Spelling Rules

1. If a word ends in *e*, drop the *e* when you add a suffix that begins with a vowel.

   save + ing = saving

   Keep the *e* when you add a suffix that begins with a consonant.

   hope + ful = hopeful

2. If a word ends in a vowel and *y*, keep the *y* when you add a suffix.

   pay + ing = paying

3. If a word ends in a consonant and *y*, keep the *y* when you add *-ing*.

   try + ing = trying

   Change the *y* to *i* when you add other suffixes.

   try + es = tries   **busy + ly = busily**

4. Many words end in one vowel and one consonant. Double that consonant when you add a suffix that begins with a vowel.

   swim + er = swimmer

5. When you choose between *ie* and *ei*, usually choose *ie*.

   pie   field

   Use *ei* after *c* or for the long *a* sound.

   ceiling   eight

50 Words Often Misspelled

1. again	18. every	35. some
2. always	19. forty	36. sometime
3. among	20. guess	37. sugar
4. answer	21. hear	38. sure
5. anything	22. heard	39. their
6. been	23. here	40. there
7. break	24. knew	41. they
8. busy	25. know	42. threw
9. children	26. laid	43. through
10. color	27. many	44. tired
11. coming	28. much	45. together
12. cough	29. often	46. too
13. could	30. pretty	47. two
14. doctor	31. raise	48. very
15. done	32. said	49. where
16. early	33. shoes	50. writing
17. easy	34. since	

PRACTICE

Read the words below. They are often misspelled. Each pair of words sounds alike, but their spellings and meanings are different. Write a sentence for each word. You may use a dictionary if you are not sure of the meaning of a word.

1. hear, here
2. their, there
3. threw, through
4. too, two

Handwriting Models

a b c d e f g h i
j k l m n o p q r
s t u v w x y z

Circle letters
a b d o p q

Curved letters
c e f h m n r u

Double-curved letter
s

Straight-line letters
b d h i k l t

Slant-line letters
k v w x y z

Below-the-line letters
g j p q y

A B C D E F G H I
J K L M N O P Q R
S T U V W X Y Z

Handwriting Models

a b c d e f g h i

j k l m n o p q r

s t u v w x y z

Upward-loop letters

b e f

h k l

Rounded letters

m n v

x y z

Oval letters

a c d

g o q

Pointed letters

i j p r

s t u w

A B C D E F G H I

J K L M N O P Q R

S T U V W X Y Z

Used with permission from Zaner-Bloser *Handwriting: Basic Skills and Application.*
Copyright © 1984, Zaner-Bloser, Inc., Columbus, Ohio.

6 Tips for Taking Tests

1. **Be prepared.** Have several sharp pencils and an eraser.

2. **Read or listen to the directions carefully.** Be sure you know what you are to do.

3. **Answer the easy questions first.** Quickly read all the questions on the page. Then go back to the beginning. Answer the questions you are sure you know. Put a light check next to those you are not sure of or don't know.

4. **Next try to answer the questions you are not sure you know.** You may have a choice of answers. If so, narrow your choice. Get rid of answers you know are wrong. Then mark the answer you think is right.

5. **Answer the hardest questions last.** If you can't answer a question at all, go on to the next.

6. **Plan your time.** Don't spend too much time on just one question. If you do, you won't have time to answer the others. You will also need to save some time to check over your answers.

Thesaurus

What Is a Thesaurus?

In a thesaurus, words are listed in alphabetical order. These are called entry words. Under each entry word, synonyms and antonyms are shown.

Below is part of a thesaurus entry from this book.

Entry word ➛ **like**— to be pleased with; to have a good feeling for. Carol and her friends <u>like</u> to play computer games.

Synonym ➛ *enjoy*— to get pleasure from; to be happy with. If you <u>enjoy</u> historical places, you should visit Williamsburg.

Antonym ➛ ANTONYM: dislike

An entry word is always in dark type: **like**
The synonyms are always in slanted type: *enjoy*
The antonyms are always in blue type: dislike

How to Use the Thesaurus Index

To find a word, use the Thesaurus Index. If the word is an entry word, it will look like this in the Index:

like 379

If the word is a synonym, you need to find its entry word. Here is how the synonym *enjoy* is shown:

enjoy **like** 379

The two words and the number mean "To find *enjoy,* look under **like**. The entry for **like** begins on page 379."

If the word is an antonym, you also need to find its entry word. Here is how the antonym dislike is shown:

dislike **like** 379

The two words and the number mean "To find dislike, look under **like**. The entry for **like** begins on page 379."

To learn more about a thesaurus, turn to the lesson "Using a Thesaurus" on page 30.

THESAURUS INDEX
A list of all the words in this thesaurus

A

abandon **keep** 378
abandon **leave** 378
abrupt **quick** 382
accurate **right** 383
admire **like** 379
admit **let** 379
advance **go** 376
advise **help** 377
afraid 373
aid **help** 377
alarming **scary** 383
all **part** 381
alone 373
alter **change** 374
amazing **funny** 376
amble **run** 383
amiable **nice** 380
ancient **old** 381
antique **new** 380
antique **old** 381
anxious **afraid** 373
appreciate **like** 379
arid **wet** 384
arrive **go** 376
arrive **leave** 378
ascend **fall** 375
ask **tell** 384
assemble **join** 377

assist **help** 377
attach **join** 377
authorize **let** 379

B

bad 373
ban **let** 379
bar **let** 379
barbeque **cook** 374
beginning **end** 375
benefit **help** 377
big 373
big **small** 384
bit **part** 381
blast **noise** 381
bold **afraid** 373
boring **funny** 376
bound **jump** 377
boundary **end** 375
brave **afraid** 373
bright 374
brilliant **bright** 374
brisk **cool** 374
budge **move** 380

C

captain **leader** 378
change 374
charming **nice** 380

chase **run** 383
cheerful **happy** 376
chief **leader** 378
chuckle **laugh** 378
clamor **noise** 381
clasp **join** 377
clean **dirty** 375
climb **fall** 375
cloudy **bright** 374
collage **picture** 381
collapse **fall** 375
combine **join** 377
combined **alone** 373
come **go** 376
come **leave** 378
comical **funny** 376
commander **leader** 378
component **part** 381
concede **let** 379
conclusion **end** 375
conductor **leader** 378
congenial **nice** 380
connect **join** 377
consent **let** 379
construct **make** 379
contented **happy** 376
convert **change** 374
cook 374
cool 374

correct **right** 383
courteous **nice** 380
crawl **run** 383
create **make** 379
creepy **scary** 383
cry **laugh** 378
current **new** 380
current **old** 381

D

dally **hurry** 377
damp **wet** 384
dark **bright** 374
dash **hurry** 377
decrease **grow** 376
delay **hurry** 377
delayed **quick** 382
delighted **happy** 376
demonstration **show** 383
depart **go** 376
descend **fall** 375
describe **tell** 384
design **make** 379
destroy **make** 379
detached **alone** 373
detain **hurry** 377
detest **like** 379
diagram **picture** 381
dim **bright** 374
dirty 375
disagreeable **nice** 380

discard **keep** 378
disconnect **join** 377
discontent **happy** 376
dishonest **right** 383
dislike **like** 379.
disregard **look** 379
divide **join** 377
doze **rest** 382
drag **pull** 382
drop **fall** 375
dry **wet** 384
dull **bright** 374
dull **funny** 376

E

eerie **scary** 383
elderly **old** 381
end 375
enjoy **like** 379
enlarge **grow** 376
enormous **big** 373
entirety **part** 381
examine **look** 379
excellent **bad** 373
exhibit **show** 383
expand **grow** 376
explain **tell** 384

F

faded **bright** 374
fall 375
false **right** 383
fearless **afraid** 373

filthy **dirty** 375
fine **bad** 373
finish **end** 375
flee **leave** 378
follower **leader** 378
forbid **let** 379
fragment **part** 381
fresh **new** 380
frightened **afraid** 373
frown **laugh** 378
frosty **cool** 374
fry **cook** 374
funny 376

G

giant **small** 384
gigantic **big** 373
giggle **laugh** 378
glance **look** 379
glowing **bright** 374
go 376
good **bad** 373
grand **big** 373
grant **let** 379
great **big** 373
great **small** 384
grow 376

H

happy 376
harm **help** 377
harmful **bad** 373
hasty **quick** 382

hate **like** 379
haul **pull** 382
help 377
hilarious **funny** 376
hinder **help** 377
historical **old** 381
horrifying **scary** 383
huge **small** 384
humid **wet** 384
humorous **funny** 376
hurdle **jump** 377
hurry 377
hurt **help** 377
hush **noise** 381
hustle **hurry** 377

I

ignore **look** 379
inch **move** 380
increase **grow** 376
inform **tell** 384
inquire **tell** 384
instant **quick** 382
invent **make** 379
isolated **alone** 373

J

jaunt **trip** 384
jerk **pull** 382
jog **run** 383
join 377

joint **alone** 373
jolly **happy** 376
journey **trip** 384
jubilant **happy** 376
jump 377
just **right** 383

K

keep 378

L

labor **rest** 382
landscape **picture** 381
large **small** 384
laugh 378
leader 378
leave 378
lessen **grow** 376
let 379
like 379
limit **end** 375
linger **hurry** 377
lingering **quick** 382
listen **tell** 384
little **big** 373
little **small** 384
loathe **like** 379
loiter **hurry** 377
long **quick** 382
look 379

lose **keep** 378
lounge **rest** 382
lull **noise** 381

M

make 379
manufacture **make** 379
massive **big** 373
mean **nice** 380
mention **tell** 384
mild **cool** 374
miserable **happy** 376
miss **look** 379
mistaken **right** 383
modern **new** 380
modern **old** 381
moist **wet** 384
mount **fall** 375
move 380
multiply **grow** 376
mural **picture** 381

N

nap **rest** 382
naughty **bad** 373
new 380
new **old** 381
nice 380
noise 381
novel **new** 380

O

obstruct **help** 377
old 381
old **new** 380
old-fashioned **new** 380
onset **end** 375
opening **end** 375
original **new** 380
outdated **old** 381
outing **trip** 384
overlook **look** 379

P

pageant **show** 383
parched **wet** 384
part 381
part **join** 377
past **new** 380
pause **rest** 382
peek **look** 379
performance **show** 383
petite **small** 384
picture 381
pocket-sized **small** 384
polluted **dirty** 375
poor **bad** 373
portrait **picture** 381
pounce **jump** 377
prefer **like** 379

preserve **keep** 378
prevent **let** 379
private **alone** 373
proceed **go** 376
program **show** 383
progress **go** 376
prompt **quick** 382
proper **right** 383
public **alone** 373
pull 382
pure **dirty** 375
push **move** 380
push **pull** 382

Q

question **tell** 384
quick 382
quiet **noise** 381
quit **leave** 378

R

race **run** 383
racket **noise** 381
recent **old** 381
recite **tell** 384
refuse **let** 379
relax **rest** 382
remain **change** 374
remain **go** 376
remain **leave** 378
reserve **keep** 378
rest 382

retain **keep** 378
retreat **go** 376
right 383
right **bad** 373
rise **fall** 375
roar **laugh** 378
rude **nice** 380
ruin **make** 379
ruler **leader** 378
rumble **noise** 381
run 383
rush **hurry** 377

S

sad **happy** 376
saunter **run** 383
save **keep** 378
scan **look** 379
scared **afraid** 373
scary 383
scowl **laugh** 378
scramble **hurry** 377
secluded **alone** 373
section **part** 381
separate **alone** 373
separate **join** 377
serious **funny** 376
sever **join** 377
severe **bad** 373
share **part** 381
shift **change** 374
shining **bright** 374

shivery **cool** 374
shove **move** 380
shove **pull** 382
show 383
shrink **grow** 376
silence **noise** 381
simmer **cook** 374
sink **fall** 375
slight **big** 373
slow **quick** 382
small 384
small **big** 373
smudged **dirty** 375
snicker **laugh** 378
soaked **wet** 384
soar **fall** 375
soggy **wet** 384
soiled **dirty** 375
sorrowful **happy** 376
spotless **dirty** 375
spring **jump** 377
sprint **run** 383
stained **dirty** 375
stare **look** 379
start **end** 375
startling **scary** 383
stay **change** 374
stay **go** 376
stay **leave** 378
stillness **noise** 381

stir **rest** 382
stop **go** 376
store **keep** 378
stroll **run** 383
sunny **bright** 374
superior **bad** 373
support **help** 377
swell **grow** 376
swift **quick** 382
switch **change** 374

T

tell 384
terrified **afraid** 373
timid **afraid** 373
tiny **big** 373
tiny **small** 384
tip **end** 375
toast **cook** 374
toil **rest** 382
tour **trip** 384
tow **pull** 382
transfer **move** 380
trip 384
trot **run** 383
tug **pull** 382
tumble **fall** 375

U

unafraid **afraid** 373
unfair **right** 383

unfriendly **nice** 380
unhappy **happy** 376
unpleasant **nice** 380
uproar **noise** 381
used **new** 380

V

vacate **leave** 378
valid **right** 383
value **like** 379
vault **jump** 377
vivid **bright** 374
voyage **trip** 384

W

walk **run** 383
warm **cool** 374
warm **nice** 380
washed **dirty** 375
weak **small** 384
wet 384
whole **part** 381
witty **funny** 376
work **rest** 382
wreck **make** 379
wrong **bad** 373
wrong **right** 383

Y

young **old** 381

THESAURUS

A

afraid—feeling fear. Some people are afraid of flying in airplanes.

anxious—uneasy from fear of what may happen. Everyone became anxious as flood waters continued to rise.

frightened—filled with sudden fear. The frightened campers heard another noise in the bush.

scared—suddenly becoming afraid. A scared animal will run from danger.

terrified—filled with great fear of danger. The terrified swimmer yelled for help.

timid—easily frightened; afraid to do something. The timid child would not ride the pony.

ANTONYMS: bold, brave, fearless, unafraid

alone—being away from or left without others. The rider was alone on the trail.

detached—standing alone. The house has a detached garage.

isolated—kept apart from others, usually for a certain reason. The isolated patient has the mumps.

private—away from the public. The club's meeting place is private.

secluded—removed and shut off from others; undisturbed. The secluded cabin is hidden by trees.

separate—not connected or joined; apart from others. The new books are on a separate shelf.

ANTONYMS: combined, joint, public

B

bad—not good; not as good as it should be. It was a bad movie, and everyone was bored.

harmful—causing hurt or damage. Buyers were warned that the new toy might be harmful.

naughty—behaving badly; not obeying. The naughty puppy chewed on the table.

poor—not good in quality; without quality. The tennis player made a poor shot and lost the point.

severe—very harsh. Travelers need to be extra careful in severe weather.

wrong—not right. It is wrong to interrupt someone who is speaking.

ANTONYMS: excellent, fine, good, right, superior

big—large in size, amount, or number. A crowd gathered in the big room.

enormous—extremely large or great. Thousands of fans watched the game in the enormous stadium.

gigantic—huge, like a giant. A tour guide talked about the gigantic redwood trees in the national park.

grand—large and very nice-looking. The grand hotel is the oldest building in the city.

great—very big. Years after the shipwreck, divers found a great number of gold pieces.

massive—big and heavy; solid. The airplane looked tiny flying over the massive mountain.

ANTONYMS: little, slight, small, tiny

THESAURUS

bright—full of light; clear in color. We see bright stars at night.

brilliant—brighter than usual. The artist used brilliant colors in her painting.

glowing—giving off light because of heat; showing strong color. A glowing fire made the room warm and cheerful.

shining—giving off light. The shining lamp of a lighthouse guides ships at night.

sunny—bright with sunshine. The park is filled with people on a warm, sunny day.

vivid—strong and clear in color. It is easy to see the crossing guard in her vivid yellow raincoat.

ANTONYMS: cloudy, dark, dim, dull, faded

C

change—**1** to make or become different. We will change our plans if it rains. **2** to move from one place, position, or direction to another. You should change your seat so that we can sit next to each other.

alter—to change slightly. A tailor can alter the jacket to make it shorter.

convert—to change for a different use. The builders will convert the porch into a family room.

shift—to go or move in a different place, position, or direction. Gymnasts must shift their weight properly to keep their balance.

switch—to change place, position, or direction. Due to an engine problem, the passengers must switch airplanes.

vary—to change so that something is not always the same. The cafeteria should vary the food it serves.

ANTONYMS: remain, stay

cook—to use heat to prepare food. Will you please cook dinner tonight?

bake—to cook in an oven. Did the pioneers bake their own bread?

barbecue—to cook over an open fire. Wait for the coals to get hot before you barbecue the chicken.

fry—to cook in hot fat over direct heat. While you fry the eggs, I will make the toast.

simmer—to cook slowly with low heat. Put a lid on the vegetables when you simmer them.

toast—to make brown by heating. The campers will toast marshmallows.

cool—having a low temperature. The autumn air feels cool.

brisk—cool and dry; fresh. A brisk morning is a good time for a walk.

chilly—very cool, almost cold. It is too chilly outside to have a picnic.

frosty—cool enough to have frost. Can you see through the frosty window?

shivery—chilly enough to make a person quiver. Hot soup tastes good on a shivery day.

ANTONYMS: mild, warm

D

dirty—not clean; not pure. You will need a bucket of soapy water to wash the <u>dirty</u> car.

filthy—completely covered with dirt. After walking in the mud, Brian's shoes were <u>filthy</u>.

polluted—dirty from what is in something. The health department warned people about the <u>polluted</u> drinking water.

smudged—no longer clean from being smeared. The child eating a peanut butter and jelly sandwich has a <u>smudged</u> face.

soiled—needing to be washed. The <u>soiled</u> clothes are in the laundry basket.

stained—discolored in a spot, usually where something has been spilled. The <u>stained</u> tablecloth will have to be washed immediately.

ANTONYMS: clean, pure, spotless, washed

E

end—the last or final part; where something stops. Their house is at the <u>end</u> of the street.

boundary—a line or other marking that shows where something ends. The river forms the northern <u>boundary</u> of the state.

conclusion—the final part of something, such as a book or a play. The audience clapped after the <u>conclusion</u> of the children's concert.

finish—the end of something that has begun or has been started. Everyone stood up to watch the <u>finish</u> of the close race.

limit—a point beyond which something cannot or should not go. We had a two-dollar <u>limit</u> for the gift exchange.

tip—the end of something, usually something that is long and slim. The gardener clipped off the <u>tip</u> of the flower stem.

ANTONYMS: beginning, onset, opening, start

F

fall—to go from a higher place to a lower place. In autumn, leaves <u>fall</u> from the trees.

collapse—to fall in or cave in. If you put those heavy books on that box, it might <u>collapse</u>.

descend—to come down from a higher place. The airplane will slowly <u>descend</u> before landing on the runway.

drop—to fall suddenly. If you bump the table, that bottle of milk might <u>drop</u> and break.

sink—to slowly go lower and lower. A brick or a heavy rock will <u>sink</u> in water.

tumble—to fall accidentally, possibly rolling over and over. The apples will bruise if they <u>tumble</u> out of the sack.

ANTONYMS: ascend, climb, mount, rise, soar

THESAURUS

funny—causing laughter. The funny clowns delighted the circus crowd.

amusing—entertaining in a funny way. Carly told an amusing story about her vacation.

comical—funny, almost silly. The most comical hat had bananas on the top.

hilarious—extremely funny. The dancing bears were a hilarious sight.

humorous—laughable and enjoyable. Limericks are humorous poems.

witty—clever and amusing. Her witty remark made the guests feel at home.

ANTONYMS: boring, dull, serious

G

go—**1** to move or pass along. My bike will not go any faster in this mud. **2** to move away from a place; to leave. The students may go when the bell rings.

advance—to move forward. The people with tickets should advance to the front of the line.

depart—to go away; to leave. What time does your bus depart?

proceed—to continue or go on after a stop. Tomorrow Mr. Wilson will proceed with the science lesson.

progress—to go ahead. The tired runners could not progress swiftly.

retreat—to move back or backward. If the deer becomes frightened, it will retreat into the woods.

ANTONYMS: arrive, come, remain, stay, stop

grow—to become bigger in size, amount, or number. The plants will grow taller with water and light.

enlarge—to make or become larger. Will this tent enlarge to fit six people?

expand—to become larger than before. A balloon will expand from hot air.

increase—to make greater. Will my strength increase if I exercise more?

multiply—to grow in number or amount. The small group of people will multiply when the parade begins.

swell—to fill out or puff up. Paul's finger may swell from the bee sting.

ANTONYMS: decrease, lessen, shrink

H

happy—feeling glad and having a good time; not sad. The birthday party was a happy occasion.

cheerful—full of gladness; friendly and pleasant. A person with a cheerful smile greeted us at the door.

contented—satisfied with the way things are. The contented baby was soon asleep.

delighted—greatly pleased; very glad. After the spelling bee, the delighted winner accepted his prize.

jolly—full of fun; merry. The jolly singers clapped their hands to the beat of the music.

jubilant—showing much joy and happiness. The jubilant team celebrated their victory.

ANTONYMS: discontent, miserable, sad, sorrowful, unhappy

THESAURUS

help—to do or give what is needed; to be useful. I will help you carry that heavy box.

aid—to help by giving relief. The money will aid needy families.

assist—to give help, usually by working with another person. The art teacher will assist the classes with their projects.

advise—to help by giving a suggestion or an opinion. Before the game, the coach will advise the players.

benefit—to bring good to; to be good for. Good eating habits will benefit a person's health.

support—to help with comfort and encouragement. Friends support each other.

ANTONYMS: harm, hinder, hurt, obstruct

hurry—to move or act quickly; to move or act more quickly than usual to save time. We will not be late for the show if we hurry.

dash—to move quickly for a short distance. The children always dash into the kitchen at lunchtime.

hustle—to do something fast. When the storm begins, the farmer will hustle the cows into the barn.

rush—to go or do something with speed. If you rush when you do your homework, you may make careless mistakes.

scramble—to move quickly using the hands and feet. A frightened bear cub may scramble up a tree.

ANTONYMS: dally, delay, detain, linger, loiter

J

join—to put or bring together in order to make or become one. The neighbors will join us for dinner.

assemble—to put the parts or pieces of something together. Did Carla assemble this jigsaw puzzle?

attach—to fasten one thing to another. Can you attach the bike to the top of the car?

clasp—to join in order to hold or keep together. Clasp arms with someone so you do not fall on the ice.

combine—to put or bring together to form a new whole. The cook will combine the salad ingredients.

connect—to join one thing to another. First connect the two wires.

ANTONYMS: disconnect, divide, part, separate, sever

jump—to go into the air from the ground; to leap. He must jump up to reach the high cupboard.

bound—to jump lightly and quickly along. Frogs often bound from one lily pad to another.

hurdle—to jump over a barrier, usually while running. The young colt would not hurdle the fence.

pounce—to go up suddenly and come down on something. Watch the kitten pounce on the ball.

spring—to move or rise quickly and suddenly. Fire fighters spring into action when the alarm rings.

vault—to leap over something using the hands or a pole. They will vault the wall and take a shortcut.

THESAURUS

K

keep—to have or to hold on to, sometimes for a long time or forever. Ann should keep the shells that she finds on the beach.

preserve—to keep from change; to keep safe from harm. The paint will preserve the wood.

reserve—to hold back, usually for a short time only. The librarian will reserve the book for you.

retain—to continue to have. She will retain her part-time job when school starts.

save—to set aside for a special use. Our teacher will save our papers for a bulletin-board display.

store—to put away for later use. You can store your bicycle in the basement.

ANTONYMS: abandon, discard, lose

L

laugh—to make sounds that show joy or amusement. Do you laugh at elephant jokes?

chuckle—to laugh quietly. They chuckle over funny cartoons.

giggle—to laugh in a silly or nervous way. Did you giggle when the ride spun you in circles?

roar—to laugh loudly. You will roar when you see the hilarious show.

snicker—to make slight or covered laughing sounds in trying not to laugh aloud. Please do not snicker when someone makes a mistake.

ANTONYMS: cry, frown, scowl

leader—a person who guides or tells others what to do; the person in charge. The leader assigned each camper to a cabin.

captain—the head of a group or a team. Marcia is the captain of our team.

chief—the person who has the highest rank. A new police chief will be chosen next month.

commander—a person who gives orders to others. The commander ordered the troops to stand at attention.

conductor—a person who directs music performers. The conductor lifted his baton.

ruler—a person who makes decisions and has control over others. The country honored its new ruler.

ANTONYM: follower

leave—to go from; to go away. Our visitors must leave after lunch.

abandon—to go away from, planning never to return. The crew must abandon the sinking ship.

flee—to run away from in a hurry. The animals will flee the burning barn.

part—to leave and separate. My friend and I part on the corner when we walk home from school.

quit—to give up and go away from. She will quit the basketball team and join the band.

vacate—to go away from and leave empty. All swimmers must vacate the pool during a storm.

ANTONYMS: arrive, come, remain, stay

let—to allow something to be done or to happen. The teacher will let the students go outside for recess.

admit—to allow to enter or join. They will not admit people into the gym during the rehearsal.

authorize—to give formal permission. Do you think the principal will authorize the field trip?

concede—to give in so something can happen or be done. Did your sister finally concede to helping us with the puppet show?

consent—to agree and give approval or permission. If her father does not consent, she will not be able to go swimming with us.

grant—to give or allow what is asked. Imagine if someone could really grant you three wishes!

ANTONYMS: ban, bar, forbid, prevent, refuse

like—to be pleased with; to have a good feeling for. Carol and her friends like to play computer games.

admire—to think of with respect or approval. A good citizen is a person whom people admire.

appreciate—to understand and enjoy. Do you appreciate that artist's work?

enjoy—to get pleasure from; to be happy with. If you enjoy historical places, you should visit Williamsburg.

prefer—to like better than another or others. Some people prefer to live in big cities.

value—to think highly of; to like very much. She will always value the ring given to her by her mother.

ANTONYMS: detest, dislike, hate, loathe

look—to turn the eyes to see or watch something. People go to a zoo to look at the animals.

examine—to look at closely and carefully. The doctor will examine Ling's sprained ankle.

glance—to take a quick, almost uninterested look. I'll only glance at the menu, because I'm not hungry.

peek—to look quickly and secretly. Did Tom peek at the present hidden in the closet?

scan—to pass the eyes over quickly, usually to find a certain thing. Everyone should scan the list by the door to find their seat number.

stare—to look directly at for some time. Sometimes I stare out the window and think of faraway places.

ANTONYMS: disregard, ignore, miss, overlook

M

make—to form or put together; to bring into being. Will you make some paper flowers for my vase?

construct—to make by putting together; to build. Chris will construct a model car for the contest.

create—to make something new or different. Can we create our own flavor of ice cream?

THESAURUS

make (*continued*)

design—to work out and draw plans for. Mr. McCormick will design the new shopping center in North Carolina.

invent—to think of or make for the first time. Did the Wright Brothers invent the airplane?

manufacture—to make, usually in large amounts, using machines. Many companies manufacture the parts for this computer.

ANTONYMS: **destroy, ruin, wreck**

move—to change from one place or position to another. Move the plant closer to the window.

budge—to move even a little bit. I tried to open the window, but it did not budge.

inch—to move a very short distance at a time. The drivers must inch their way through the deep snow.

push—to move something by using force against it. I will push my bike across the street.

shove—to move by pushing from behind. Can two people shove that heavy crate up the stairs?

transfer—to move or send from one place or person to another. If the closet gets too full, transfer some things to the attic.

N

new—**1** recently made; not old. He showed his new roller skates to his friends. **2** having not existed before. The new highway will go past the airport.

current—having to do with the present time. The newspaper informs readers of current events all over the world.

fresh—not known, seen, or used before. We put a fresh coat of paint on the doghouse.

modern—up-to-date. The modern building is made of glass.

novel—new and unusual. Clare thought of a novel costume to wear to the party.

original—thought of or done for the first time. We need original ideas for our science projects.

ANTONYMS: **antique, old, old-fashioned, past, used**

nice—kind, thoughtful, or friendly. Some nice people stopped to help us fix the flat tire.

amiable—pleasant and agreeable. She is an amiable person who has many friends.

charming—attractive and delightful. The guest speaker was a charming person with many interests.

congenial—getting along well with others. She was elected team captain because she is congenial.

courteous—thoughtful of others; showing good manners. The courteous child asked to be excused from the table.

warm—showing affection or much interest. He wrote a warm letter telling us how much he missed us.

ANTONYMS: **disagreeable, mean, rude, unfriendly, unpleasant**

noise—a sound that is neither pleasant nor musical; a loud or sharp sound. I cannot read with all that <u>noise</u> in the next room.

blast—a sudden, loud noise. The trumpet player let out a <u>blast</u> with her horn.

clamor—loud, continuing noise, usually voices. The <u>clamor</u> of the party lasted for hours.

racket—clattering noise that is disturbing. The <u>racket</u> outside woke everyone up.

rumble—a deep, heavy, rolling sound. The thunder made a <u>rumble</u> that seemed to shake the windows.

uproar—very loud and mixed-up noise. There was an <u>uproar</u> when the movie star walked into the room.

ANTONYMS: hush, lull, quiet, silence, stillness

O

old—**1** having lived or been for a long time; not young. We were afraid to go into the <u>old</u>, deserted house. **2** from long ago; not new. I wore my <u>old</u> shoes because it was raining.

ancient—belonging to times long past; very old. Rome is an <u>ancient</u> city.

antique—very old but still existing or being used. This store sells <u>antique</u> furniture.

elderly—somewhat old in age. The <u>elderly</u> man rides a bicycle to work to keep fit.

historical—having to do with the past. I wrote about a <u>historical</u> event.

outdated—old-fashioned. The people in the photograph were wearing <u>outdated</u> clothing.

ANTONYMS: current, modern, new, recent, young

P

part—not the whole; a piece. A leg is one <u>part</u> of the body.

bit—a small piece. Only a <u>bit</u> of his sandwich was left on the plate.

component—a main or necessary part of something. Joe's radio did not work because one <u>component</u> was missing.

fragment—a piece broken off of something. The scientist examined a <u>fragment</u> of a moon rock.

section—a part that is separated or divided from the whole. My garden is planted in one <u>section</u> of the yard.

share—the part belonging to one person. Each person received an equal <u>share</u> of the reward money.

ANTONYMS: all, entirety, whole

picture—a painting, a drawing, or a photograph. The travel poster has a <u>picture</u> of Hawaii on it.

collage—a picture made by pasting different materials on a surface. We made a <u>collage</u> with pieces of felt, yarn, and tile.

diagram—a drawing that shows the important parts of something and how they work. It would be difficult to assemble the bike without a <u>diagram</u>.

THESAURUS

picture *(continued)*

landscape—a picture of a scene on land, which someone might see from one spot. The artist painted a beautiful <u>landscape</u> of wildflowers in a field.

mural—a large picture painted on a wall. You will see the <u>mural</u> as soon as you walk into the room.

portrait—a picture of a person. That is a <u>portrait</u> of my grandfather when he was very young.

pull—to move something toward the person or thing giving the force. Let's <u>pull</u> the wagon up the hill.

drag—to pull along the ground. Your coat will get dirty if you <u>drag</u> it.

haul—to pull with much force. Can you <u>haul</u> the sacks into the shed by yourself?

jerk—to pull quickly and suddenly. The lamp may fall if you <u>jerk</u> the cord.

tow—to use a rope or a chain to pull something. The truck will have to <u>tow</u> the car out of the mud.

tug—to pull hard, usually more than once and stopping between pulls. If the door gets stuck again, <u>tug</u> on it.

ANTONYMS: **push, shove**

Q

quick—fast or sudden. I made a <u>quick</u> trip to the store to buy milk.

abrupt—changing suddenly with no warning. The animal made an <u>abrupt</u> turn when it spotted danger.

hasty—done quickly and in a hurry, often without thinking first. Leslie wrote a <u>hasty</u> note on her way out the door.

instant—without a delay; immediate. The bright student gave an <u>instant</u> answer to the teacher's difficult question.

prompt—quick and on time. This flower shop has lovely gifts and <u>prompt</u> service.

swift—moving or happening very fast. Ben can get the job done because he is a <u>swift</u> worker.

ANTONYMS: **delayed, lingering, long, slow**

R

rest—to be still or quiet, especially after work; to sleep. Let's <u>rest</u> after we wash the dishes.

doze—to sleep lightly. The audience may <u>doze</u> during a long, boring speech.

lounge—to pass the time relaxing. They will <u>lounge</u> in the backyard on their vacation.

nap—to sleep for a short time. My cats usually <u>nap</u> outside on a sunny afternoon.

pause—to stop and rest briefly. If you are tired, <u>pause</u> at the top of the hill.

relax—to take a rest from work. You should <u>relax</u> and let me finish this job.

ANTONYMS: **labor, stir, toil, work**

THESAURUS

right—1 being good or fair. He did the right thing when he told the truth. **2** not wrong; true. What is the right way to solve this problem?

accurate—exactly right. The reporter's story was accurate.

correct—with no mistakes. Allison raised her hand and gave the correct answer.

just—fair and honest. The judge made a just decision.

proper—right for a certain time or place; fitting. Will it be proper to wear shorts to the party?

valid—true according to the facts. Did they have a valid reason for being late?

ANTONYMS: dishonest, false, mistaken, unfair, wrong

run—to move or go along by using quick steps. Lucy must run to catch her bus.

chase—to run after and try to catch. In the game of tag, one person must chase the other players.

jog—to run with a slow, steady pace. Many people jog in the park.

race—to run very fast. The children should not race on the playground.

sprint—to run with as much speed as possible, usually for a short distance. The runners will sprint to the finish.

trot—to run, but not very fast. The two children trot behind their father when they go shopping.

ANTONYMS: amble, crawl, saunter, stroll, walk

S

scary—causing fright or fear. I cannot sleep after listening to a scary story.

alarming—causing sudden fear of danger. The animal ran when it heard an alarming noise.

creepy—having a strange feeling from being frightened. The silence in the house made me feel creepy.

eerie—scary because something is odd or strange. Those shadows on the wall are eerie.

horrifying—causing terror. Did anyone scream during that horrifying monster movie?

startling—surprising and frightening. The startling siren awakened us.

show—something presented for people to see or watch. The third-grade class is having a talent show.

demonstration—a showing of how something works or is done. The cooking instructor will give a demonstration next week.

exhibit—a show in which things are displayed for people to look at. Would you like to go to the arts-and-crafts exhibit with me?

pageant—an entertaining show about historical events. Rose played the part of a pilgrim in the pageant.

performance—a show, like a circus or a ballet, given for an audience. What time is the performance tonight?

program—a scheduled show on radio or television. I have been waiting to watch my favorite program.

THESAURUS

THESAURUS

small—not big in size or number; the opposite of large. She saw a <u>small</u> kitten in the tree.

little—small in size or number. Have you seen my <u>little</u> notebook?

petite—small in body size or height. Some clothes come in <u>petite</u> sizes.

pocket-sized—small; miniature. He carries a <u>pocket-sized</u> radio in his book bag.

tiny—very small in size; not giant. That <u>tiny</u> bird makes a soft sound.

weak—small or soft. Her voice sounded <u>weak</u>.

ANTONYMS: big, giant, great, huge, large

T

tell—to say in words to another person. The children begged, "Please <u>tell</u> the story again!"

describe—to tell all about something. Can you <u>describe</u> the jacket that you lost?

explain—to tell so that someone will understand. The science teacher will <u>explain</u> the experiment.

inform—to tell the facts. The report I wrote will <u>inform</u> readers about sharks.

mention—to say or refer to briefly. Did she <u>mention</u> her new pet to you?

recite—to repeat something that has been learned or memorized. My younger brother can <u>recite</u> the alphabet.

ANTONYMS: ask, inquire, listen, question

trip—a traveling about from one place to another. We are excited about our <u>trip</u> to the mountains.

jaunt—a short trip for enjoyment. Don asked his friend to join him on a <u>jaunt</u> downtown.

journey—a long trip. The travelers were tired from their <u>journey</u>.

outing—a pleasurable time spent away from home. Everyone agreed that the picnic was a nice <u>outing</u>.

tour—a trip to many different places. A guide took the group on a <u>tour</u> of the famous sites.

voyage—a long trip by water. The ship needs to be repaired before the next <u>voyage</u>.

W

wet—covered with water or another liquid; not yet dry. Gina used a <u>wet</u> cloth to wipe the sticky table.

damp—having some water. These clothes are still too <u>damp</u> to wear.

humid—having water vapor in the air. If the kitchen is <u>humid</u>, turn on the fan.

moist—slightly wet. Newly planted seeds should be kept in <u>moist</u> soil.

soaked—wet throughout. We had <u>soaked</u> feet because we forgot to wear boots.

soggy—heavy from being wet. This <u>soggy</u> oatmeal tastes awful!

ANTONYMS: arid, dry, parched

Index

A, an, the, 240–241, 245, 260, 298, 342, 344–345

Abbreviations
common, 360–361
definition of, 88
of names of states, 352–353
of titles, 88–89, 98, 114, 150, 360–361

Action verbs, 154–155, 168, 188–189, 206, 326–327, 336

Addresses
on envelopes, 352
in heading of friendly letter, 176–177, 185, 349

Adjectives, 232–233
articles, 240–241, 245, 260, 298, 342, 344–345
definition of, 232
that compare, 238–239, 244–245, 260, 298, 342–345
that tell how many, 234–235, 244, 260, 298, 342–345
that tell what kind, 236–237, 244, 260–261, 298, 342–345
with *-er* or *-est*, 238–239, 244–245, 260, 298, 342–345
writing with, 246–247

Adverbs, 268–269, 278, 294, 299, 346–347
definition of, 268
with *-ly*, 270–271, 346–347

Advertisements, writing, 288–291, 295

Agreement
of noun and verb, 156–157, 194–195, 328–329
of pronoun and verb, 158–159, 169, 194–195, 326, 328–329

Alphabetical order, 24–25
in dictionary, 26–27
in encyclopedia, 216–217, 227

Antonyms, 30–31, 242–243, 245, 260
definition of, 30, 242
See also Thesaurus.

Apostrophes
in contractions, 202–203, 274–275, 359
in possessive nouns, 54–55, 56–57
See also Contractions.

Articles (*a, an, the*), 240–241, 245, 260, 298, 342, 344–345

Audience for writing, 34–37

Be, 192–193
agreement with subject, 334–336
forms of, 194–195
past tense of, 194–195, 206, 226
present tense of, 194–195, 206

Biography, 212–213, 227

Body language, 138–139, 147

Book reports
form for, 286–287, 351
writing, 286–287, 351

Books
index in, 214–215
parts of, 214–215
table of contents in, 214–215
titles of, 286–287, 357, 359, 361

Building Bridges
to art, 145
to health, 293
to mathematics, 79
to science, 43, 183, 259
to social studies, 113, 225

Calendar words, 92–93, 99
See also Capitalization.

Capitalization
of abbreviations, 88–89, 98, 114, 150, 360
in addresses, 176–177, 185, 358

in book titles, 286–287, 357–358
of calendar words, 92–93, 99, 114, 150, 228, 296, 356, 358
of dates, 176–177
first word of sentence, 8–9, 20, 44, 82, 148, 296, 306–309
in friendly letter, 176–177, 185, 349
of initials, 88–89, 98, 150, 296
of place names, 90–91, 99, 114, 150, 228, 296, 356
in poem titles, 357–358
of pronoun *I*, 126–127, 357
of proper nouns, 86–87, 90–91, 98–99, 114, 150, 228, 296, 356–358
in story titles, 357–358
of titles for people, 88–89, 98, 114, 150, 356, 358, 360–361
Classifying, 38
Commands, 10–11, 20, 306–309
Commas
after name of person spoken to, 94–95, 99, 115, 151, 228, 359–360
after *yes* or *no*, 94–95, 99, 115, 151, 228, 359–360
in dates, 176–177, 185, 349
in the greeting and closing of friendly letters, 176–177, 185, 349
separating city and state, 176–177, 185, 349
in a series, 272–273, 279, 294, 299, 358, 361
Common nouns, 86–87, 98, 114, 149–150, 228, 320–321
Comparisons
of adjectives, 238–239, 244–245, 260, 342–345
listening for, 104–105
similes, 106–107, 115
writing, 106–107
Composition. *See* Writing.
Compounds, 58–59, 61, 81
Content areas, language in. *See* Building Bridges.
Context clues, 96–97, 99, 115
Contractions
apostrophe in, 202–203, 274–275
definition of, 202
forming, 202
with pronoun and verb, 202–203, 207, 226, 229, 299, 361
with verb and *not*, 274–275, 279, 294, 299, 361

Dates
capitalization of, 176–177, 185
commas in, 176–177, 185
in friendly letters, 176–177, 185, 349
Description
with adjectives, 250–251, 252–253, 261
details, 248–249, 250–251, 252–253, 261
writing, 254–257
Details, 32–33, 45, 248–249, 250–251, 252–253, 261
Dictionary, 26–29, 45
alphabetical order in, 26–27
entry words, 28–29, 45
guide words, 26–27, 45
See also Thesaurus.
Directions
following, 172–173, 183
giving, 172–173, 185
listening to, 172–173
writing, 178–181

Editing. *See* Revising.
Editing marks, 354
See also Writing Projects.
Encyclopedia
finding information, 216–217, 227
using information, 218–219, 220–221, 227
Entry words. *See* Dictionary.
Envelope, addresses on, 352
Exclamation marks, 10–11, 20, 306–309
See also Punctuation, end marks.
Exclamations, 10–11, 20, 306–309

Fact and Opinion
definition of, 282
in commercials, 282–283, 295
Fiction and nonfiction, 212–213, 227
Friendly letter
parts of, 176–177, 185, 349
writing, 176–177, 185, 349

Glossary, definition of, 43
Grammar and Writing Workshops
Sentence Combining, 22–23, 280–281
Writing with Adjectives, 246–247
Writing with Nouns, 62–63
Writing with Pronouns, 132–133
Writing with Proper Nouns, 100–101
Writing with Verbs, 170–171, 208–209

Grammar Handbook, 302–347
Guide words. *See* Dictionary.

Handwriting models, 364–365
Helping verbs, 196–197, 206, 226, 229, 297, 334, 337
  definition of, 196
Homographs, 276–277, 279, 295
Homophones, 128–129, 131, 146

Indenting, 32, 348
Index, using an, 214–215
Information
  gathering, 134–135, 136–137
  reporting, 218–219
  See also Encyclopedia.
Invitations, 350
Irregular verbs. *See* Verbs, irregular.

Letter. *See* Friendly letter.
Library
  biography, 212–213, 227
  fiction and nonfiction, 212–213, 227
  reference materials, 212–213, 227
Listening
  for comparisons, 104–105
  to directions, 172–173
  for fact and opinion, 282–283
  to poetry, 102–103, 104–105
  sharing opinions, 284–285, 295
  on telephone, 174–175
Literature. *See* Poems, Stories.

Main idea, 32–33, 348
Main verb, 196–197, 206, 226, 229, 297, 334, 337
Make-believe. *See* Real or make-believe.
Media awareness, 72–73, 81
Mystery story, writing, 140–143

Names, 88–89, 98, 114, 356
Nonfiction. *See* Fiction and nonfiction.
Nouns
  agreement with verbs, 156–157, 194–195, 328–329

  common, 86–87, 98, 114, 149–150, 228, 320–321
  compound, 58–59, 61, 81
  definition of, 48
  identifying, 48–49, 314–315
  plural, 50–51, 52–53, 60, 80, 83, 149, 228, 296, 316–317
  plural possessive, 56–57, 61, 80, 83, 149, 228, 296, 318–319
  proper, 86–87, 88–89, 90–91, 92–93, 98–99, 100–101, 114, 150, 228, 320–321
  as simple subject, 264–265, 278, 294, 299
  singular, 50–51, 60, 80, 83, 149, 316–317
  singular possessive, 54–55, 60, 80, 83, 149, 228, 296, 318–319
  writing with, 62–63, 100–101

Object pronouns, 122–123, 130, 146, 151, 229, 297, 322–325
Opinion. *See* Fact and opinion.
Opinions, sharing, 284–285, 295
Oral language. *See* Speaking.

Paragraphs
  indenting, 32, 348
  topic sentence of, 32–33, 348
  writing, 32–33, 38–41, 45, 348
Paraphrasing, 218–219, 227
Periods
  after abbreviations, 88–89, 98, 114, 150, 360
  after initials, 88–89, 98, 114, 150
  ending sentences, 8–9, 10–11, 20, 306–309
Photo essay, "The Writing Process," 34–37
Poems
  "A Modern Dragon" by Rowena Bastin Bennett, 104
  "April Rain Song" by Langston Hughes, 102
  "At the Seaside" by Robert Louis Stevenson, 230
  "Buried Treasure" by Aileen Fisher, 2
  "Central Park Tourney" by Mildred Weston, 105
  "Frog" by Valerie Worth, 104
  "George Washington" by Winifred Catherine Marshall, 84
  "Grandmother's Brook" by Rachel Field, 262
  "Grownups" by William Wise, 186
  "How to Eat a Poem" by Eve Merriam, 102

"I See a Thousand Roofs" by James S. Tippett, 113

"I Speak, I Say, I Talk" by Arnold L. Shapiro, 152

"Knitted Things" (excerpt) by Karla Kuskin, 103

"Little" by Dorothy Aldis, 116

"Moon" by William Jay Smith, 46

"The Rains of Spring" by Lady Ise, 104

untitled poem by Onitsura, 105

"Whispers" by Myra Cohn Livingston, 106

"Who Has Seen the Wind?" by Christina Georgina Rossetti, 103

Poetry
    comparisons in, 104–105, 106–107, 115
    reading aloud, 102–103
    rhyming words, 103, 115
    writing, 108–111

Possessive nouns, 54–55, 56–57, 60–61, 80, 83, 149, 228, 296, 318–319

Possessive pronouns, 124–125, 130–131, 146, 151, 322, 324

Predicates
    complete, 12–13, 16–17, 21, 44, 82, 148, 228, 296, 310–313
    definition of, 12
    simple, 266–267, 278, 294, 299

Prefixes
    re-, 166–167, 169, 184
    un-, 166–167, 169, 184

Problem solving, 136–137, 147

Pronouns
    agreement with verbs, 158–159, 169, 194–195, 326, 328–329
    contractions with, 202–203, 226, 229, 361
    object, 122–123, 130, 146, 151, 229, 297, 322–325
    plural, 118–119
    possessive, 124–125, 130–131, 146, 151, 322, 324
    singular, 118–119
    subject, 120–121, 130, 146, 151, 229, 297, 322–323, 325
    using *I* and *me*, 126–127, 131, 146, 151, 322, 325
    writing with, 132–133

Proofreading, 355
    See also Writing Projects.

Proper nouns, 86–87, 88–89, 90–91, 92–93, 98–99, 100–101, 114, 150, 228, 320–321

Punctuation
    apostrophes, 54–55, 56–57, 202–203, 274–275, 359
    commas, 94–95, 99, 115, 151, 176–177, 185, 228, 272–273, 279, 294, 299, 349, 359–361
    end marks, 44, 82, 148, 296
    exclamation marks, 10–11, 20, 306–309
    periods, 8–9, 10–11, 20, 88–89, 98, 114, 150, 306–309, 360
    question marks, 8–9, 20, 306–309
    quotation marks, 359, 361
    underlining, 286–287, 351, 359, 361

Purpose for writing, 38, 74, 108, 140, 178, 220, 254, 288

Question marks, 8–9, 20, 306–309

Questions, 8–9, 20, 306–309

Quotation marks, 359, 361

Real or make-believe, 72–73, 81

Reference materials, 212–213, 227

Reports
    choosing a topic, 210–211
    preparing for, 212–219
    writing, 220–223
    See also Book report.

Review and Practice Handbooks
    Grammar Handbook, 302–347
    Young Writer's Handbook, 348–366

Revising, 39–40, 75–76, 110–111, 142, 180, 222, 255–256, 290

Sentences
    combining, 22–23, 280–281
    commands, 10–11, 20, 306–309
    complete, 4–5, 21, 44, 82, 148, 302–305
    definition of, 4
    detail, 32–33, 45
    exclamations, 10–11, 20, 306–309
    predicates, complete, 12–13, 16–17, 21, 44, 82, 148, 228, 296, 310–313
    predicates, simple, 266–267, 278, 294, 299
    punctuation of, 8–9, 10–11, 20, 44, 82, 94–95, 115, 148, 296, 306–309
    questions, 8–9, 20, 306–309
    statements, 8–9, 20, 306–309
    subjects, complete, 12–13, 14–15, 21, 44, 82, 148, 228, 296, 310–313

subjects, simple, 264–265, 278, 294, 299
topic, 32–33, 45, 348
word order in, 6–7, 20, 44, 82, 148, 302–305
writing, 7, 9, 11, 13, 15, 17, 22–23, 280–281
Simile. *See* Comparisons.
Speaking
complete sentences, 5
giving directions, 172–173
reading poetry aloud, 102–103
sharing opinions, 284–285, 295
telephone, 174–175
Spelling
of plural nouns, 50–51, 52–53, 60
rules for, 362
of verbs in past tense, 164–165, 169, 184,
188–189, 330–331, 333
of verbs in present tense, 162–163, 168, 184,
188–189, 330, 332
words often misspelled, 363
Statements, 8–9, 20, 306–309
Story
"The Practical Princess" by Jay Williams
64–69
Story
reading, 64–69
time order in, 70–71, 81
writing, 74–77, 140–143
Study skills
alphabetical order, 24–25
choosing and narrowing a topic, 210–211
dictionary, 26–27, 28–29, 45
encyclopedia, 216–217, 227
library, 212–213, 227
paraphrasing, 218–219, 227
parts of a book, 214–215
taking tests, 366
thesaurus, 30–31, 45
Subject pronouns, 120–121, 130, 146, 151, 229,
297, 322–323, 325
Subjects
complete, 12–13, 14–15, 21, 44, 82, 148, 228,
296, 310–313
simple, 264–265, 278, 294, 299
Subject-verb agreement, 156–157, 158–159,
169, 194–195
Suffixes
-*er* and -*est*, 238–239, 244–245, 260, 298,
342–345
-*er* and -*or*, 204–205, 207, 226, 362
-*ly*, 270–271, 247

Synonyms, 18–19, 21, 30–31, 44
See also Thesaurus.

Table of contents, using, 214–215
Telephone
listening, 174–175
messages, taking, 174–175
speaking, 174–175
Thank-you notes, 350
Thesaurus, 367–384
using, 30–31, 45, 63, 101, 133, 171, 209, 247
Thinking skills
asking questions, 134–135
classifying, 38
fact and opinion, 282–283, 295
nonverbal communication, 138–139, 147
solving problems, 136–137, 147
Titles
of books, stories, poems
capitalization of, 286–287, 357–358
quotation marks in, 359, 361
underlining, 286–287, 351, 359, 361
for people
abbreviation of, 88–89, 98, 114, 150,
360–361
capitalization of, 88–89, 98, 114, 150, 356,
358, 360–361
Topic, choosing a, 210–211
Topic sentence, 32–33, 45, 348

Underlining, book titles, 286–287, 351,
359, 361
Usage
articles (*a, an, the*), 240–241, 245, 260,
342–345
be, 194–195, 206, 226
comparison of adjectives, 238–239,
244–245, 260, 342–345
irregular verbs, 198–199, 200–201, 207, 226,
229, 338–341
See also Verbs, irregular.
pronoun-verb agreement, 158–159, 169,
194–195, 326, 328–329
verbs in present tense, 156–157

Verbs
action, 154–155, 168, 188–189, 206,
326–327, 336
agreement with nouns, 156–157, 194–195,
328–329

agreement with pronouns, 158–159, 169, 194–195, 326, 328–329

be, 192–193, 194–195, 206, 226, 334–336

contractions with, 202–203, 207, 226, 229, 274–275, 279, 294, 299, 361

definition of, 154

helping, 196–197, 206, 226, 229, 297, 334, 337

irregular

   come, came, come, 200–201, 207, 226, 338–341

   come, comes, came, 190–191, 226, 334–335

   do, did, done, 198–199, 207, 338–341

   do, does, did, 190–191, 226, 334–335

   draw, drew, drawn, 200–201, 338–341

   eat, ate, eaten, 198–199, 207, 229, 338–341

   give, gave, given, 198–199, 207, 338–341

   go, goes, went, 190–191, 226, 334–335

   go, went, gone, 198–199, 207, 229, 338–341

   grow, grew, grown, 200–201, 338–341

   have, has, had, 190–191, 226, 334–335

   know, knew, known, 200–201, 207, 226, 338–341

   run, ran, run, 200–201, 207, 338–341

   run, runs, ran, 190–191, 226, 334–335

   see, saw, seen, 198–199, 207, 338–341

linking. *See* Be.

main, 196–197, 206, 226, 229, 297, 334, 337

past tense, 160–161, 164–165, 168, 169, 184, 188–189, 198–199, 200–201, 229, 297, 330–331, 333

present tense, 162–163, 168, 184, 188–189, 229, 297, 326, 330–332

as simple predicates, 266–267, 278, 294, 299

spelling of, 162–163, 164–165, 168–169, 184, 188–189, 330–333

writing with, 170–171, 208–209

Vocabulary

antonyms, 242–243, 245, 260

compounds, 58–59, 61, 81

context clues, 96–97, 99, 115

homographs, 276–277, 279, 295

homophones, 128–129, 131, 146

prefixes, 166–167, 169, 184

suffixes, 204–205, 207, 226, 362

synonyms, 18–19, 21, 30–31, 44

Who, What, When, Where, and *Why,* 134–135, 145, 147

Word order in sentences, 6–7, 20, 44, 82, 148, 302–305

Worktables

A Class Dictionary, 42

A Collage, 258

A Concrete Poem, 112

A Paper-Plate Mask, 78

A Picture Riddle, 144

A Puzzle Greeting Card, 182

A Safety Poster, 292

"What's the Answer?" 224

Writing

advertisements, 288–291

book reports, 286–287, 351

descriptions, 254–257

directions, 178–181

friendly letters, 176–177, 349

invitations, 350

mystery stories, 140–143

paragraphs, 32–33, 38–41, 45, 348

poems, 108–111

reports, 220–223

sentences, 7, 9, 11, 13, 15, 17, 22–23, 280–281

stories, 74–77

thank-you notes, 350

Writing Process

editing. *See* Writing Projects.

four steps of (prewriting, writing, revising, publishing). *See* Writing Projects.

Photo Essay, 34–37

proofreading. *See* Writing Projects.

Writing Projects (Prewriting, writing, editing, revising, proofreading, and publishing are taught in each Writing Project listed below.)

Writing an Advertisement, 288–291

Writing a Description, 254–257

Writing Directions, 178–181

Writing a Mystery Story, 140–143

Writing a Paragraph, 38–41

Writing a Poem, 108–111

Writing a Report, 220–223

Writing a Story, 74–77

Young Writer's Handbook, 348–366